Social and Cultural Depictions of India

Social and Cultural Depictions of India

C.1700-1850

(The Memsahibs' Narrations)

Shalini Awasthi

SWATI PUBLICATIONS

DELHI

First Published 2013

ISBN : 978-93-81843-04-8

Published by:
For Swati Publications
34, Central Market, Ashok Vihar
Delhi - 110 052
Tel.: 011-27212195, 65688806-7
Fax: 91-11-27212195
Email: agambooks@gmail.com, agambook@yahoo.com
www.agamkala.com

Composed by:
Aman Printographics
Delhi - 110 052
Mobile: 9891395309

Printed by:
Chawla Offset Prenters
Wazirpur Village, Ashok Vihar
Delhi-110 052

Printed in India

Acknowledgements

The Memsahibs on the threshold of India must have experienced trepidation and anxiety as they took their first tentative steps on the Indian soil. A similar churning is being experienced by me, as I put the final touches to this first venture of mine. The present work is largely based upon the Research Project, undertaken by me for the Indian Council of Historical Research. I have no words to thank the organization who awarded the research grant, which enabled me to pursue research in an area which had aroused keen interest. My heartfelt thanks go out to Shri. Ishrat Alam, Member-Secretary, ICHR; Shri. Pandeya, Director, Research, ICHR; for instilling faith in my ability to undertake the work. Special thanks go out to Shri. Upamanyu Basu who directed me towards undertaking the research project through ICHR. I am thankful to my colleagues at the Delhi Institute of Heritage Research and Management for their unstinted support and encouragement.

The staff at the India International Centre Library, New Delhi; the National Archives of India, New Delhi, and the library at the Delhi Institute of Heritage Research and Management, New Delhi, are deserving recipients of deep gratitude for their seamless assistance in locating books and research material. I am thankful to my parents-in-law, and my parents, especially my father Shri. R.C. Tripathi, who out of affection, went minutely through the draft, and made invaluable improvements to the manuscript. Special thanks are due to my husband Sanjay, whose encouraging attitude, spirit and advice sustained me through the rough passages during the time this work was being completed. I cannot forget my daughters, Lavanya and Devashri, for their understanding and cooperation about my work, despite encroaching upon the time which rightfully belonged to them.

My thanks are also due to those who helped me during this period through advice and guidance in research, and also in the typing, setting, proof-reading, printing and publishing of the book, whose names I cannot give for want of space.

Shalini Awasthi
July, 2012, New Delhi

Contents

Chapter I

Introduction: Empire, Women and Narratives

On the last day of the 16th century, the London East India Company was formed at the house of Alderman Godard, or Founders' Hall, where the parties assembled determined upon measures to equip certain vessels "upon purely mercantile bottom." In the year 1600, the consent of the Government was obtained to equip a fleet of five ships for an Indian voyage under Captain James Lancaster who commanded the fleet; thirty-six factors on salaries varying with their different trusts, accompanied the fleet. In the same year John Maidenhall, a merchant, was deputed to the court of Akbar. No records are left of the results of that embassy beyond the fact that he obtained a *firman*, was well received in the court, and that he returned in a few years to England, and that subsequently, while revisiting India, he died at Agra.

On 2nd May 1601, the vessels set sail from Torbay, and reached Sumatra and Java, and in 1603 returned to

England. The reign of Jehangir witnessed two missions from England to his court. The first by the East India Company was conducted by Captain Hawkins for the purpose of opening up a commercial intercourse with India. The second was by Sir Thomas Roe, as the ambassador for King James I, who arrived at Agra on the 16th of April 1609, and quitted Agra at the end of two and a half years. It was Hawkins' voyage in which was alluded the promise of the establishment of a factory at Surat on the west coast. This was established in 1611 by a daring mariner named Best, despite the Portuguese resistance.

These maritime expeditions of the British were the results of the two earlier expeditions; (a) the first by Sir Francis Drake and Sir John Hawkins, in 1567, from Plymouth to Java by the Pacific Ocean; and (b) the second by Thomas Cavendish on 21st July 1586, on the route of Sir Francis Drake. These two expeditions fired the ambition of the Englishmen and led to the coalition of the company of merchant adventurers who first undertook to lay the scheme before the public of trading on an extensive scale with India. In August 1608, *Hector*, the first East India Company ship arrived in India, after a voyage of seventeen months, under the command of William Hawkins. Hawkins carried with him a letter from James I to the Mughal court asking for trade with India. After landing, within a period of two and a half months, Hawkins reached the court of Jahangir, and obtained licenses to trade in India.

The maritime expeditions and the contact with India, generated a vast repertoire of literature on India, initially by the men, and later by the intrepid women from Britain who accompanied their spouses, family, brothers, on their sojourn to a new land, a great distance away from the umbilical safety of the mother-country. In the period that saw the foundation and growth of the of the East India Company, the most influential accounts of India which appeared were Samuel Purchas four folio volumes entitled, *"A History of the World in Sea Voyages and Lande Travells"*, (1625), along with the Indian travel accounts collected by Purchas predecessor, Richard Hakluyt's "*Voyages*." In these writings, cultural difference is generally elided through comparison, or registered in terms of deviation from the European norm.

The next phase of writings belong to that of Sir Thomas Roe, the first English ambassador to the Mughal court and the work of the French traveler, Francois Bernier whose contemporary account, *"History of the Late Revolution of the Empire of the Great Mogol"* after a twelve year long stay in the Mughal court, which was published in 1670-71. All these writers were directly or indirectly involved in exploring trading possibilities with India. Their accounts convey a sense of dependable authority since they were written to indicate commercial opportunities to their employers' or patrons, and to serve as sources of practical information, so much so that Hakluyt's "*Voyages*" became the standard issue on all East India Company expeditions.

In 1608 English merchants received permission to settle for trade. They built the first factory in 1618 at Surat and established a hierarchy and precedence of their community. At Surat, the Englishmen dressed in extravagant European costumes, which always impressed the Indians with awe- as the ruffs "of twelve, yea sixteen lengths, set three or four times double", the slashed silks and heavy folds of lace, enormous Caroline wigs. The Englishmen were interested in their clothes being closest in their approximation to the latest fashions at home, and begged their friends in London for advice on dress. But "It must often, however have seemed a sad waste of all this male finery that there were so few women to admire the feathered hats and watered silks and lace cuffs. English women were rare and though on festive occasions the local Armenian and Portuguese ladies might sit at the table with the English merchants, such reunions were not encouraged, for there was no knowing when some Englishman might wish to marry a Portuguese and then the children "thro' their father's neglect, brought up in the Roman Catholic principles to the great dishonor and weakening of the Protestant religion.........the Portuguese Government, in its concern for the morals of its employees in the East, used to send out annual batches of women who had failed to find husbands at home and, that the obedient officials might not cavil at such trifles as lack of physical attraction, sent them substantial dowries. These women, however, as often as not were provided by fate with other husbands in other parts of India, their ships being captured by Musulman pirates and themselves dispatched to the slave-market at Surat.................Senior members of the English Company discussed the dangers of these Papist women and warned susceptible juniors against their seductive charms."[1]

The advent of these European women in India gave rise to the new nomenclature of the *'memsahib'*. The Merriam Webster Dictionary describes the word as the

---

[1] Kincaid, Dennis. *British Social Life in India, 1608-1937*; p.25-26

conjunction of the English word 'ma'am', with the Hindi /Urdu term 'sahib'. This union of words gave rise to the category of the 'memsahibs', who were defined as "a white foreign women of high social status living in India; especially the wife of a British official." According to the Merriam Webster dictionary, the first known use of the term is assigned to the year 1852. The Hon. Emily Eden in a letter dated February 13th 1838 alludes to the use of the term memsahib for the English women in India. She writes,[1] "yesterday the Baboo of Mr. B.'s office stalked into my tent with a pair (of earrings) precisely the same, and a necklace like that I had bought at Lucknow, and said his '*Mem Sahib*' (so like the East Indians calling their ladies 'Mem Sahibs') had sent him to show me those, and ask if they were the same as mine." The Rev. T. Acland has also referred to the use of the term "*meem Sahib*" in a journal entry of August 7th, 1843 while giving an account of the *moufassil* society of Cuttack.[2] It is apparent that while the use of the term 'memsahib' was popular among the British populace residing in India, its official entry into the lexicons, is of a later date.

The writings' of the women travellers have been regarded by many generations of critics who would have us believe are less- entertaining and less-valid, a view which was postulated in June edition of *The Punch*, in 1893.

"A Lady an explorer? a traveler in skirts?

The notion's just a trifle too seraphic:

Let them stay and mind the babies, or hem our ragged shirts:

---

[1] Eden, Emily. *Up the Country.* Vol. I. p.133

[2] Rev. Acland, T. *A Popular Account of the Manners and Customs of India.* p.81

But they musn't, can't, and shan't be geographic."

The difference in the account's of the women travellers as compared to the account's of the writings of men lie in the nature of their preoccupation, which has to be duly acknowledged. The women wandered along in her husband's footsteps, scribbling down whatever fancy happened to flit into her homely head. And because women were writing for their friends and family back home, belonging to the same sex, they could afford to be more discursive, more impressionable, and more ordinary, but none the less, informative.

In chartering the course of the memsahibs in India, it is said that the first British women to undertake the voyage to India was, perhaps, a Mrs. Hudson and her maid, Francis Webb, who went as companion to an Armenian lady who had been born in India.[1] But, it was much later, in the eighteenth century that a British woman first put to paper her thoughts on her interface with India. Thus began what was to be the beginning of a most fruitful relation of the British women writings on India. Jemima Kindersley landed in Madras in 1765, and settled at "Allahabad, where she became one of the British India's earliest official memsahibs by settling with her husband, for a few years' residence. And ...... one of the first Englishwomen to publish an account of it....."[2]. Jemima Kindersley nee Wicksteed, was a great beauty, who in April 1762 married Lieutenant Nathaniel Kindersley. In 1764 , the Kindersley's, with their infant son, set out for India, where Lieutenant Kindersley was to join the Bengal Artillery of the East India Company. They spent

---

[1] MacMillan, Margaret. *Women of the Raj*; p.16.

[2] Robinson, Jane. *Angels of Albion* p.2.

the next four years, mostly at Calcutta (now Kolkatta) and Allahabad. In 1769 Jemima Kindersley returned to England, on account of her son's ill health; and, her husband died in the same year at Calcutta. In 1777 her *Letters from the Island of Teneriffe, Brazil, the Cape of Good Hope, and the East Indies* were published, giving a popular account of Indian life, religion, and culture; and this work established a genre of travel writing, which the memsahibs increasingly adopted.

Jemima Kindersley's position as the first memsahib writing about India from personal experiences has been challenged and the credit is now accorded to Jane Smart, who is said to have authored the first known publication in 1743, when her "original letter to her son describing the visit she and her two daughters had paid to the wife of the 'Nabob' of Madras was published in London."[1] Jane Smart spent the years 1740-1743 in Madras with her husband Jonathan, and daughters Elizabeth and Jane. In 1742, she and her two daughters accompanied Mrs. Frances Benyon, wife of the Governor of Madras, to call upon the wife of the Nawab. The slim eight-page *Letter From a Lady at Madras* was an account of this meeting, written for the edification of her son in London and that was published in 1743. Jane Smart, later, moved with her husband to Calcutta, where she died in September 1753.

The entire genre of British writings on India in the eighteenth and the first half of the nineteenth century were either a summary of sea voyages to India, or the cataloguing of the history, legal codes and the fauna and flora of India. In the list of women authors who have left behind narratives based on their personal experiences

---

[1] Raza, Rosemary. *In Their Own Words*; p.2.

in India, one name that cannot be omitted, and that is of Mrs. Katherine Gyfford, née Cooke, who although has not left behind any account on her own, but "to her belongs the distinction of being the first Englishwoman to earn a place in the Company's history."[1]

In the next few pages, a brief introduction is being provided to the 'memsahib' authors, whose works are being chiefly relied upon in the present study. It is, of course, well- known that many English women came to India during the colonial period, and some of them have left interesting accounts of their experiences in India. Since these accounts were written by women, they allow us in exploring the role of the feminine gender in India as colonialism progressed. As far as possible, their opinions have been quoted *in-extenso*, to provide an insight into their mind-set, without clouding them in the guise of a psycho-analytical, ideological-interpretative analysis of data. The objective behind this being, to present their ideas and opinions in original, in a coherent and thematic study from a bare narrative of reminiscences/ memoirs before they were evolved in a kind of sacred folk myth. This anthology aims to eliminate the studied official positions and bring forth the attitudes of mind and perception revealed through personal narratives which will give this proposed work its relevance.

The above narratives were soon followed by the *Original Letters From India; Containing A Narrative of a Journey through Egypt and the Author's Imprisonment at Calicut by Hyder Ally, to which is added an Abstract of Three Subsequent Voyages to India*, by Eliza Fay. These were letters written by Eliza Fay to her sister, and later to

[1] Kaey, John. *The Honourable John Company*. p.256.

her friend, in the style of a journal. The letters commence from 18th April 1779 and are a contemporary work which throws light on the social life of Calcutta, of the time of Warren Hastings and Sir Philip Francis. These were first published in 1817. Eliza Fay was married to Anthony Fay, a barrister, but their marriage was unsuccessful, and Eliza separated from her husband, while residing at Calcutta. Eliza Fay arrived at Calicut on 8th November 1779, to "sufferings, which have been extreme, both in mind and body for fifteen weeks which were spent in wretched confinement, totally in the power of the barbarians" because she and her husband along with others were taken into captivity by Sirdar Khan, a potentate of Hyder Ally, only to be released in February 1780. Soon after this, her experiences of a less adventurous nature and an exploration of the inestimable variety afforded by India commenced and Eliza Fay began their detailing for the reading pleasure of family and friends, back home in England. These begin with her impressions of the city of Cochin. "Here we were welcomed by the two wives of Issac who were most splendidly dressed to receive us, rather overloaded with ornaments yet not inelegant. Indeed I think the Eastern dresses have infinitely the advantage over ours. They are much more easy and graceful; besides affording greater scope for display of taste than our strange and unnatural modes".[1] Unusual for a woman of her time, Eliza Fay made three journeys to India. The dates of Mrs. Fay's journeys are as follows: the first trip began on 18th April 1779 and she returned in February 1783; her second sojourn in India was from

---

[1] Fay, Eliza. *Original Letters from India.* 19th February 1780, Cochin, p.114.

March 1784 to September 1794; but by July 1795 Mrs. Fay was in America. The dates of her third and last trip to India are not clear, but she was buried on 10th September 1816, at Calcutta. Her return to Calcutta was guided by the motive of setting up a dress making business, as a means to economic independence, while she simultaneously was preparing her letters for publication. Unfortunately, Eliza Fay died in 1816 and her letters were published posthumously, in the subsequent year, 1817.

Maria Graham, later Lady Callcott, came to India in early 1809, with her father; and married Lieutenant Thomas Graham, R.N. in Bombay (now Mumbai) in December 1809. The first few months of her residence were spent at Bombay, from where she most frequently visited Elephanta; the island of Salsette; the recently excavated archaeological discovery of the caves at Carli (modern Karle); Poonah (now Pune); Ceylon (Sri Lanka); Trincomale; Madras (now Chennai); and finally arrived at Calcutta, which marked the last leg of her travels within India. In the beginning of early 1811, Maria Graham returned to the Coromandel Coast to embark for her return journey to England. She reached back home to England in the same year, travelling via the Cape of Good Hope and St. Helena. Her reminiscences of her stay in India were written solely for the amusement and reading pleasure of an intimate friend. This journal was prepared for publication in 1812 under the title of, *"Journal of a Residence in India"* merely by omitting private details and anecdotes of individuals which would have exceeded the limits of propriety had they been made public so recently. In 1814, Maria Graham also published the *Letters on India,* which extended her account of India and its culture.

Of the early nineteenth century, Mrs. Meer Hassan Ali has left her account the *Observations on the Mussulmauns of India: Descriptive of Their Manners, Customs, Habits and Religious Opinions Made During a Twelve Years' Residence in Their Immediate Society*, a work she penned down owing to her marriage into a noble Muslim family of Lucknow. Nothing is known of her background or her maiden name, and she was reticent about details concerning herself and her husband. She apparently met her husband Meer Hassan Ali, while he was a Professor of Hindustani at the Oriental Department at Addiscombe, the East India Company's Military College in England, between 1812 and 1816[1]. They married in March 1817, shortly after which they left for India, disembarked at Calcutta, and reached Lucknow via Patna. After living in India for some twelve years, she left for England, in 1829, never to return. As Mrs. Meer Hassan Ali writes in her Introductory Letter to her *Observations*, she "was induced to write the principal number of the following Letters ......at first designed merely for the perusal of private friends; who viewing them with interest, recommended my bringing them before the public, considering that the information they contained would be acceptable from its originality, as presenting a more familiar view of the opinions and domestic habits of the Mussulmaun community of Hindoostaun than any hitherto presented though other channels". In the course of her work, Mrs. Meer Hassan Ali gives only one date, September 18, 1825, when her husband held the post of Tehsildar, or the sub-collector of revenue, at Kannauj. However, a secondary date can also

[1] W. Crooke asserts that Mir Hasan Ali was in fact appointed assistant to the well known Oriental scholar, John Shakespear, a Professor of Hindustani, at the Military Co!lege at Addiscombe, from 1816-130.

be assigned to her stay in India on the basis of a private correspondence between Nawab Hakim Mehndi, while he was living at Fategurh, and invited Bishop Heber to visit him. The Bishop was assured by the former, "that he had an English housekeeper, who knew perfectly well how to do the honours of his establishment to the gentlemen of her own nation. (She is, in fact, a singular female, who became the wife of one of the Hindustani Professors at Hertford, now the Hukeem's Dewan, and bears, I believe, a very respectable character." According to initial reports, Mrs. Meer Hassan Ali's departure from India was on account of her health, but later reports hint to the reason that she could not tolerate her husband's other wives, as Hassan Ali had no children from her, but had a daughter and two sons, by his Indian wife(s)?

Mrs. Colonel Anne Katherine Elwood, penned the details about her residence in India, in letters which were originally written for her sister Mrs. Elphinstone, which were later dedicated to Edward Jeremiah Curtis, Esq. of Windmill Hill, M.P. for the County of Sussex (her father) in July 1830. Her work is titled *Narrative of a Journey Overland from England by the Continent of Europe, Egypt, & the Red Sea to India; including a Residence there, and Voyage Home in the years 1825, 26, 27 and 28."* Her objective in putting to paper her thoughts are reflected in the Preface of the Narrative where; "She begs to state that in doing so, she is likewise complying with the wishes of several friends, who have frequently expressed themselves desirous of being informed of the particulars of her journey to, and residence in India........ But, since she can safely affirm that she has given a true and faithful description of what she saw and felt, in the very peculiar circumstances she found herself, and in the singular countries which it was her fate to visit, and since, if she may judge from her own feelings, women naturally take a lively interest in what concerns their own sex, she flatters herself, that the following account of the adventures of the first and only female who has hitherto ventured overland from England to India, may at least prove not wholly unacceptable to the fair part of the reading community. She, likewise hopes, that it is not impossible some future over-land traveler may benefit from her experience, which has already enabled her to give hints, and to furnish suggestions and information, that have been found useful by parties proceeding to and returning from India."

In the interregnum, from the turn of the nineteenth century to the pre-Mutiny years, a large number of works were penned down by the memsahibs. A singular work is *The Golden Calm* edited by M.M. Kaye, about *'An English Lady's Life in Moghul Delhi: Reminiscences by Emily, Lady Clive Bayley, and by her father Sir Thomas Metcalfe'.* Emily Annie Theophila, later Lady Emily Clive Bayley was Sir Thomas Metcalfe's eldest daughter by his second wife, Felicity Anne. Sir Thomas Metcalfe administered Delhi as its Resident, and also in his position as Agent to the Governor-General at the Court of the King of Delhi. Emily was born in India, in 1831, at Meerut, a garrison town less than fifty miles or eighty kilometers from Delhi. In February 1836, she and her younger sister Georgie were sent to England where they spent their childhood with their grandmother. By January 1848, after attaining the age of seventeen, Emily rejoined her father in Delhi, and, two years later she married Sir Edward Clive Bayley, the then Under-Secretary to the Foreign Department, at St, James Church, Delhi. Her reminiscences cover the period from her early childhood and abruptly end at the event of Sir Thomas' death in 1853, from subtle poison.

An intrepid traveler, who has left behind a voluminous account of her residence and travels within India, is Frances Susannah Parks nee Archer (Fanny Parks) who sailed for India with her husband Charles Crawford Parks, a Writer in the East India Company in 1822. On 30th October 1822 she had her first brush with exotic India as her ship the 'Marchioness of Ely' made a three day brief stopover at Nicobar Island. Fanny Parks first introduction was to set the tenor for her stay in India, as they first landed on the island of Car-Nicobar on 30th October 1822 and quitted the island on 2nd November 1822. Her brush with the 'exotic' was to fuel her innate curiosity to know India and her inhabitants better. Of her experiences at Car-Nicobar she writes, "The Island where we landed was covered to the edge of the sand of the shore with beautiful trees; scarcely an uncovered or open spot was to be seen. Off the ships the village appeared to consist of six or eight enormous bee-hives, erected on poles and surrounded by high trees; among these, the cocoa-nut, to an English eye, was the most remarkable".[1] She later writes, "Little did I think it would ever have been by fate to visit such an uncivilized island, or to shake hands with such queer looking-men; however, we agreed very well, and they were quite pleased to be noticed.........I cannot refrain from writing about these people, being completely island struck".[2] The Andaman

[1]Parks, Fanny. *Wanderings of a pilgrim.* p.14,Vol.I

[2] *Ibid.*p.18,Vol.I

Islands were bypassed as the inhabitants of these islands were regarded as "Cannibals" who were "reported to have a fondness for strangers of a nature different from the Carnicobarians". Subsequently, their ship anchored on 10th November 1822 at Saugor (Sagar) on the Hoogly and they finally landed at Fulta. The Parks returned to England in 1846, and throughout those twenty-four years Fanny Parks kept a diary. During their long stay in India Fanny Parks gives an account of the metropolitan centre of Calcutta, from 1822 to 1826. There on the focus shifts to life in a *mufassil* town of Allahabad, till the end, except for a brief interlude at Cawnpore (Kanpur). Fanny Parks travelled widely over North India, visiting Fategarh, Khasgunge, Lucnow (Lucknow), Agra, Delhi, Meerut and visited areas seldom visited by other memsahibs as Gaur, Kannauj, and the Himalayas. With her fluent Hindustani, she was able to penetrate the Indian life, and shared a close rapport with Indian women, especially Baiza Bai, the deposed Maratha queen, with whom she shared a close and intimate friendship. Her diary was written for her mother, and sent home in installments. Fanny Parks missives taper off after her mother's death in 1842. She prepared her journal for publication and edited it carefully, adding a few information avaliable to her as the death of Prince Dara Bukht in 1849, and that of Baiza Bai; a glossary; list of Oriental Proverbs and Sayings. Twenty-five years before her demise in 1875, Fanny Parks record of her life and times in India were published as the *Wanderings of a Pilgrim in Search of the Picturesque, During Four-and -Twenty Years in the East; with Revelations of the Life in the Zenana.*

Another source consulted for the present study is the *Letters from Madras: during the years 1836-1839* written by Julia Maitland. Born on 21st October 1808, Julia Maitland nee Barrett, at the age of nearly twenty-eight years married James Thomas, a Writer who had risen to become a Senior Merchant (the highest civil service grade) from India in 1836, a widower with three small daughters. James Thomas died in January 1840, and Julia married Charles Maitland, her second husband, in 1842. The *Letters* of Julia Maitland are record of her life and stay in India, with James Thomas, her first husband, written for her mother and her family, back in England. Soon after her marriage in the summer of 1836, Julia set sail for India, and arrived at Madras in December 1836. By August 1837 James Thomas had taken up his post as a Judge dealing primarily with civil and criminal matters, at Rajamundry, where they were to stay for nearly for a year and half. By July 1839 they had moved to Madras, and in the October of 1839, the Thomas's were residing in Bangalore. While in India, Julia wrote prolifically to her mother in England, and those letters, which Julia called 'journal letters' along with extracts to her grandmother, her brothers Richard and Arthur, and her cousin and friend Minette Raper Kingston, were published in 1843, anonymously, as her mother had objections to her publishing under her own name. Before publication, the letters were edited by Julia, who edited nearly all details pertaining to her family; to her family at home in England; to her children born in India; and to the children of James Thomas from his previous marriage; the details regarding her husband's career in India; his family and the friends she made in India. Due to the heavy editing, the work turns out to be an exercise in the personal opinion of the writer, on the dominant issues of the times, such as English education and missionary activity, rather than an insight to India.

Around the same time, the Eden sisters, Emma and Frances, accompanied their brother, George, (Lord Auckland) to India in 1835, the country to which he was appointed Governor-General. Emma was the seventh of eight daughters and the twelfth of the fourteen children; while Frances (or Fanny) was the youngest child of the brood. Both the sisters were intrepid keepers of journal, however in posterity, Emily Eden is better known than her younger sister Frances Eden, "whose response to India was more positive than one of Emily."[1] Frances (Fanny) made copious and entertaining entries of her impressions of India for her closest friend Eleanor Grosvenor. Fanny's first journal, *The Trip to the Rajmahal Hills*, commences in February 1837, when she set out with her nephew William Osborne, on a tiger-shooting trip to the Rajmahal Hills, 150 miles north-west of Calcutta. Her second journal, *The Progress Through the Upper Provinces* resumes in October 1837, when she embarked with her brother George, the Governor-General, her elder sister Emily, and nephew William, accompanied by 12000 members of the Governor-General's entourage over North India, with two ends to achieve; one, being that George wanted to visit the Upper Provinces of India to see whether they were being well administered, and, secondly to strengthen ties of friendship with Ranjit Singh, the Lion of Punjab, in order to secure the protection of India's northwest borders. The third journal was titled, *To the Court of Ranjit Singh.*

---

[1] Dunbar, Janet. *Tigers, Durbars and Kings.* p.4

Emily Eden's letters during her residence and sojourns in India were published in May 1866, as a two volume work, titled *Up the Country: Letters written to her sister from the Upper Provinces of India*. The first volume starts on October 21st, 1837, when aboard the '*Megna*', she set off with her brother, Lord Auckland, sister Frances, and their entourage on "eighteen months of travelling by steamers, tents, and mountains", on an extended tour, in which the itinerary covered vast tracts of North India, including towns as Cawnpore, Lucknow, Delhi, Simla, etc., to name a few, and the native state of Punjab, under Ranjit Singh. The first volume terminates on 8th December 1838, while the Governor-General was at Umritzar (Amritsar), confabulating with Maharaja Ranjit Singh, the ruler of Punjab. The second volume resumes a day later on the 10th of December 1838, culminating on the 13th of March 1839, at the Governor-General's house at Barrackpore, having touched down at Calcutta on the 1st of March. These letters, written largely to her sister Mary Drummond, were subsequently dedicated, out of nostalgia, by an affectionate Aunt, Emily Eden, to her nephew Lord William Godolphin Osborne, as "she, to whom they were written, have all passed away, and you and I are now almost the only survivors of the large party that in 1838 left the Government House for the Upper Provinces." In dedicating these letters to her nephew, the Hon. Emily Eden has deliberately omitted "many of the passages" which were "written solely for the amusement of my own family". The merit of this work, as acknowledged by the authoress herself, is that "not a word has been added to the descriptions which have little merit, but that they are true and that they were written on the spot".

Marianna Postans was another memsahib recording her reminiscences of her residence in India. Her work *Cutch or Random Sketches taken during a residence in one of the Northern Provinces of Western India, interspersed with Legends and Traditions* commences from the 29th September 1837, and was published two years later in 1839. Marianna Postans was married to Thomas Postans, an officer with the East India Company's Bombay Native Infantry, in February 1833, whom she accompanied to India. This work is of singular importance in that it records the "general and domestic manners of the population in its various castes" of a province generally not visited by the memsahibs, who were securely ensconced in the towns of Calcutta, Bombay, Madras or the moufassil towns. The author has herself acknowledged this fact when she introduces the objective behind her work. She writes, "General acquaintance with the remote stations which form a considerable part of our Indian possessions is very limited; and as Cutch from its maritime importance, is likely to become connected with the favourite and apparently feasible plan of steam-navigation on the Indus, it will perhaps be deemed more deserving of attention than any other stations not likely to be in any way affected by the progress of commercial civilization." Marianna Postans has also, in the course of her writing ventured to "offer such reflections as were suggested by the occasion."

Another work cited from secondary sources, has been authored by Vicountess Amelia Cary Falkland, born Amelia Fitzclarence, the youngest of the ten children of Dora Jordan and her lover, the Duke of Clarence, later William IV. In 1831, Amelia married Lucius Bentick Cary, the 10th Viscount Falkland, who was the Governor of Bombay from 1848 to 1853. Lady Falkland called her journal, containing a medley of impressions, ranging from Bombay's social life, to the excursions of the author to famous sights, the Ch*ow-Chow; being Selections from a Journal kept in India, Egypt, and Syria. 2 vols*. The title of the work was derived from the term used for the odds and ends sold by the travelling peddlers of India.

The fascinating thing about the memsahibs writings are that they are full of surprises. Some women authors are capable of displaying a warm affection for the women inhabitants of the *zenana,* a minority, in the writings of the memsahibs. The majority of the memsahibs expend page upon page in describing the picturesque landscape of India, and encounters with the Indians—which other than the army of servants employed by them—are rare. The works alluded to have been selected on the singular criteria that they derive their source material from original travel and exploration, and refrain in the large measure, from the recycling of popular entertainment contained in articles and novels, which were widely subscribed to, in the contemporary historical time-line.

Chapter II

First Impressions: Introduction to Life in India c.1700-1800

In the two centuries beginning from the 1600's, the burgeoning British hegemony in India the Women were honoured in their absence as the founders of the empire suffered prolonged separation from their wives and families. To rephrase a catch-phrase, it is said that the "empire was not acquired in a fit of absence of mind, so much as in a fit of absence of wives[1], as the East India Company was looking for marines who had to be able men unmarryed and approved saylors". This hypothesis is questioned, where it is stated that "Such abstinence was dictated by prudence and lack of opportunity rather than by any weird theory that the empire builders sublimated their sexual desires in order to conserve the energy needed to build empires. A few may have risked brothels in the cities, a few more or less discreetly have

[1] Neville, Pran. *Rare Glimpses of the Raj*. p.1

kept native mistresses, and a few had occasional flings with memsahibs in the hill stations. But most of them stayed celibate in their most sexually potent decade—and celibate in a very monastic way: not only did Assistant Magistrates seldom have sex, many of them seldom saw women with whom they might wanted to have sex."[1]

The Europeans trading in India had their settlements scattered along the coast of India. "These trading centres had, to some extent been protected by guarantees from the central government, but, with the collapse of the empire, officials intent upon and creating and preserving their own independence now disregarded the immunities and privileges for Europeans which had been extracted—often with much difficulty—from the Mughal emperor. In self-defense, the Europeans began to fortify their settlements. But defense was to bring a measure of involvement, for there is an interior logic essential to the maintenance of simple security; it is always necessary to occupy a little more territory than one actually needs in order to defend the area one actually holds."[2] The Mughal emperor Jahangir had given permission to the British to establish a post at Surat (1612) in the face of stiff opposition from the Portuguese, who had been the first of the European trading powers to arrive in India. After Surat, 'factories' were further set up at Ahmedabad, Burhanpur, Ajmer, Agra, and by 1647 had increased to twenty-three establishments. By 1699, the East India Company had by virtue of acquiring territories in India, now become an Indian landowner. The Company's possessions were listed four in number;

---

[1] Gilmour, David. *The Ruling Caste.* p.279-280

[2] Edwards, Michael. *British India 1772-1947.* p.6-7

(i) Fort St. George, Madras (ii)Bombay (iii)Calcutta (iv) Fort St. David opposite the town of Cuddalore on the Coromandel Coast.[1] These British territories, where the memsahibs would put their first steps on the Indian soil, were provided with a modicum of British governance by the Letters Patents granted to the United Company of Merchants of England, Trading to the East-Indies, by George III, in the year 1726. Thereafter Richard Higginson, Esq. was made the first modern mayor of the town and factory of Madraspatnam. Likewise, William Henry Draper, Esq. was made the first Mayor of the town and factory of Bombay; and John Sainsbury, Esq. the first modern Mayor of the town of Calcutta, at Fort William, in Bengal.

By the grant of August 1639, Mr. Francis Day had obtained permission from the Naik prince, Damala Venkatappa Nayak, a local chieftain ruling the Coromandel Coast, on behalf of the Raja of Chandragiri, the permission "out of the our spetiale love and favour to the English to build a fort and Castle in or about Madraspatam".

Meanwhile along the Konkan Coast, in 1688, King Charles II had transferred Bombay, which he had received as dowry from his wife, Catherine of Braganza, to the East India Company for a loan of £50,000 at six percent, charging an annual rent of £10 per annum, which the East India Company paid till 1730. Bombay became a safe haven for the Hindus who were under the constant threat of the anti-Hindu policies of Aurangzeb; for the

[1] Fort St. David had been acquired from the Marathas in September 1690, under the 'ye randome shott of a piece of ordinance', for which the English called from Madras the gun with the longest range and the most expert gunner. The villages within the radius of the site were called 'cannonball villages'.

Christians fleeing from the Inquisition in Portuguese Goa; and for merchants of Surat facing depredations of the Marathas on (as of 1664), made these groups look for safety towards Bombay, which was taken up for fortifications as the new headquarters for the Company's interests in India.

In Bengal, Job Charnock, the East India Company's agent, declared war on the Mughal Empire over a quarrel over custom dues in 1686, but Charnock and the English were forced to seek shelter in Madras. By 1690, following a treaty, the Company's ships were moored in the Hooghly river near a spot where Charnock founded Calcutta. In 1692, Calcutta was made independent of Madras, and four years later, in 1696, the English were allowed to fortify Calcutta. Fort William was constructed in1699, in honour of the Dutch king of England. In the same year, the three villages of Chutanati, Govindpur, and Calcutta were rented from the Nawab of Bengal.

It was against the backdrop of these political settings that the British women ventured out from the shores of England to set up a home and life in an alien and unknown country. These women were not merely confined to Madras, Bombay and Calcutta, but moved to the smaller towns and settlements outside of these Presidency towns.

In the 1600's few British women came to India, deterred by the long and torturous voyage. Another deterrent was that the original Charter of the East India Company, which forbade women on its posts. The Portuguese, who had preceded the British in India, used to send out annual batches of women for marriage to their officials in Goa. British settlers at first married widows and daughters of the Portuguese Catholics, which did not find favour the East India Company. So, towards the end of the seventeenth century, the Company emulated the Portuguese practice and shipped out batches of young women divided into 'gentlewomen' and 'others' for matrimonial objectives solely. These were provided with free boarding and lodging for one year. As the demand for wives was far in excess of supply, some women took to prostitution as a more lucrative and pleasant vocation than marriage. Letters from the President and Council to Deputy Governor of Bombay, of December 18th 1675, and January 17th 1676, state that, "Whereas some of these women are grown scandalous to our nation, religion and Government interest, we require you to give them faire warning that they do apply themselves to a more sober Christian conversation." And, when these injunctions were ignored, "the sentence is that they shall be confined totally of their liberty to go abroad and fed with bread and water," and shipped back home to England. An example of the scandalous behaviour of the English women is narrated thus, "Of course if women arrived in the marriage-market with dowries of their own, there was no longer any question of prevailing on the Government to support them if they failed to find husbands; the difficulty was to prevent senior Government servants interesting themselves in the dowries. A Miss Ward had actually £3,000 of her own and the Governor, Sir John Gayer (1697-1698), decided a lady with that capital was just the wife for his son. Unfortunately before he made known this decision she had fallen in love with, and married, a junior clerk. The Governor declared this marriage void and succeeded in marrying her to his son.

But presently she had an affair with the schoolmaster, 'who was ordered to teach her to write good *English*, but neglecting these Orders, he taught her something else, and was discovered Practising, by a watchful Mother-in-law; and the poor Husband's Head aked as long as he lived', in spite of his father causing the schoolmaster to be arrested and sent home in chains".[1]

Meanwhile the Madras Government, which had spent a great fortune on dressing up their troops, and after having expanded vast monies in this exercise, were not in the least desirous to follow the costly Bombay experiment of importing women for their white subjects. Instead they decided to "induce by all means our Soldiers to marry with the Native women because it will be impossible to get ordinary young women to pay their own passages"[2] out from England to India. Despite the acute shortage of white women public events and festivals, such as the news of the marriage of the Prince of Orange with Princess Mary; the accession of James II; etc. were celebrated at Madras with great fanfare and magnificence. On the occasion of the reception of the ambassadors of Persia and Siam by the President of Madras there was hosted a 'Banquet and Dancing'. This occasion was marked by the 'gentlemen from the President down, posturing, pointing a toe, bowing and retreating, and the ladies in their broad Caroline shoulders and high scarcely-hid breasts, smirking and quizzing behind their tinseled fans.' In contrast to the staidness and conservative attitudes of the British, their French rivals had adapted themselves more easily to the Indian habits, which was evident at

---

[1] Kincaid, Dennis. *British Social Life in India, 1608-1937*. p.44-45.

[2] *Ibid*. p.58.

the French settlement of Pondicherry. The young men fresh from France were appalled to find that all the ladies of Pondicherry had copied the Indian custom of chewing betel-nut which stained their lips bright-red, and that they would testify to their favourable reception of a compliment by offering the new arrival a pinch of their own powdered betel-nuts from silver comfit boxes, putting the youth to the uncomfortable choice of giving offence to a lady of himself tasting the repulsive-looking stuff. As the young men naturally chose the latter course, they soon adopted the habits themselves.[1]

After the death of Aurangzeb, south-eastern India was worked up by the intrigues of the English and the French; and the merchants at Madras were concerned with the good sale of cloth they were able to effect with the different commanders for their soldiers' equipment. The Council, on the other, hand was deeply disturbed over some recent unsuitable marriages of Englishmen in Madras.[2] Many of these kept slave-girls, as mistresses, but this did not cause concern; it was the marriages that were unfortunate, especially when the "Young Gentlemen were of good families in England". For instance "one Crane, was married to a Frenchman's daughter of this place on Sunday last", and "one Dutton, an ordinary fellow, married Ann Ridley", who was a Catholic, so, "for preventing the like practices for the future" it was enacted, after considerable discussion, that no Christian should be married in Madras without leave from the Government. It was these unsuitable marriages, to which the authorities objected to; they connived at less regular unions. These

[1] *Ibid.* p.59 ff.

[2] *Ibid*. p.68-69.

were so common that no stigma was attached to them, and sometimes they brought great happiness. Henry Crittleton, a Company's officer, kept a Brahmin girl called Raje; and in his will he refers to her with obvious sincere gratitude and devotion, leaving to her all his property. General Pater was so fond of his mistress Arabella that when, on her death, the chaplain refused to bury her in the consecrated ground, he had her body interred in a field and then built a church over it, the church of St. Mary's, so that inspite of the chaplain she should lie in consecrated ground. These were men of means, but many a poor sailor and soldier showed a similar affection for their mistresses. The sailor, James Buller left his slave-girl Noky, her freedom and fifteen Arcot rupees a month; and William Stevenson left his Maria a third of his "estate" provided she remained virtuous.

As the British women began arriving on the Indian shores their character was under severe doubt. Katherine Gyfford, was perhaps the first Englishwoman whose exploits are recorded in the East India Company's history. The narrative of her exploits in India is reproduced below.[1] "It all began at Karwar in the year 1709 when the *Loyal Bliss*, outward bound for Bengal and carrying the family of Gerrard Cooke, a Fort William gunner, had put in for fresh supplies and water. Twelve days later the *Loyal Bliss* resumed her voyage minus Katherine, the eldest Cooke daughter. 'A most beautiful lady not exceeding thirteen or fourteen years of age', she was also a paragon of virtue for 'to oblige her parents' she had accepted the offer of marriage from John Harvey. Harvey was the chief of the Karwar factory, he was also 'in years'—so probably

---

[1] Kaey, John. *The Honourable John Company*. p.256ff.

old enough to be her grandfather—and 'deformed'. Such sudden and suspect pairing was not uncommon. For bringing to India an English girl who was past puberty there was only one possible reason, to find a husband. In the Company's settlements suitors swarmed around a fresh faced beauty as thickly as mosquitoes. Had little Miss Cooke been twice as old and half as pretty, she would still have been eagerly courted; but the twelve-day conquest, and of such a senior factor,[1] may be taken as testimony that her charms were indeed exceptional. Happily they were not long lavished on the repulsive Harvey. Within a couple of years the child-bride was a child-widow and within a couple of months the child-widow had remarried. This time the lucky suitor was a young factor newly arrived in Karwar called Thomas Chown. Harvey had left an estate large enough to enable the sixteen-year old to choose a more attractive partner; but as was ever the case, Harvey's personal affairs were hopelessly confused with those of his office. The Company was therefore laying claim to his estate and the Chown's were determined to contest the matter. With Katherine already 'heavy with child' (presumably Chown's), they sailed for Bombay in 1712. As was usual, the waters were infested with 'pirates' (i.e. the Marathas), and the Chown's ketch, the *Anne*, sailed in a convoy with two other vessels. A day out from Karwar, the small fleet was attacked by four Maratha 'grabs' (*ghurabs* or square-rigged frigates). Chown was immediately hit in the shoulder by a canon ball; and he bled to death in his wife's

[1] The hierarchy at the East India Company was Apprentice (until 1694), Writer, Factor, Junior Merchant, Senior Merchant (or Chief Agent), Councillor, President and Governor. There were also Chaplains, Surgeons and Masters.

arms. The *Anne* and her consorts were then boarded and the twice-widowed Katherine consigned to captivity in the Maratha stronghold of Colaba, about fifty miles down the coast from Bombay. It must have been with some trepidation that she learnt that she was the first European female to be a prisoner of the dreaded Kanhoji Angrey,[1] otherwise 'Connajee' or 'Angria', the man destined to be the scourge of the Company for the next twenty years and the founder of a naval power that would last half a century. .....The plight of the delectable Mrs. Chown was provoking Bombay to no end and Kanhoji was ready to discuss terms if an 'Englishman of credit' would come to Colaba to discuss terms. .....Mindful of Mrs. Chown, a young Scots lieutenant offered his services. With 30,000 rupees by way of ransom, the volunteer made his way to Colaba, found Kanhoji a man of his word, and duly returned with all the prisoners.....Mrs. Chown had 'most courageously withstood of all of Angria's base usage and endured his insults beyond expectation'........the young widow was discovered in such a state of undress that the Scots lieutenant, well named Mackintosh, 'was obliged to wrap his clothes about her to cover her nakedness'. The whole experience does not, though, seem to have greatly disconcerted Mrs. Chown. A few weeks later she duly gave birth to Chown's son. The tide of sympathy persuaded the Bombay Council to grant her an allowance from Harvey's estate; and within a few months she was remarried to the

---

[1] Kanhoji Angrey, in 1712 had been appointed the Surkhail, or Grand Admiral of the Maratha fleet, and the Viceroy of Konkan. Kanhoji had been building a naval fleet from 1707, and in the same year he had sunk a Company frigate by using fast sailing fleet of 'grabs' and many-oared 'gallivats', thus becoming the scourge of the Company free-traders.

hot-headed young Gyfford. When the latter was posted to Anjengo, she no doubt heaved a becoming sigh of relief. A new husband, a new home, a new life, she must have thought." By now Katherine was already a celebrity, twice-widowed, once captured, had by now learnt to make the most of adversity, as later events were to show. In 1721 Gyfford and his emissaries numbering over a hundred were ambushed and killed. "The young Mrs. Gyfford and two other Englishwomen were quickly bundled aboard a native longboat. Four weeks later they came ashore in Madras, disheveled and destitute. Their plight excited great sympathy and even wrung from the Fort St George Council a small compensatory allowance. There was, however, some doubt whether Mrs. Gyfford would accept charity. Although barely twenty-six years old she had had the presence of mind to come away from Anjengo with the factory records and a useful sum of money which she claimed as belonging to her late husband. She knew better than to let grief get the better of business and she had every intention of extracting more than charity from her husband's employers." The scene now shifts to Calcutta, in the year 1772. Here Commodore Matthew, incharge of the Royal Squadron "was approached by a distraught but still pretty widow who was being detained in India pending payment of £9000 from her late husband's estate. Matthew listened to her long and heart-rending story with interest; and convinced that no one who heard it could fail to condemn the Company's ingratitude, promptly took the young lady under his wing and into his cabin. She was, of course, none other than Mrs. Katherine Gyfford, previously Harvey and Chown, née Coke, lately of Karwar, Colaba, and Anjengo. Together the Commodore and the widow sailed to Bombay, where old acquaintances were duly scandalized by Mrs. Gyfford's new liaison, and then to England. Years of litigation over the tangled affairs of Anjengo followed, their outcome unknown. But evidently Mrs. Gyfford returned to India for she died in Madras in 1745."

At Bombay, the exploits of Mrs. Draper[1] (Eliza Draper), and her association with Sterne, made her more famous with the English reader than all the generals and presidents who were her contemporaries in Bombay. Mrs. Draper was born in 1744, as Eliza at Anjengo,[2] in Malabar, where her father was employed in the English store. An ugly, yet an extraordinarily gifted women, the tree under which she rested after her evening stroll on the beach came to be known for about a century as "Eliza's Tree". Eliza married Daniel Draper, Secretary to Government at Bombay, twenty years her senior while he was on a visit to Anjengo. While on a trip to England she became intimate with Lawrence Sterne, from the literary circle in London, and went on to exchange letters consisting of formal expressions of interest. Following Sterne's death, his widow and her daughter, threatened to make the letters public, but Eliza was grateful that her husband was transferred to Tellicherry, seven miles from Mahe. Unfortunately for Eliza's virtuous declarations and resolve, her husband was recalled to Bombay and

---

[1] The life and times of Mrs. Draper are recorded by Dennis Kincaid, and extracted from the text.

[2] Anjeno had been acquired in 1693 by arrangement with the local *rani*, or queen, at nearby Attingal. She is said to have fallen in love with a 'beautiful' young English emissary who, although rejecting the chance of a royal wedding, 'satisfied her so well' that she could scarcely refuse his countrymen anything.

appointed Member of Council, where they lived in a house at Mazagaon, called Belvidere. Once more Eliza attracted admiration when she appeared at the balls at Government House in hoop and farthingale; factors and cadets besieged her for dances. There was not much competition, as there were only thirty-nine ladies on the station, thirty-three married, five widows, and one 'Winnifred Daries, Unmarried Women' as she was described on an invitation list. Cadets and factors would call on the Drapers in the morning (morning calls were then fashionable), but Daniel Draper's sudden interest and middle-age infatuation with their house-keeper Mrs. Leeds, compelled Eliza to seek solace in the ardent suit of a naval officer called Clark, eventually forcing her to let herself out from her house by a rope from her bedroom window, and seek refuge in Clark's ship. Eliza was received in the literary circles of London with much enthusiasm, not troubled by scruples on the impact of her flight on 'poor Draper'; she also authorized the publication of Sterne's letters to her. Eliza Draper died in 1778 and was buried at Bristol. The memory of Eliza's exploits were still fresh in the memory of the British population at Bombay, so much so, that Maria Graham writes in August 1809, that at "Mazagong , a dirty Portuguese village" which is "beautifully situated on the shore between two hills, on one of which is Mazagong house, a leading mark into the harbor. It is interesting to the admirers of sentimental writings, as this is the house from which Sterne's Eliza eloped, and perhaps may call forth the raptures of some future pensive traveler, as strongly as the sight of Anjengo does to those of the Abbé Raynal, when he remembers "that it is the birth place of Eliza."[1]

The English women coming to India were not simple damsels but resourceful individuals, as is evident from yet another episode, featuring a Miss. Elizabeth Mansell. Miss. Elizabeth Mansell's charges against Captain Cummings were investigated at great length in solemn proceedings by the President and the Council of Madras, and which formed the subject of gossip for over a year. The episode is described as follows:[2] "Miss. Mansell, the niece of a Member of Council, had come out to stay with her uncle. As soon as she landed she made a formal charge of rape against the commander of the East Indiaman in which she sailed. This was, of course, a capital charge, and Captain Cummings was arrested and confined to prison till the first hearing of the case. The captain conducted his own defence and cross-examined the prosecution witnesses with some skill. His case was an admission of intimacy with Miss. Mansell; but he alleged that from her arrival on board she had not ceased to pester him with her attentions, and when Mrs. Cummings was seeing her husband off at Portsmouth she was so alarmed at Miss. Mansell's manner towards her husband that she "burst out into tears, which he had much ado to overcome by promises of prudent behaviour". Rather early in the session Miss. Mansell's character began to suffer; one witness admitted that at Portsmouth she was caught "playing Tagg with a couple of footmen". Miss. Mansell's chief witness was a Mrs. Mary Coales who deposed that she had often seen Miss. Mansell cry and exclaim

[1] Graham, Maria. *Journal of a Residence in India*; p.5.

[2] Kincaid, Dennis. *British Social Life in India, 1608-1937.* p.70-71.

"She could never be happy" on account of the captain's behaviour. Captain Cummings put to her this subtle question: "Did she not fall into a passion *whenever I took any notice of you*?" Simpering complacently, Mrs. Coales admitted this was so. Other witnesses, cited to prove Miss. Mansell's distress and despair, made increasingly damaging admissions. Mark Romney, for instance, saw her sitting on a chair beside the captain at eleven o'clock one night, and she suddenly put her arm around his neck, called him "her dear captain" and gave him a kiss. Mark Romney thought this entertaining that he "beckoned to a midshipman, who was a small distance off, to come and look; who put his finger to his nose but would not come". Other witnesses admitted that Miss. Mansell had been intimate with two other young men on the boat, so that at this stage the Council broke up the trial and formally acquitted the captain. Obviously Miss. Mansell ought to have been prosecuted for perjury, or the captain awarded some compensation for his imprisonment; but then the prosecutrix was related to a Member of Council and so the Captain while being acquitted was treated to a severe lecture to the effect that his "relation to this young woman would be a perpetual Blot on him", since he had taken away her character. And when the wretched man exclaimed that she had no character even before she came on board, he was "stopped from proceeding in this sort."

The British dominions began to spread over India. The Battle of Plassey, fought on 23rd June 1757 marked a milestone as, the East India Company began to exercise power in Bengal, as the *zamindars* of the Twenty-Four paraganas[1] and interfered and improvised upon the administration there. With the occupation of Bengal, for the East India Company, trade now had taken a second place to acts of revenue-collection and the transformation of revenue-surplus into dividends for the Company's stockholders in Britain. The British success in the battle of Buxar,[2] in October 1764 inaugurated the phase of direct intervention in revenue arrangements[3] and administrative affairs of India, whereby 'the Company ceased to be a company of merchants and became a formidable political force.' While down South the Nizam of Hyderabad, was guaranteed the continuance of his dynasty by the Treaty of Mauslipatnam in 1768 by the Company, but the Sultan of Mysore, Haider Ali, and his son Tipu Sultan, were able to dictate their own terms to the British at Madras.

By 1772, the financial state of the East India Company was such that, failing to extract a loan from the Bank of England, it approached the government with a request for a million pounds. Parliament appointed a committee of investigation, and its startling disclosures of the 'presents' received by the Company's servants between 1757 and 1766 led to the Regulating Act of

---

[1] Territory nearly nine hundred square miles south of Calcutta which was yielding substantial revenue.

[2] The Company's forces defeated the combined forces of the Mughal Emperor Shah Alam, the Nawab of Bengal Mir Kasim, and the Nawab of Oudh.

[3] By the treaty of Allahabad, the East India Company acquired the *diwani* rights of Bihar, Bengal and Orissa, an appointment which was granted by the Mughal Emperor, who was now a pensioner of the Company.

1773. This marked the beginning of the decline of the Company as a trading power. The Act, while reorganizing the constitution of the Company, appointed a Governor-General, and established the supremacy of the parliament over the Company. A Supreme Court, consisting of a Chief Justice and three judges, was to be set up. In England, the Directors were to supply parliament with copies of all their correspondence and half-yearly accounts. A second Act authorized a loan to the Company. Warren Hastings, the Governor of Bengal from April 1772, proposed his own name for the post of Governor-General, a charge that he assumed on 20th October 1774, and was designated as the first Governor-General in Bengal, with authority over Madras and Bombay- though how it was to be exercised remained obscure. Under his administration the outlines of British India were formed. He attempted for the first time to establish the concept of a central authority, to introduce a system based not on exigencies of the moment but upon considered policy and organization. Above all, he was the first to suggest that the Company's territories in India were not just a place of investment for the shareholders, but a responsibility, an obligation requiring sympathy, understanding and good government. Hastings' relations with his Council, where he was in a minority, were difficult. His administrative reforms were carried through like a battle at sea, in a continuous running fight, until the death of a member of the council put him in a majority of one.[1]

The next important phase in the expansion of British power in India, as opposed to the Company's influence was the Pitt's India Bill of 1784. This bill established a

[1] Edwards, Michael. *British India 1772-1947.* p.24.

Board of Control comprising impartial notables. The Governor-General was invested with the power to overrule his council, as well as the Governors of Madras and Bombay. The Directors were left with only the power of patronage.

Warren Hastings left India in 1785, and was succeeded after a twenty –month interregnum by Sir John Macpherson, who acted as Governor –General from 8th February 1785 to 12th September 1786, and whose rule was described by his successor Lord Cornwallis, as a 'system of the dirtiest jobbery'.

Under Lord Cornwallis' rule, the civil service was divided into executive and judicial branches, salaries were increased, and a revenue settlement was imposed. Cornwallis went to war with Tipu Sultan and the Marathas. Towards the end of the eighteenth century the easy social relations that the British had with the Indians began to decline, though first only in Calcutta. In other parts of India, where English society was numerically small and fashionable attitudes slow to arrive, the old relations with Indians continued. The change in social atmosphere was a by-product of the policies of Lord Cornwallis, who in his desire to rid the Company officialdom of corruption and nepotism inevitably excluded Indians from the higher positions of government. Cornwallis on18th April 1789 wrote to the Court of Directors that, "I think it must be universally admitted that without a large and well-regulated body of Europeans, our hold on these valuable dominions must be very insecure." Convinced that every 'native of Hindustan' was corrupt, he replaced native judges with English judges, forcing the old Indian governing classes into isolation, leaving behind them only the Indian servant, the clerk, the merchant and the banker as representatives of India and the Indian culture. The British community took its lead from senior officials and, in particular, the Governor-General. As they withdrew from contact, so did the lesser beings. Lord Cornwallis was succeeded by Sir John Shore in1795.

Jemima Kindersley, was among the earliest English ladies to maintain her record of stay in India, and she writes about 'Madrass, or Fort St George, June 1765',[1] "You will congratulate me on being at last arrived in India, and in an English settlement; but it is only for a few days, I shall then return again to the stormy ocean: in the mean while I could not omit giving you some little, though imperfect account it must be, of this town; which it would be unpardonable to pass over without saying something in praise of, as it is without exception the prettiest place I ever saw. Madras is built entirely by the English.......The town is laid out in streets and squares; the houses neat and pretty, many of them large; in all the good houses the apartments are upstairs, and all on one floor; the rooms are large and very lofty; most of the houses are built with a *varendar*, which is a terrace on a level with the room in the front, and sometimes in the back part of the house, supported by pillars below, and a roof above supported likewise by pillars, with rails around to lean on. The *varendàrs* give a handsome appearance to the house on the outside, and are of great use, keeping out the sun by day, and in the evening are cool and pleasant to sit in. But what gives the greatest elegance to the houses is a material peculiar to the place; it is a cement or plaster call'd *channum*, made of shells of

[1] As quoted in Jane Robinson, *Unsuitable for Ladies*; p.241-242.

a very large species of oysters found in this coast; these shells, when burnt, pounded and mixed with water, form the strongest cement imaginable: if it is to be used as plaster, they mix it with whites of eggs, milk, and some other ingredients; when dry, it is as hard, and very near as beautiful as marble; the rooms, stair-cases, &c. are covered with it......"

Eliza Fay, recording her first impressions of Madras in April 1780, wrote uncannily echoing Jemima Kindersley, "There is something uncommonly striking and grand in this town and the whole appearance charms you from novelty as well as beauty. Many of the houses and public buildings are very extensive and elegant. They are covered with a sort of shell-lime which takes a polish like marble, and produces wonderful effect. I could have fancied myself transported into Italy, so magnificently are they decorated, yet with utmost taste. People here say that *chunam*, as it is called, loses its properties when transported to Bengal, where the dampness of the atmosphere prevents it from receiving that exquisite polish so much admired by all those who visit Madras".[1] She further adds about the intermingling of architectural styles and ornamentation which created a unique impact. "The free exercise of all religions being allowed, the different sects vie with each other in ornamenting their places of worship, which are, in general, well built; and from their great variety and novel forms afford much gratification, particularly when viewed from the country, as beautiful groups of trees intermingle their tall forms and majestic foliage, with which the *chunam* and rising spires, communicating such harmony, softness and elegance to the scene as to

[1] Fay, Eliza. *Original Letters from India*. p.121.

be altogether delightful—rather resembling the images that float on the imagination after reading fairy tales or the *Arabian Nights'* entertainment than anything in real life. In fact Madras *is* what I conceived Grand Cairo to be before I was so unlucky as to be undeceived". During her stay at Madras, Eliza Fay recorded the historical event of the process of the expansion of the city. She records, "(Mr. Popham) is at present laying plans for building what is called Black Town[1] .... (which) is that part of Madras which was formerly inhabited wholly by the natives, but of late many Europeans have taken houses there, rents being considerably lower than Fort St. George, which is a strong garrison built by the English, and where since have been constructed many fine houses, etc. This is considered, of course, a more fashionable place to reside in. Between the Black Town and the Fort lies Choultry Plain,[2] which being covered entirely with a whitish sand, reflects such dazzling light and intolerable heat as to render it a terrible annoyance, especially to strangers".[3]

The wonderous raptures of Eliza Fay were soon overtaken in the next fifty years by a dismissal of the city. "You ask what kind of scenery we have round Madras. Flat plains of sandy ground, covered with a little harsh

---

[1] Julia Maitland writes in the letter dated 11th January 1837, that on a Sunday evening they attended a sermon in a chapel in the Black Town. The chapel was "originally intended for the half-castes", but the present preacher, Mr. Tucker, was so good that "the Europeans will go there too."

[2] Choultry Plain was the open plain or maidan, once existing south-west of Madras. It was a residential site, the headquarters of the Madras Army. Choultry in Tamil signifies a rest-house or travelers bungalow.

[3] Fay, Eliza. *Original Letters from India.* p.124.

dry grass; half-cultivated gardens with high hedges; and large dilapidated-looking houses. Here and there we see very curious and picturesque native buildings, chiefly pagodas; but in general there is very little beauty either of architecture or scenery. Indian colouring is not for a moment to be compared with Italian for lightness, softness, or brilliancy. The sunsets are sometimes exceedingly beautiful, but in general I think the colouring is rather heavy and glaring....The number of open fields and gardens must be healthy, but there is never any fresh feeling in the air: it is all as dead and close as the air of a street. The flowers have no perfume, except the pagoda-flowers, and those are sickly, like withered jessamine; and at every turn in the road one meets with the smell of native cookery, fried cocoa-nut oil, and nasty messes of the same kind."[1]

Calcutta by the eighteenth century had become the greatest of the British Presidency towns. This city was described by Robert Clive as, "one of the most wicked Places in the Universe. Corruption , Licentiousness and a want of Principle seem to possessed the Minds of all the Civil Servants, by frequent bad examples they have grown callous, Rapacious and Luxurious beyond Conception, and the Incapacity and Iniquity of some of the Youth of others.........." It was against the backdrop of this city that Mrs. Sherwood described the social practices of the English, "...the splendid sloth and the languid debauchery of European Society in those days—English gentlemen, overwhelmed with the consequences of extravagance, hampered by Hindoo women and by crowds of olive-coloured children, without either the will or the power

[1] Maitland, Julia. *Letters from Madras.* 9th January 1837, p.47-48.

to leave the shores of India...... Great men rode about in State coaches, with a dozen servants running before and behind them to bawl their titles; and little men lounged in palanquins or drove a chariot for which they never intended to pay, drawn by horses which they had bullied or cajoled out of the stables of wealthy Baboos............."[1]

The town of Calcutta, in 1780, is described through the eyes of Eliza Fay as: "Calcutta, you know, is on the Hooghly, a branch of the Ganges; and, as you enter Garden Reach, which extends nine miles below the town, the most interesting views that can possibly be imagined greet the eye. The banks of the river are, as one may say, absolutely studded with elegant mansions here, as at Madras, garden-houses. These houses are surrounded by groves and lawns, which descend to the waters' edge, and present a succession of whatever can delight the eye or bespeak wealth and elegance in the owners. The noble appearance of the river also, which is much wider than the Thames at London Bridge, together with the amazing variety of vessels continually passing on its surface add to the beauty of the scene..................The town of Calcutta reaches along the eastern bank of the Hooghly. As you come up past Fort William and the Esplanade it has a beautiful appearance. Esplanade Row, as it is called, which fronts the Fort, seems to be composed of palaces. The whole range, except what is taken up by the Government and Council houses, is occupied by gentlemen in the settlement. No person being allowed to reside in Fort William but such as are attached to the Army gives it greatly the advantage over Fort St. George, which is so incumbered with buildings of one kind or the other

[1] Kincaid, Dennis. *British Social Life in India, 1608-1937.* p.90-91.

that it has the more the look of a town than a military Garrison. *Our* Fort is also so well kept, and everything in such excellent order, that it is quite a curiosity to see it. All the slopes, banks, and ramparts are covered with richest verdure, which completes the enchantment of the scene". [1]

In a span of less than fifty years, the Presidency town of Calcutta had expanded vastly and grown in magnificence. Fanny Parks writes "Calcutta has been styled the City of Palaces, and it well deserves the name. The Government House stands on the Maidan, near the river; the city, and St. Andrew's Church,[2] lie behind it; to the left is that part called Chowringhee, filled with beautiful detached houses, surrounded by gardens; the verandahs, which generally rise from the basement to the highest storey, give, with their pillars, an air of lightness and beauty to the buildings, and protecting the dwellings from the sun, render them agreeable for exercise in the rainy season".[3]

The routine in the Presidency towns, more or less remained unchanged for the British women during their long stay in India. A glimpse into this routine is found, early in Eliza Fay's account from Calcutta, in a letter written in December 1780.[4] "The dinner hour ...is two, and it is customary to sit a long while at table, particularly during the cold season: for people here are mighty fond of grills

[1] Fay, Eliza. *Original Letters from India.* 22nd May 1780. p. 131-133.

[2] The beginning of the plan of this church to provide for Divine Services was pointed out in the letter of Eliza Fay written on 5th September 1781.

[3] Parks, Fanny. *Wanderings of a pilgrim* . November 1822, p.20, Vol.-I

[4] Fay, Eliza. *Original Letters from India.* p. 147-148.

and stews[1], which they season themselves and generally make very hot.....During dinner a good deal of wine is drunk, but a very little after the cloth is removed, except in bachelor's parties as they are called. For the custom of reposing, if not sleeping after dinner is so general that the streets of Calcutta are from four to five in the afternoon, almost as empty of Europeans as if it were midnight. Next come the evening airings. To the Course every one goes, though sure of being suffocated with dust. On returning from thence, tea is served and universally drunk here even during the extreme heats. After tea, either cards or music fill up the space till ten when supper is generally served." The amusements in the evenings generally consisted of 'five-card Loo', Trédille and whist were also in fashion, but the ladies did 'seldom join the latter, for, though the stakes were moderate, bets frequently ran high among gentlemen—which renders those anxious to sit down for amusement lest others should lose by their blunders. Formal visits were paid in the evening. They are generally very short, as perhaps each lady has half a dozen to make and a party waiting for her besides. Gentlemen also call to offer their respects, and if asked to put down their hat, it is considered as an invitation to supper".

The women kept themselves busy, as is evident from the routine of ladies in Madras of the eighteenth century, by buying furniture, either directly from London or bought from East Indiamen captains, to furnish the enormous rooms in which they spent long languid hours, on sofas drawn close to the doors hung with moistened grass screens through which the wind came cool and

[1] Special mention has been made of the Burdwan stew, which has been compared with the Spanish Olla Podrida.

damp. In 1754 the catalogue of the Madras library had few books which could appeal to the female heart, and their main recreation was 'repairing their complexions with rogue, with Venus Bloom and Mareshell Powder, freshening their hands and shoulders with Hungary water, lavender, and bergamot and changing their jewels and dresses. Even visitors fresh from the raffish extravagance of London commented on the gaudy ostentation of the ladies' diamonds and on the extraordinary colours and designs of their dresses.'[1] While the men were busy with their work in the factories, courts, etc. the women were forced to while away their time till dinner, which was at two or three o'clock and yet they had to wear "fashionable undress and large caps" for fear an acquaintance should call.

The memsahibs who had come to recreate a home enviournment, in an alien land, witnessed many a strange paradoxes, especially in the religious and cultural arena. The memsahibs strongly commented upon the lack of places for worship for them, even in the Presidency town of Calcutta. In September 1781, Eliza Fay writes that 'how indifferently we are provided with respect to a place of worship, Divine Services being performed in a room (not a very large one) at the Old Fort—which is a disgrace to the Settlement. They talk of building a church, and have fixed a very eligible spot whereon to erect it, but no further progress has been made in the business." Singularly, the celebration of English festival acquired an Indian idiom, which is especially evident in the celebration of Christmas. "The external appearance of the English gentleman's houses on Christmas Day is really

[1] Kincaid, Dennis. *British Social Life in India, 1608-1937.* p.76-77.

pleasing from its novelty. Large plantain trees are placed on each side of the principal entrances, and the gates and pillars, being ornamented with wreaths of flowers fancifully disposed, enliven the space. All servants, from the *Banian* down to the lowest menial, bring presents of fish and fruit; for these, it is true, we are obliged in many instances to make a return perhaps beyond the real value, but still is regarded as a compliment to our burrah-*din*. A public dinner is given at Government House to the gentlemen of the Presidency, and the evening concludes with an elegant ball and supper for the ladies. These are repeated on New Year's Day and on the King's Birthday".[1] These forms of celebration continued into the next century, becoming established mores, as Fanny Parks records of the decoration of the gate-ways with plantain trees, *hars* (chaplets) and garlands of fresh flowers, and laments sorely of missing the holly and mistletoe of an English Christmas. The tradition of *bakshish* had become firmly entrenched leading to the origin of the Christmas-boxes. An amusing incident recorded, is that of the sadler, a servant, who brought five trays in honour of *kishmish*[2] (Christmas).

Half a century later Emily Eden narrates her feelings on Christmas-day, while in camp; her emotions on that day are a mixture of nostalgia for 'home', and a dislike for things Indian. The latter sentiment, becoming marked in the next century, as the novelty of India wears off, and the memsahibs arrive to recreate the domestic felicity of 'home', with lessened desire to intermingle and interact

---

[1] Fay, Eliza. *Original Letters from India.* 27th January 1781, from Calcutta.

[2] Kishmish is the Indian term for Sultana raisins.

with the Indian populace. "This is our third Christmas-day, so, however appearances are against it, time does really roll on. I don't know why, but I am particularly *Indianly* low to-day. There is such a horrid mixture of sights and sounds for Christmas. The servants have hung garlands at the doors of our tents, and (which is very wrong) my soul recoiled when they all assembled, and in their patios wished us, I suppose, a happy Christmas. Somehow a detestation of the Hindustani language sounding all round us came over me in a very inexplicable manner. Then, though nothing could be better than the way in which Mr. Y. performed the service, still it was in a tent, and unnatural, and we were kneeling just where the Prince of Lucknow and his son, and their turbaned attendants, were sitting on Saturday at the durbar, and there was nobody except G. with whom I felt any real communion of heart and feelings. So, you see, I just cried for you and some others, and I dare say I shall be better after luncheon."[1]

Life in Calcutta, and other towns, was made comfortable for the memsahib by the army of servants. William Hickey, a bachelor English lawyer of Calcutta, and not a wealthy man by Calcutta standards, in his Memoirs while giving a picture of late eighteenth century Calcutta, writes that he employed sixty-three servants; including eight whose only duty was to wait at the table, three men were employed to cut the grass in the garden, four grooms and one coachman, two bakers, two cooks, a hairdresser, and, nine valets. The richer denizens employed servants above hundred. The wig-barber was a necessity in every fashionable house hold, as was the *hookaburdar*, who

[1] Eden, Emily. *Up the Country*. Vol-I, p.77-78.

not only tended the gentleman's hookahs at home, kept the silver chains and rosettes brightly polished, blew on the charcoal and renewed the rose-water, and also accompanied his master abroad even to the dinners at Government House. To the lady of the house, it was with these very servants that a war of attrition was inevitable, as they tried to establish the English rules for hired help in alien surroundings. Eliza Fay remarked that the servants were 'a set of thieves', who unlike their English counterparts had no 'sense of shame'. This she illustrates with two examples, the first being that of her experiences with her *khansaman*. "My *khansaman* (house-steward) brought in a charge of a gallon of milk and thirteen eggs for making scarcely a pint and half of custard. This was so barefaced a cheat that I refused to allow it: on which he gave me warning. I sent for another, and, after I had hired him, said I: "Now take notice, friend, I have enquired into the market price of every article that enters my house and will not submit to imposition. You must, therefore, agree to deliver in a just account to me every morning". What reply you think he made! Why, he demanded double wages. You may be sure that I dismissed him, and have since forgiven the first, but not till he had salaamed to my foot: this being the most abject token of submission." Once aware of the habits of the servants, the lady of the house would slip into an uneasy truce so that the house could be run smoothly: "I know him to be a rogue, and so they are all: but, as he understands me now, he will perhaps be induced to use rather more moderation in his attempt to defraud. At first, he used to charge me with twelve ounces of butter a day for each person: now he grants that the consumption is only four ounces".[1]

As the memsahibs settled into their households, they displayed their superior command in the gendered domain of the private spaces, by introducing economy, a measure which was not appreciated by the Indian servants who tended to avoid employment in tight-fisted households. Eliza Fay laments the fact that the 'servants have no profit by staying with me', as at the other gentleman's house they made 'a rupee a day at least besides his wages, but here, if he only charges an *anna* or two more, it is sure to be taken off'. The grouse of the chatelaine of the home was with the *banias*, who took advantage of the prevalent custom whereby 'no one pays or receives money but through the medium of these people, who have their profit on everything that comes into the house'. These *banias* were the scourge of the British women's attempts to economize as it was remarked that the facility of obtaining credit was beyond what one could have imagined. "The European shopkeepers are always ready to send in goods, and the *banias* are so anxious to get into employment that they outbid each other. One says: 'Master had better take me: I will advance five thousand:' another offers seven, and perhaps a third ten thousand. A Company's servant particularly will always find numbers ready to support his extravagance. It is not uncommon to see Writers within a few months after their arrival dashing away on the course four-in-hand. Allowing for the inconsiderateness of youth, it is surprising if some become deeply embarrassed? Several have been pointed out to me who in the course have of two

[1] Fay, Eliza. *Original Letters from India*. Letter of 29th August 1780, from Calcutta. p.138-139.

or three years have involved themselves almost beyond hope of redemption. The interest on money being twelve percent, and the *bania* taking care to secure bonds for whatever he advances, making up accounts yearly and adding the sum due for interest,[1] his thoughtless *master* (as he calls him—but in fact his slave) soon finds his debt doubled, and dares not complain unless he has the means of release which alas! are denied to him".[2]

Not only were the servants 'difficult', but their religious prejudices hampered in the efficient discharge of duties. Eliza Fay remarked that none of the 'Mahomedan servants on account of an old custom.....would not touch a plate in which pork had been laid. So that, whenever we had any at our table, our plates remained till the cook or his mate came up to change them. This being represented as a religious prejudice[3], I felt it right to give way, however ridiculous it might appear". She goes on to narrate the episode that in order to get rid of this inconvenience the Europeans at Calcutta decided to follow the example set by the Army at Fort St. William, 'who had emancipated themselves from any such restraint'. The Muslim servants employed in civilian households were given the ultimatum of 'doing the same as those of the officers of the Fort or quitting their places'; within four days of quitting, the very same servants begged for reinstatement, as the only penalty incurred by touching the plates was 'the necessity of bathing afterwards'. And thus was a problem resolved which had agitated the minds of the British

---

[1] The precise interest to the greatest exactitude were maintained, as cowries were used , where 5120 cowries went into making a rupee.

[2] Fay, Eliza. *Original Letters from India.* p.141.

[3] According to Muslim traditions pigs are considered polluting.

ladies. Despite measures adopted by the memsahibs in Calcutta towards the close of the eighteenth century to resolve this very issue, it appears that these measures had only limited success. The practice of religious prejudice of house-servants continued even till the close of the nineteenth century, as noticed by a female traveler, who was in India for barely three months. She noticed at Bombay, that "Miss P—y's "*hamal*" or housemaid, (only he is a man!) is of a rather good caste, and would not touch our food, or do several things that the other servants would not object to do so".[1]

The early sense of understanding the services which could be rendered by the Indian servants evolved into a system of profiling them. Muslims were preferred as bearers, perhaps as a consequence of the British view, widespread after the Mutiny, that Muslims were more loyal than the Hindus—and more straightforward, a quality which was often attributed to the fact that they worshipped only one God and were 'people of the book' just like the Christians. In the North, the servants were more likely to be Muslims because there were more of them around. Hindu servants could come from any caste. The sweepers, by the nature of their task, were bound to be untouchables. Brahmins did not generally act as cooks because the ingredients employed in European cooking would have had a defiling impact on their caste standing. The poorer Brahmins, of whom there were many, frequently worked as gardeners. Indian Christians were mostly disliked, despite the civilizing impact of the Christian religion, on the ground that they were

---

[1] Ford, Helen C. *Travels in India and Ceylon*.p.25.

insincere in their conversion, and hence made dishonest servants.[1]

In Calcutta, of the eighteenth century, as there were more ladies as compared to other British settlements, much space in the local newspapers was taken up by allusions of present gossip. There is a reference to Miss Wrangham's charms on a member of the Government, "Counsellor Feeble now constantly drinks a sort of cordial dram which he calls W-g-h eye-water and of which he drinks so freely that he, d'ye see, retires tipsy—he, he!". "*March 1781—Lost* on the Course, last Monday evening, Buxey Clumsey's heart whilst he stood simpering at the footstep of Hooka Turban's carriage."[2] Arising out of the fact of that there were very few British women in any town, as compared to the British men, there were few unmarried men without a mistress, who were often Indian women, or half-caste mistresses. Such irregular unions were seldom a secret, as is evident from the satiric poem "The Grand Master", which is an account of the birth of *Qui Hi's* son. Fanny Parks provides the episodic idea behind *Qui Hi.* She recollected in her journal,[3] "In India we use nobells to call servants; but as the chaprāsis are always in attendance just without the door, if you want one, you say "*Qui hy*?" i.e. "is there any one?"-----or "*Kon hy*?"-"who is there?" When a servant appears. For this reason old Indians are called *Qui hys*.

Poor *Gulab* now was in *that* way,
That those who "love their lords" should be;
And in a week, to *Qui Hi's* joy,
Produced our youth a chopping joy.

[1] Mac Millar, M. *Women of the Raj.* p.144.

[2] Kincaid, Dennis. *British Social Life in India, 1608-1937.* p.104.

[3] Parks, Fanny. *Wanderings of a pilgrim.* August 4th 1830, p.45, Vol.-I

The duce! said *Qui Hi* with a curse;
It's well, however, it's no worse;
For what the d—l could he do,
If he had manufactur'd two'
Like other ladies that he knew?
Our hero now, without pretence,
Thought himself of *some consequence*;
A child he'd got, and what was curious,
He knew the infant was not spurious;
For though *Qui Hi* was never tied
By licence to his Indian bride,
Yet he was confident that she
Had acted with fidelity,
But now he finds that he must submit
To European damsel's wit.
Wherever *Qui Hi* did appear,
The spinsters titter, chat and jeer.
"O dear, Miss *Pinchback* , have you heard,
La! what a scandal—on my word."
"What", (said Miss Pinchback) "prithe say?
Tell us the scandal of the day?"
"The fellow! But we'll send him out
Of our society, no doubt;
There is sweet Miss *Wabina Stocking*,
She can repeat it—'tis so shocking;
That *Qui Hi's* creature, it is said,
The other day was brought to bed."
"Oh heaven!" exclaimed Miss Indigo
"And could he have us'd me so?
And with a *black one* too connected—
A precious precedent's begun,
A mistress first, and then a son."

This satirical poem, 'The Adventures of Qui Hi' (1816), in fact touched a raw nerve of every memsahib who came to India in the eighteenth and nineteenth century, as the majority of the Englishmen were likely to have a *bibi* (i.e. a common law wife or a long term consort, of Indian origin, of an Englishman), complete with her separate establishment, and off-springs, the by-products of this union. This state of affairs came to arise from the fact that the experiment of importing British women to India was abandoned by the East India Company in the eighteenth century, leaving the members of the John Company to find women/wives for themselves. What is more, the British men normally expected that they would spend the rest of their days in India, and that, coupled with the fact that their own society was very small, meant that they were thrown into closer contact with India and Indians. Until the end of the eighteenth century, the number of European women was so small that every spinster and widow was snapped up at once, irrespective of her physical charms. Around 1790, there were only 250 European women in Calcutta, but 4,000 men. Therefore it was a normal practice for *sahibs* to keep Indian *bibis* and maintain *zenanas*, as a solution to their sexual isolation. Resorting to native mistresses was not only a piece of erotic expediency, but these 'sleeping dictionaries' were considered a delightful method of learning the language, customs, manners of the country and its inhabitants. Captain Williamson, who spent twenty years in the Company's service in India, in his famous guidebook *East India Vademecum* (1810) justified the practice of keeping Indian mistresses as being far more economical than maintaining European wives and as demanded by the exigency of the situation of the expatriate bachelor. He observes, "young men attach themselves to the women of the country and acquire a liking or taste for the society and customs which soon supersedes every other attraction." Williamson further adds for the native mistresses that, "they will depend upon the circumstances and the disposition of the gentleman, generally speaking---a certain sum to be paid monthly: the pay of two or three female attendants, an allowance for betel; tobacco, shoes, clothes and gold and silver ornaments." The total estimated cost of which according to Williamson was forty rupees a month, "which must certainly be considered no great price for a bosom friend, when compared with the sums laid out upon the British damsels."[1]

The genesis of these 'irregular unions', of the British men with women of non-British origin, can trace its antecedents to William Hawkins and Job Charnock. Hawkins, as the British representative at the court of Jahangir, impressed the latter so much that, the former was offered a *mansabdari* of 400 horses, which was accepted by him. As the rank was accompanied by an enormous salary, Hawkins wrote to the East India Company justifying this act of his, "I should feather my nest and doe you service". Jahangir also insisted that Hawkins should marry, the latter however insisted on marrying only a Christian girl. Jahangir brought forth a Christian girl from Armenia, from his palace and the nuptials were solemnized. Hawkins was "married" by his English servant Nicholas, and this marriage was later legalized by a Chaplain at Surat. Hawkins died en-route,

[1] Neville, Pran. *Rare Glimpses fo the Raj*. p.6-7.

while on his return journey to England. Mrs. Hawkins arrived in London, made a considerable nuisance of herself to the Company and married Gabriel Towerson, a senior servant of the Company. [1]

Job Charnock, the founder of a fort at Kalikatta (a village, which was later to become Calcutta), too had a *bibi*. She was a Brahmin widow, Leela, who had been rescued by Job Charnock, while she was about to commit *sati* at Patna, Bihar. Charnock renamed her Maria, and they enjoyed together for twenty-five long years, their association ending with Maria's death in 1687. Together they had four children; one son (who would predecease Charnock), and three daughters, Mary, Elizabeth and Katherine, who were baptized at Madras. All three daughters married Englishmen, the eldest Mary was married to the first President of Bengal, Sir Charles Eyre, who was also Charnock's successor.

The civilians and soldiers alike were thus encouraged to take native wives and mistresses (*bibis*), who were spoken about in hushed whispers among the memsahibs. Fanny Parks friend writes to her about one such personality, in a note of high pitched horror. "Did you ever hear of Colonel Gardner? he is married to a native princess.........His son's wife is the sister of the *legal* queen of our present worthy sovereign of Oude....... Colonel Gardner, who is a very gentlemanlike person, I hear, of the old school, was educated in France some fifty years ago."[2]

The famous earliest account of an association with a *bibi* is that of William Hickey, the attorney in Calcutta

---

[1] Gardner, Brian. *The East India Company,* p.33

[2] Parks, Fanny. *Wanderings of a pilgrim*. October 1828, p.90, Vol.-I.

in 1790's who through his memoirs has made immortal the 'lovely Jemdanee, as gentle and affectionately attached a girl as ever a man was blessed with." The acknowledgement of these bonds was universally known and accepted, and even the Governor-General, Sir John Shore (1793-1798), and the Governor of Bombay and members of his Council, publicly kept native women. David Ochterlony, the British Resident of Delhi (1803), lived like a royal prince and used to take air in the evening accompanied by his thirteen *bibis* riding elephants.

These irregular unions between the British and the Indian women created a breed of "half-castes". There is a rather an unkind legend which was current in the last decades of the nineteenth century, of a street urchin transported to Calcutta who said, " God made white men, and God made coloured men, but the English Tommy, he made d—d half-castes". Emily Eden following an interaction with James Skinner, writes, "He is a native of this country, a half-caste, but very black, and talks broken English. He has had a regiment of irregular horses for the last forty years, and has done all sorts of gallant things,......has made several fortunes and lost them; has built himself very fine houses; and has his zenana and heaps of black sons like any other native."[1] Till the middle of the nineteenth century, the offspring's of these mixed unions were not ostracized. In 1848 Emily Metcalfe, while staying with her father, who was a senior official at Delhi, called on happily at families, with mixed Indian blood. She records in her journal, "both Mrs. Foster and her sister Mrs. Fuller were enormously stout people, and being half-castes, were dark in complexion and spoke

[1] Eden, Emily. *Up the Country*. Vol.-I, p.136.

English with a very curious accent. And as both were dressed in white cotton dresses made like bedgowns, they presented a very curious spectacle to a newcomer. They were, however, excellent old ladies, and their sons and daughters were all connected with the British Army in India."

In the third decade of the nineteenth century, and with the introduction of the overland route, English girls started coming to India in large numbers to hunt for husbands, the practice of keeping *bibis* came under the severe attack and criticism from the memsahibs, who viewed the *bibis* as a threat to themselves and scandalous to the position of the ruling class. The memsahibs were jealous of the *bibis*, the average British lady, and even a memsahib even if in sympathy with her Indian women, was wont to be dismissive of their Indian counterparts. "I once saw two apparently very beautiful women: they use so much art, however, as it renders it difficult to judge what claim they really have to that appellation. Their whole time is taken up in decorating their persons. The hair, eye-lids, eyebrows, teeth, hands, and nails all undergo certain processes to render them more completely fascinating. Nor can one seriously blame their having recourse to these or the like artifices, the motive being to secure the affections of a husband or to counteract the plans of a rival".[1]

Mrs. Mary Martha Sherwood, a prolific author of stories with religious content, wrote that "many an English wife lost her life from the jealousy of the native favourites". This sentiment, extreme in its interpretation, apparently discounts the memsahibs' subtle advocacy

[1] Fay, Eliza. *Original Letters from India*. p.165.

of ideas to undermine the position of their gender adversaries, and the offsprings of this union. It was recorded by Mary Frances Billington, that as a race (i.e. the half-castes) "they seem to possess the faculty of uniting the worse qualities of both sides. Here and there they may be found one superior to the usual attributes, and in the case of women, those who overcome their tendencies to a backboneless, flabby inertia generally have energy and perseverance enough to carry them through the course of their study (i.e. education).[1] From sympathy arising out of the Christian sentiment of helping the down-trodden and charity, the half-caste women were trained for tasks as *ayahs,* which were deemed most suitable for them. "My new *ayah*, Mary O'Neil, is a very attractive person, a half-caste; she was brought up at the Military Orphan School—was married at twelve years to a man forty years older than herself who came and ***chose*** her from the school as was the custom—she is a little more than twenty now. He went home to England leaving her here. She had six sisters who all married in the same way, most of them happily."[2]

By the beginning of the twentieth century, there were several tens of thousands of what were called by the Government of India, the Domiciled Europeans, and, the Eurasians[3]. The distinction was between those of pure European blood and those of mixed descent. The latter were the cynosure of the contempt of the Europeans. The Eurasians were not wanting to be Indians and they were

---

[1] Billington, M.F. *Women in India*. p.94

[2] Eden, Fanny. November 14th 1838; *The Third Journal*; p.161

[3] During the nineteenth century the British living in India were known as Anglo-Indians, while the people of British Indian descent were called Eurasians.

left in a state of suspense, as the Europeans did not accept them as being part of the ruling class. The Eurasians were not asked to join the Clubs nor invited to the best parties; and the English nannies refused to mix with them. The British society laughed at their sing-song accent; at the names they gave to their daughters—Blossom, Honeydew, Hyacinth; and at the way they talked of a Home they had never seen. So open was the contempt of the Europeans, that the Eurasian girls, who were very often beautiful, tried all means of obliterating any hint of Indian blood with powder and patent preparations, which promised "Four shades whiter in four weeks". Their universal dream was to marry a British husband and go Home.[1] The antecedents of this contempt were already evident, even in the attitude of the officials, by the middle of the nineteenth century. Calcutta society was affronted by the way in which Lord William Bentinck, the Governor-General of India (1827-1835), and his amiable scatter-brained Irish wife—whose advise he always sought before taking any decision—threw open the doors of the Government House to all and sundry, even to the ships' stewards and the "less elevated" Indians; though they tended to draw the line at Eurasians.

A reverse scenario was distressing to the British population in India, when it appeared that some British women might encourage the prospect of marriage to Indian men. When the Maharajah of Patiala, in 1893, expressed the desire to marry Miss Florry Bryan, a music hall entertainer, the Government of India took steps to discourage him. These initiatives were not because the prospective bride came from the wrong class but

[1] Mac Millan, M. *Women of the Raj*. p.47.

because she came from the ruling race of India, and was happy to marry a man, no doubt of aristocratic lineage, but who belonged to the class of the ruled. The British Government wrote to the Maharajah that the marriage will "render your position both with Europeans and Indians most embarrassing."[1] The Maharajah, however, ignored the warning and went ahead with the marriage.

For memsahibs at Calcutta, during the tenure of Warren Hastings, an agitation was brewing within their small community on the issue of etiquette, as the incumbent Governor-General's would become spouse was a Franconian baroness awaiting divorce, to become the legally wedded wife of the first Governor-General. Warren Hastings, on his return to India for a second time, met the wife (Marian Imhoff) of a noble German portrait-painter, whom he apparently conquered. She was to become his constant companion, and with whom he was to live. In 1777, she obtained her divorce; it is alleged that Warren Hastings bought off the husband of his prospective bride (Marian Imhoff), who became Mrs. Hastings in the very same year. The first problem of etiquette was 'what was the Governor-General's wife to be called?' The foreigners, for whom she had a decidedly marked preference despite her English marriage called her 'milady Hastings' or 'Lady Hastings', while the English called her 'Lady Governess', was due to some inapposite comparison was with Margaret of Parma. Gradually the procedure of etiquette became settled. When the Lady Governess entered a drawing-room she was welcomed by a general cry of greeting from all the ladies. Then each lady set herself to catch the eye of the Lady Governess.

---

[1] Ibid. p.106.

Mrs. Fay was instructed that "You must fix your eyes on her and never take them off till she notices you." So the ladies sat round in a circle, staring. The Lady Governess would select one lady and acknowledge her stare with a 'complacent glance' to which the lady replied with a 'respectful bend'. A brief conversation followed, of almost royal banality; while the other ladies continued their purposeful stares, each expecting to be the next honoured with notice. But where there were no precedents for such a lofty situation, it was inevitable that Mrs. Hastings, a foreigner, should offend many. Her every action was spied upon and criticized by the faction opposed to her husband. Acceptance of an invitation was sneered at, a refusal caused mortal offense. Even in the Lady Governess's relations with her personal friends the critics insisted on unearthing extravagant motives. Thus when Mrs. Hastings sat for some time talking to Lady Impey, Philip Francis was revolted and scribbled in his diary: "*Vulgo.* Toad-eating." Then Lady Impey invited Mrs. Hastings to supper to meet Mrs. Wheeler who had recently arrived from England. Mrs. Hastings pleading an indisposition declined, but no one believed the indisposition. Mrs. Wheeler had brought some new clothes with her from London, in particular a hoop of astounding size concerning which all drawing-rooms had been agog. It was assumed that in any ordinary circumstances, Mrs. Hastings would be as anxious as anyone to see Mrs. Wheeler's wardrobe. There must be some sinister reason behind the refusal. Had she quarreled with Lady Impey? Francis put it about that she had and exclaimed in his diary that Mrs. Hastings' letter was 'an intended slight'.

Probably the real reason, apart from the indisposition, was that Mrs. Hastings was disappointingly uninterested in Calcutta fashions. She dressed to please herself; and her knowledge of Paris fashions and styles were far in advance of the Calcutta ladies. She had many correspondents in England and France who regularly reported to her each new fad and fashion. A friend wrote to her that smart women in London "are grown so Young as not only to appear in their Sashes but their Shifts". And presently the Lady Governess startled Calcutta by the juvenile air of her clothes. Mrs. Fay tittered at this 'infantile simplicity' and breathlessly complained of 'her whole dress being at variance with our present modes which are certainly not so, perhaps for that reason she has chosen to depart from them'. But when Mrs. Hastings appeared at a ball without powder, her beautiful hair brushed back in artfully calculated disorder like a Greuze milkmaid's, the contrast with the toppling head-dresses of the other guests was so remarkable that Mrs. Fay could only grumble that Mrs. Hastings' 'rank sets her above the necessity of studying anything but the whim of the moment'. Fuel to this fire was added by James Augustus Hickey, an eccentric Irishman, who was a contemporary of Warren Hastings in Calcutta, and wrote articles criticizing the activities of Lady Hastings in his newspapers, the *Bengal Gazette* or the *Calcutta General Advertiser*, the first English language newspapers to be printed and published in the sub-continent.

In the light of the disdain which was heaped on Lady Hastings, it is generally held that "Lady Moira (wife of the Marquess of Hastings) was the first Lady Sahib to reign at

Government House (from 1813 to 1815)"[1]. This is so held as Lady Cornwallis, wife of Lord Cornwallis (1786-1793) was prevented from joining her husband in India, due to family cares. Sir John Shore (1793-1798), the Governor-General of India, had a native wife. Lord Wellesley (1798-1805),while he was the Governor-General of India, had only one regret, that he was unable to take his wife with him. They had been married only for three years, but she had had five of his children before that. Wellesley's friends advised him that such a situation might cause embarrassing difficulties for the new Governor-General, even in the loose moral climate of Calcutta. Wellesley adored his children. He told a friend, named as guardian in his will: "Whatever may have been the folly which produced these little children, I am sure you have too much real feeling not to agree with me that they are a charge as dear and sacred as if they had been born under a most solemn engagement." He decided to leave his wife and family at home, with regret. "The voyage, the climate, might injure her health, and it is my duty not to separate her from her children". Lady Minto, like Lady Cornwallis, was unable to join her husband while he was the Governor-General of India from 1807-1813.

Lord Cornwallis himself led a very spartan life, as he described to his son a working day as getting on "horseback just as the dawn of the day begins to appear, ride on the same road and the same distance, pass the whole forenoon after my return from riding in doing business, and almost exactly the same portion of time every day at the table, drive out in a phaeton a little before sunset, then write or read over letters or papers

[1] Bence-Jones, Mark. *The Viceroys of India*. p.12.

on business for two hours; sit down at nine with two or three officers of my family to some fruit and biscuit and go to bed soon after the clock strikes ten". Despite Cornwallis' dull routine, society life at Calcutta blossomed under him, as never before. With an increase in shipping, the British were able to live as much as home as possible, and now, the adoption of Indian life-styles were looked down upon with askance, although not with horror. Much after the departure of Mrs. Eliza Fay from Calcutta, it was during the tenure of Lord Cornwallis that dancing was established as a form of entertainment. This was achieved by the simple dictum of Cornwallis' insistence that his guests should not merely indulge in drinking, but also engage in dancing at dances organized by him. "Before the coming of Cornwallis there had seldom been any dancing after supper. The gentlemen-dancers were too far gone in drink to venture upon any experiments of activity demanding the preservation of the perpendicular". Now the local newspaper, The *Calcutta Gazette*, reported on the minuets at Government House and their dancers on official functions. At the New Year ball of 1788 it was reported that, "Lady Chambers and Colonel Pearse led the first minuet, and the succeeding ones continued till about half-after eleven o'clock, when the supper tables presented every requisite to gratify the most refined epicurean. The ladies soon resumed the pleasures of the dance, and knit the rural braid, in emulation of the poet's sister graces, till four in the morning". From then on, dances became a regular feature, and the details of which are recorded in the newspapers of Calcutta: on the celebration of His Majesty's birthday on 6th December 1792, the ball was opened by Lady Jones, wife of Sir

William Jones, the eminent orientalist; then on the first anniversary of the victory at Seringapatnam on 6th February 1793 a superb entertainment was given at Calcutta Theatre, where at 11o'clock the ball commenced with a figure dance elegantly performed by Mrs. Haldane, Mrs. Montgomery, Mrs. Barlow, Mrs. Peter Murray, Mrs. Collins, Miss Mackintosh and Miss Frail. Later, on March 27th 1793, another ball was held; and, on the evening of 3rd December 1793 a ball was held on the occasion of the King's birthday, and the ball at the Calcutta Theatre was opened by Mrs. Chapman and Sir George Leith, and the minutes continued till near 12 o'clock, when the company retired to a very elegant supper, and, after supper country-dances commenced, which were continued with great spirit till 4 o'clock in the morning. By 1793, the ladies were accustomed to dancing from 9 in the evening till 5 o'clock in the morning, and by the beginning of the nineteenth century, the ladies according to Lord Valentia,[1] were in the habit not unfrequently of dancing themselves into the grave. Lord Valentia wrote, "Consumptions are very frequent among the ladies, which I attribute, in a grand measure, to incessant dancing even during the hottest weather. After such a violent exercise they go into the verandas and expose themselves to a cool breeze and damp atmosphere".

While the dances gained popularity, rules were devised for them, and, for the first time a set of rules appear for dances at the Calcutta Theatre in 1792.[2] These rules were detailed, and they provide a glimpse into the

[1] George Annesley, 2nd Earl of Mountnorris, was styled the 8th Lord Valentia. In 1802 he started on a trip to India, returning to England in 1806, and produced a work "Voyages and Travels to India."

[2] Carey, W.H. *The Honourable John Company*. p.82.

intricacies of the most popular form of the prevailing entertainment, amongst the ladies of the British society in India. And in some of these rules we can draw a glimpse into the rules of precedence, which was to animate the social etiquettes of the memsahibs in the next century. The rules listed were as follows:

(1) that minuets be danced on the nights of dress assemblies only.

(2) that ladies be taken out to dance minuets according to the rank their husband's hold in the King's or Hon'ble Company's service.

(3) that ladies whose husband's are not in the King's or Hon'ble Company's service, be taken out to dance minuets in the order they came into the room, and that this regulation holds good with regard to unmarried ladies. (In preservation of this rule, ladies are to receive tickets as they enter the room).

(4) that all ladies draw lots for places in country dances.

(5) that any lady allowing the first couple to pass the place corresponding with the number of her ticket shall stand the last couple for that dance.

(6) that ladies having gone down a country dance shall stand up for all the couples who are to follow, or not dance any more that night.

(7) that hookers be not admitted to the ballroom during any part of the night (but hookers might be admitted to the supper rooms, to the card rooms, to the boxes in the theatre, and to each side of the assembly room, between the large pillars and the walls).

Dancing had become so popular an entertainment that lessons were offered to the interested. An advertisement of 1795 in a newspaper of Calcutta states that, "Mr. Macdonald presents his respects to the ladies and gentlemen amateurs of dancing, and informs them that he will instruct any lady or gentlemen, who are in the habit of dancing, in the fashionable Scotch step, and its application to the country dancing, for *sicca* rupees 100. Besides the fashionable step, the athletic and agile, may be taught a variety of Scotch steps, equally elegant, but more difficult in the execution, for an additional charge".

The fact that the presence of English ladies was scarce had an impact on the patterns of dance, making a ball a different affair from the same scene in England. "In the first place, the company includes no ladies—at least, of the softer sex; for doubtless there are the usual proportions in breeches. The absence of elderly persons in Indian society is one of the first things that strike a new arrival. At a certain age, people usually leave the country, and thus there is always degree youthfulness about the company one meets. But, strange to say, young unmarried ladies are as scarce as old ones, and naturally more in demand: consequently, a lady's dancing days last as long as she remains in India, and a man has the satisfaction of seeing the mother of his six children as much in request, even among young sparks, as before he married her, while any damsel not yet wedded has as many partners on hand as she could accommodate in a week. Hence, the light fantastic toe has enough to do, and has to keep up the steam to the end of the chapter..."[1]

---

[1] Carey, W.H. *The Honourable John Company*. p.83.

The memsahibs in their first brush with the exotica of India were attracted to documenting the caste system, the social rituals and festivals, and the picturesque details of the monuments of India, but it was ornamentation and display of the marriage ceremonies and customs, that attracted them the most. Eliza Fay writes, "I had the opportunity of witnessing the marriage procession of a rich Hindoo. The bride, as I was told, sat in the same palanquin with the bridegroom which was splendidly ornamented. They were accompanied by all the relations on both sides, dressed in the most superb manner—some on horseback, some on elephants. Bands of dancing girls and musicians (I understand) preceded them. In the evening there were fire-works at the bride's fathers house, and the appearance of much feasting, but no European was present. This wedding was of a nature by no means uncommon here. A rich man had an only daughter, and he bargained to dispose of her, or rather to take for her a husband out of a poor man's family, but of his own *caste*: for this is indispensible. In this case the bridegroom is brought to the home of his father-in-law's house and becomes a member of the family. So that, although the law prohibits a man from giving dowry with his daughter, yet, you see, he does it in effect, since he gives a house to a man who wants one—in fact a fortune saddled with an encumbrance. In a few years perhaps the old man may die, and the young one having fulfilled the wishes of his parents and provide for his wants may employ some of his female relations to look around the poorer families of his caste for a pretty girl, whom he will take as second wife, tho' the first always retains the pre-eminence and governs the house; nor can the husband devote more of his time to one than the other, the law compelling him to live with them alternatively. You may be sure that the account is strictly kept".[1]

In 1798 when Richard Wellesley became the Governor-General of India (1798-1805), he came accompanied by his brother Arthur, (later Duke of Wellington), empire building in India began in right earnestness. Tipu Sultan was defeated at the battle of Seringpatnam, and the British annexed the coasts of Kanara and Malabar, followed by Tanjore in 1799. When the Nawab of Arcot died, Carnatic was also annexed. In 1803 the British forces entered Delhi and the reigning Mughal monarch conferred on General Lake the title of 'Sword of the State'. Within six years, from holding a few pockets of influence, the East India Company had expanded into a major power holding Bengal, Southern India; its troops were stationed at Poona and Hyderabad; its Residents, or Agents at every native court. Only Rajputana, Sind and Punjab remained outside the net. Wellesley's policy proved to be his undoing, as the Directors of the East India Company saw financial ruin in his wars of aggrandizement. However Wellesley's attitude strengthened the racial arrogance of the British as 'imperialism needs the backing of pride, the consciousness of superiority'. And in pursuance of the sentiment, Wellesley furthered Cornwallis's policy of keeping the Indians out from public service, but by also banning all Indians and Eurasians from official social occasions.

From the advent of the British in India till the close of the eighteenth century, the profile of the 'memsahibs' was still an enigma, arising from the fact that initially the entry

---

[1] Fay, Eliza. *Original Letters from India*. p.164-165.

of the British women, in an alien country were frowned upon, where the British had only mercantile interests. As the East India Company became a landowner in India, the British women began to gradually settle with their spouses, or accompany their family members to in India, the British women encountered a dual paradox. The first being, that they found themselves juxtaposed vis-à-vis an entrenched adversarial foes in the form of the *bibis*; the second being that, amongst the community of the British women, the feminine representatives were of two types: the likes of Katherine Gyfford and Miss. Elizabeth Mansell vis-à-vis the burgeoning tribe of Jemima Kindersley, Mrs. Eliza Fay and her ilk. The term memsahibs can be applied to the latter group of women, with hindsight, but the contours of their forms and stereotypes were not as yet formalized.

Chapter III

Stabilization and Transition: Settling down in India (1800-1850)

In the nineteenth century, the East India Company began pushing further into India, partly because it had to protect its trade, and, partly because there was no longer a great power to stop it. After 1764, the British had no European rivals in India. And after the Marathas were defeated in 1818, and the Sikhs in 1849, they had no Indian rivals either. The East India Company by now had moved a long way from being a straight forward trading company; but had become **'the Raj'**, responsible for administering large parts of India. As the British presence in India grew slowly in the nineteenth century, its appearance changed enormously. "Many of the alterations had taken place before Victoria's accession, in 1837. The nabobs had departed, along with them their concubines and their opulence and the fruits of the pagoda tree. The *hookahs* or hubble-bubbles had mostly vanished, and with them the *hookah-burdar*, the servant especially employed to prepare the compound of tobacco, spices and molasses which his master would inhale through his water-pipe. The nabobs and their sartorial vulgarity had been replaced by men in black frock coats who wished to emphasize their Britishness and to demonstrate the moral and cultural superiority of their civilization. They had come not to revel in the Orient but to improve it—and in the process to limit its revelry."[1]

The character of the East India Company's employees started to change as well: free-wheeling traders and soldiers of fortune were replaced by earnest administrators. The British "men looked forward to going 'Home', when their tenure in India was over. They had no reason 'for going native', which had been widely done in the previous century. Neither did they want Indian wives; but they desired middle-class British girls who could share the high purpose of the Empire. As a consequence of this sentiment, more and more British women ventured into India, and British communities established themselves in larger cities. It, therefore, was no longer desirable, nor necessary, to get along with the Indians. The British men rarely questioned the justice of the British rule, and it was much less likely that their wives would do so."[2] The young memsahib-brides to India soon learnt the singular most important principle of being a good wife: "It meant joining the team, chanting its slogans, cheering it on." Thus from Madras to Bombay, from Punjab to Bengal, British society became remarkably similar, its preoccupations much the same. It is against this background that the role, philosophy, and

---

[1] Gilmour, David. *The Ruling Caste*. p.11.

[2] Mac. Millan. *Women of the Raj*. p14.

the sentiments of the memsahibs are to be regarded. And every where it was the same, the memsahibs concerns were less with the Raj, and more with the details of everyday life. In going about the learning of the expected patterns of behaviour the new memsahibs were guided by the senior ladies. In the process of their learning, they were to discover that the most important thing they had to learn was not about India at all, but about the British society in India.

As the first steamer sailed into Bombay harbor in 1830 through the Suez, at the head of the Red Sea, this momentous technological advance would have an impact on the social scene in India. On 20th March 1830 the *Hugh Lindsay*, a small steamer, left Bombay harbor, arriving in Suez in thirty-two days and on her next voyage reduced the time to twenty-two. Thus, before year 1836, despatches from London arrived in Bombay in two, instead of six months; and were reduced by the year 1919 to twelve days. In 1840, the Peninsular and Oriental Steamship Company signed an agreement with the Government of India to provide a regular service between the Suez and certain Indian ports. The P&O, in times to come was to become almost synonymous with the journey to India. There were other lines also, as the Anchor and Clan Lines, which ran between Liverpool and Bombay. The Calcutta Star Line made sea-journey between Liverpool and Colombo, and the Italian Rubatino Line from Genoa and Naples to Bombay. These marked improvements in sea transportation and communication between Europe and India meant that more women were able to travel out to India in less time, and the whole experience become enjoyable and more comfortable.

The cosmopolitan character of nineteenth century British India was in part due to the conditions of service and the connections of many of the Company's servants with the political circles in England. They neither desired nor expected to stay long in India. Their interests therefore remained those of the richer classes in London. But when fortunes could no longer be picked up in five years and a return to Europe was the final reward of long service, narrowness of outlook and a philistine suspicion of culture became the rule, not only in Calcutta or Bombay, but in the attitude of the British in India.

In the early decades of the nineteenth century, British women started arriving in India in increasing numbers, which contributed to the growing estrangement between the Indians and the British. The basis of this estrangement lay in the prevailing sentiment, which regarded India as a temporary abode, reflected in the writings of the women. *"Home always means England; nobody calls India home—not even those who have been here thirty years or more, and are never likely to return to Europe; even they still always speak of England as home."*[1] The British women always felt themselves as exiles, a feeling which was reinforced by the rigours of the Indian climate. A British lady writing in 1827 says, "Among the Europeans in India there are scarcely any old persons as almost everybody is a temporary resident. Here, if you search the well tenanted burying grounds of the large cities, you will discover few besides the graves of the youthful, who have been cut off by some violent disease amid the buoyancy of health, or the tombs of those of middle age arrested by death when just about to reap the fruit of long toil and

[1] Maitland, Julia. *Letters from Madras.* 11th August 1837, p.66.

privation by retiring to their native land. It is this which renders our Indian cemeteries so peculiarly melancholy: for though we bow to the decree which summons away the aged and the infirm, yet, humanly speaking, and in our blindness we are apt to pronounce the death of the young to be premature, and a fit subject of aggravated regret." [1] The atmosphere in which the land itself was an enemy affected the judgment of many, reinforcing their dislike for India, explaining the outbursts of hysteria among the British population.

It was the British ladies, who perceived themselves as temporary residents in India, and wrote about India with the irritation and nostalgia for 'Home'. This is evident when Miss Eden scribbled acidly—[2]"Miss Fane is again laid up with mosquito-bites. Mrs. Fane and Mrs. Beresford were part of Sir Henry's party, and the most conversable of the ladies we have seen—a slight tinge of London topics about them, or at least of London readiness to talk. After dinner all the ladies sit in a complete circle round the room, and the gentlemen stand at the farther end of it. I do not suppose they would have anything to say if they met but it would look better.......There are five long years before us". Another note from one of her letter says: "How some of these young men must detest their lives! Mr.__ was brought up entirely at Naples and Paris, came out in the world when he was quite a boy, and cares for nothing but society and Victor Hugo's novels, and that sort of thing. He is now stationed at B. (Beanleah), and supposed to be very lucky in being appointed to such a station. The whole concern consists of five bungalows,

[1] Mrs. Lushington. *Narrative of a Journey from Calcutta to Europe.* p.64.

[2] Kincaid, Dennis. *British Social Life in India, 1608-1937.* p.184-185.

very much like the thatched lodges at Lanley. There are three married residents: one lady has bad spirits (small blame to her), and she has never be seen; another has weak eyes, and wears a large shade about the size of a common verandah; and the other has bad health, and has her head shaved. A tour is not to be had here for love or money, so she wears a brown silk cushion with a cap pinned on top of it. The Doctor and our friend make up the rest of the society. He goes every morning to hear causes between natives about strips of land or a few rupees—that lasts till five; then he rides about an uninhabited jungle till seven; dines; reads a magazine or a new book when he can afford one, and then goes to bed. A lively life, with the thermometer at several hundred."[1]

This attitude combined with the increase of Puritan intolerance of other religions and customs, and the middle -class suspicion of foreigners had an inevitable effect on the relations between Englishmen and Indians. This distancing of relations would be evident in a small bit of conversation, reproduced further, when Mrs. Lushington asked a senior lady what she had seen of the country and its people since her first coming to India. These women brought with them the prejudices of their time, which were Christian, and narrowly so. The women were not interested in Indians, only in the inefficiencies of their servants. They wanted to create for themselves and their menfolk an island in the vast sea of India—and to a large extent they were successful. They brought a new sense of family life, and their arrival resulted in the expulsion of the native mistresses who had injected something of India into the world of the British. The insularity of

---

[1] Eden, Emily. *Up the Country*. Vol.-I, p.10.

the memsahibs was remarked upon by women on their arrival to India, "It is wonderful how little interested most of the English ladies seem by all the strange habits and ways of the natives; and it is not merely that they have grown used to it all, but that, by their own accounts, they never cared more about what goes around them than they do now. I can only suppose they have forgotten their first impressions. But this makes me wish to try and see everything that I can while the bloom of my Orientalism is fresh upon me, and before this apathy and listlessness have laid hold on me, as no doubt they will. *I asked one lady what she had seen of the country and the natives since she had come to India. "Oh, nothing!" said she: "thank goodness, I know nothing at all about them, nor I don't wish to : really I think the less one sees and knows of them the better!"*[1]

Sooner than later, Julia Maitland found herself under this apathy, and by early October of 1839 she was charmed by Bangalore as all things there reminded her of England; "The climate at this time of the year is delightful, equal to any in Europe. For the first two three days there was a good deal of fog, but it has now cleared away, and all is so cool, clear, and bright, that it is a pleasure to feel one's self breathing. The early mornings especially are as pleasant as anything as I can imagine: they have all the sweetness and freshness of an English summer. The air smells of hay and flowers, instead of ditches, dust, fried oil, curry, and onions, which are the *best* of the Madras smells. There are superb dahlias growing in the gardens, and today I saw a real staring full-blown hollyhock, which was like meeting an old friend from England, instead of the

[1] Maitland, Julia. *Letters from Madras.* 31st January 1837, p.41.

tuberoses, pomegranates, & c., I have been accustomed to see for the last two years. We have apples, pears, and peaches, and I really should know them one from the other, though it must be confessed there is a considerable family likeness, strongly reminding us of a potato; still they look like English fruit: and the boys bring baskets of raspberries for sale, which are like blackberries indeed. The English children are quite fat and rosy, and wear shoes and stockings."[1]

The ties with the mother- country were gaining in strength, as the fashions from there were emulated; even though off by the mother-country's standards by a few years. As Lady Amherst landed at Calcutta harbor, in 1823, and as a newcomer to India, she was surprised by the feminine styles visible in the city, and she wrote, "Surprised we were, at the well-fashioned dress and manner of most of the ladies." "In heavy coaches, lighter landaulet, or singular looking Shigrampoes, might be seen, bevies of British fair, in Leghorn hats, silk bonnets, blond caps, and Brussels lace veils. Feathers waving, flowers blooming, and ribands streaming, all the freaks and fancies of every French and English fashion, which may have prevailed in Europe during the last half dozen years. In India the veriest *adorateur des modes*, must be content always to be *one* year behind the belles of London and of Paris, and, in the out stations, at least two or three...but, however there is no deficiency of finery, whatever may be the *ton*, in the appearance and attire of the ladies of Bombay".[2]

---

[1] Maitland, Julia. *Letters from Madras.* 16th October 1839; p.191.

[2] Elwood, Anne Katherine. *Narrative of a Journey overland from England.* Vol.-I. p.376-377.

Emily Eden exults, in a letter dated January 1839,at the news of the arrival of dresses from England. "Such a pleasure! a letter from the agent at Calcutta to say a box of millinery has arrived at Custom House per 'Robert Small'. Mine, to a certainty! It has been rather more than seven months making its voyage, and will be three more months coming to the hills."[1] And despite the thousands of miles of seas separating the memsahibs from the homeland, the prevalent mores there continued to reign supreme in the Indian dominions. This is evident in the recording of a simple instance which shows that use of native china in India would not be viewed favourably. "What would the old dowagers of England, who doat so much on real china, say, if they were to hear that it is considered *mauvais ton* to use it in India. There, Worcester must be employed, because it is not so easily procured; and I have positively heard a very sensible lady apologizing for being so unfashionable as to have native china at her tea-table. How would the china-fanciers of Britain delight in the beautiful little cups in which the natives drink their coffee, but which in India, the English reject with disdain, and in the fine jars which are here used for the most ordinary purposes! However, when at Rome, one must do as they do at Rome, and no one at Bombay could venture to make use of Asiatic china, without running the risk of it being thought that he was too poor to purchase European."[2]

In their concerted effort to maintain the 'Englishness' in their existence, while in India, the memsahibs clung to the rituals of the homeland. ".......the natives have no idea

---

[1] Eden, Emily. *Up the Country*. Vol.-II, p.50.

[2] Elwood, Anne Katherine. *Narrative of a Journey overland from England.* Vol.-I, p.411.

of a walk for pleasure, I am convinced they frequently thought me a little insane, when they saw me, prompted by curiosity, or wishing for a little fresh air, issue forth to take a stroll amid the plantains of bananas, and cocoa-nut groves; but, in spite of the heat of these tropical climes, I could never become sufficiently Orientalized entirely to give up walking, which most of our countrywomen do in India,......"[1] An opinion which also found favour with Mrs. Meer Hassan Ali, who writes that "the retirement to Kannoge (i.e. the city of Kanauj) offered me so many pleasant ways of occupying time", and the one, most appreciated by her was that she could go on 'long walks'.[2] "Here I could indulge in long walks without incurring the penalty of a departure from established custom, which in most well-populated parts of Hindoostaun restrains European ladies from an exercise so congenial to their health and cherished habits. Should any English-woman venture to walk aboard in the city of Lucknow, for instance, – to express their most liberal opinion of the act, – she would be judged by the Natives as a person careless of the world's opinion. But here I was under no such constraint; my walks were daily recreations..."

Aided by advance in technology which made the sea-voyages swifter and less tiresome, but the British women were lured to India by the prize which lay at the end of this voyage, that which was dubbed 'three hundred dead or alive'. A phrase, "which passed into a proverb, and was stamped on the damsel's brow as plain as print."[3] The civil servants were called "three-hundred-a-year-

[1] *Ibid* p.369.

[2] Mrs. Ali, Meer Hassan. *Observations on the Mussulmauns of India.* Letter XIX.

[3] Carey, W.H. *The Honourable John Company.* p.83.

dead-or-alive-men" from the fact that their pay when they joined the service was £300 a year, and if they put in sufficient service, their widows, on the civilian's death, drew a pension of £300 a year. The meaning was that by marrying a member of the Civil Service, she secured a husband with at least three hundred pounds a year, and at his death, would be entitled to a pension from the Civil Fund to the same amount. The latter provision however was contingent on the husband having served a certain period. With this pecuniary greed fuelling the voyages to India, the British damsels no longer as honestly announced the motives for their trip to India, as was done in the eighteenth century, when 'Mrs. Anne Miller', as a friend wrote to the Governor of Madras, when she sailed for 'your parts to make her fortune; her father is a Vigntner and an honest man but has many children'. Despite the motivation for the trip being understood by all, nevertheless young women were generally schooled carefully by their parents to concentrate on making a good marriage. The prospective bride was admonished to look with scorn on the young and penniless, and was advised to encourage the advances of the elderly rich. Above all, the young girls were most certainly to set their cap at members of the Civil Service. Thus Miss Arabella Green,[1] when asked by her parents to repeat the lesson they had taught her before launching her in the marriage mart of India narrated:

[1] Aliph Cheem, *The Lays of Ind*. These were a collection of comic verse popular in the nineteenth century, and it makes fun of the serious purpose that lay behind the flirtation. 'Arabella Green' or 'The Mercenary Spin' gives the creed of a young British girl coming to India.

"I do believe in dress and ease,
And fashionable dash.
I do believe in bright rupees,
And truly worship cash.
I do believe in marriage quite,
But don't believe in gents,
Unless you bind them pretty tight
By way of settlements.
I do believe entirely in
The Civil Service ranks:
The best are worth a deal of tin'
And exactly blanks.
But I do believe that marrying
An *acting* man is fudge;
And do not fancy anything
Below a *pucka* Judge".

Women coming to India with this motive were called the "fishing-fleet". Julia Maitland enroute to India in 1836 notes amongst her companions "several Irish girls apparently on their promotion"[1], a euphemism for young women seeking husbands in India. Emily Eden too gives an oblique hint on this: "There are two Miss ___s come out from England to join a married sister, the wife of an officer in the lancers. She is very poor herself, but has eight sisters at home, so I suppose thought it right to help her family; and luckily, I think, they will not long hang on her hands. They are such pretty girls, and knowing-looking, and have brought out for their married sister, who is also very pretty, gowns and headdresses like their own. They are the only three young ladies at the station,

[1] Maitland, Julia. *Letters from Madras*. p.8.

so I suppose will have their choice of three regiments; but it is all a bad business when all is done."[1] Once these women landed on the Indian shores, everyone was anxious to inspect them, and the gentlemen to make acquaintance of the new arrivals. Acidic and unflattering comments on the mercenary motives of these visitors were already frequent. Hood's verses sum up the general impression of a girl's reason for a trip to India.

> "My heart is full—my trunks as well;
> My mind and caps are made up,
> My corsets shap'd by Mrs. Bell'
> Are promised ere I sup;
> With boots and shoes, Rivarta's best,
> And dresses by Ducé,
> And a special licence in my chest—
> I'm going to Bombay"[2]

The parties were generally more animated if the guests included unmarried ladies recently arrived from England. Lady Falkland noted about "The arrival of a cargo (if I dare term it so) of young damsels from England is one of the exciting events that marks the advent of the *cold season*. It can well be imagined that their age, height, features, dress, and manners become the topics of conversation, and as they bring the latest fashions from Europe, they are objects of interest to their own sex".

Those girls who succeeded in their mission were envied, while those who failed were always derided. A poem of 1813 satirised the frantic efforts of the

[1] Eden, Emily. *Up the Country.* Vol.-I, p.130.

[2] As quoted in Kincaid, Dennis. *British Social Life in India, 1608-1937.* p.164.

unsuccessful husband-hunters to retain their English freshness and bloom:

"Pale faded stuffs, by time grown faint
Will brighten though *art*;
A *Britain* gives their faces paint,
For sale at India's mart".

The disappointment at failure in the mission of these ladies was the source of verses which appeared in the *Illustrated Weekly of India* in December of 1936.

"Now sail the chagrined fishing fleet
Yo ho, my girls, yo ho!
Back to Putney and Byfleet
Poor girls, you were too slow!
Your Bond Street beauty sadly worn
Through dinking cocktails night and morn
With moonlight picnics until dawn
What ho! My girls, what ho!
You scan an old engagement book
Heigh ho! My girls, heigh ho!
Recalling scenes in ballroom nook
"Let go! My girls, let go!"
When Bill or Harry, Tom or Ray
Did Slap and Tickle with your play
Yet never *never* named the day
No go! my girls, no go!"

The unkind epithet of the 'fishing-fleet' for the British women is accurately summed up; as it was caustically observed. "One lady who came out in 1779 divided what she called 'the speculative ladies' into old maids, 'of the shriveled and dry description', and girls, 'educated merely to cover the surface of their mental deformity'. The odds were that their fishing would meet with success: as throughout the period of the British rule in India, European men outnumbered European women by about three to one."[1] Concrete proof of such a venture is alluded in the Second Journal of Fanny Eden, while she was at Dinapore on the 9th of November, 1837. She writes, "The ball was a most successful ball last night for. Oh, my dear Beadon (the young Writer, i.e. a junior civil servant with the East India Company) has proposed and we are so proud of having married our only young lady (i.e. Miss Sneyd). He is nephew to Lord Heytesbury and not of age yet......She is young, too, not pretty but ladylike, and being one of a very large family was sent out to a young uncle and aunt with children of their own, and her marriage is a great thing, and when we stop three weeks hence at Allahabad it will take place."

The presence of numerically greater number of countrywomen from Britain, led to increasingly persistent and incessant pressure for the abandonment of the Indian *bibis.* Englishwomen saw the *bibis* as a threat to their position and succeeded in persuading the men to distance themselves from their native connections. Over the years they inculcated a sense of racial superiority and by the middle of the nineteenth century, liaisons with native women were frowned upon and concubinage was morally outlawed. After 1857, the practice virtually died out. But it introduced a new element of the 'half-castes' who were placed on the fringes of the European society, being as they were the offsprings of the European father and the Indian mother. The memsahibs coming from Europe, in a spirit of Christian charity indulged

[1] MacMillan, Margaret. *Women of the Raj*. p.16.

in the efforts to train them and bring them up as good Christians. "I have been much pleased to visit a female orphan asylum. It seems admirably conducted, and the girls neat, and very expert at all kinds of needle-work. It is really gratifying to see so many poor creatures well brought up, and put in the way of gaining livelihood. There is likewise a male orphan asylum, where the boys are brought up to different trades. If such establishments are wanted anywhere, it is in India, where the number of half-caste, and therefore (if I may use the expression), half-parented children, exceed what one could imagine. I cannot but think it a cruelty to send children of colour to Europe, where their complexion must subject them to perpetual mortification. Here, being in their own country, and associating with those in the same situation as themselves, they have a better chance of being happy."[1]

[1] Graham, Maria. *Journal of a Residence in India.* p.128.

Chapter IV

Domesticity and Life in the Cities of India

Maria Graham described "the colonists", that is, the British men who had settled in India, and the women who arrived in India to ensnare the men who were the prizes of their sojourn into India. At a dinner hosted by the Governor of Bombay, in November 1809, to which all the English of the settlement were invited, she recounts, "There were a good many very pretty and well dressed women, a few ancient belles, and at least three men for every women.......I found our fair companions like the ladies of all country-towns I know, under-bred and over-dressed, and, with the exception of one or two, very ignorant and very grossiére. The men are in general, what a Hindoo would call of a higher caste than the women; and I generally find the merchants the most rational companions. Having, at a very early age, to depend on their own mental exertions, they acquire a steadiness and sagacity which prepare their minds for the acquisition of a variety of information, to which their commercial intercourse leads. The civil servants to government being, in Bombay, for the most part young men, are so taken up with their own imaginary importance, they disdain to learn, and have nothing to teach. Among the military I have met with many well-informed and gentlemen-like persons, but still, the great number of men, and the small number of rational companions, make a deplorable prospect to one who anticipates a long residence here."[1]

In less than thirty years the opinion had undergone a radical change and it was said that, "Few persons can leave Bombay without regret. It's lovely scenery, its hospitable society, and its civilized condition cannot but charm the English visitor; and when duty commands that he should resign its pleasures, the voyager does so with a sigh, and as his boat recedes from the shore, and the gay tents on the esplanade dwindle to mere specks, full many a wistful glance does he cast back to that distant scene of life and enjoyment."[2]

During the eighteenth century Bombay was a frontier outpost struggling against the might of the Marathas, and in the minute of 1825 Bombay had been dismissed as "of little Importance to the Company". The fall of the Peshwa and the annexation of the chief territories of the Maratha Empire promoted Bombay suddenly to be the capital of a great province. The second stage in Bombay's sudden rise was the opening of the overland route through Egypt, and the population of the city was said to be approximately 20,000.[3] The first steamer sailed from Suez to Bombay in 1830 and thereafter the passage round the Cape went

---

[1] Graham, Maria. *Journal of a Residence in India*. p.27-28.

[2] Postans, Marianna, *Cutch*. p.1-.2.

[3] Hall, Basil. *Travels in India: Ceylon and Borneo*. p.23.

gradually out of fashion. The ascendancy of the city of Bombay was evident in the when Marianna Postans recorded in early January of 1837 that "An additional interest is now given to the harbor of Bombay by the presence of the fine steam-packets which have lately been appointed to advance the interests dependent upon an overland communication. True, they add little to its picturesque effect, but they do far more: they afford a promise of civilization to the shores of India, such as no other means could compass; and, to the minds of her English sojourners, a hope which makes the exile's "heart sing for joy."[1]

Maria Graham after a voyage of twenty weeks from England landed on 26th May 1809 at Bombay, in a thick fog which heralded the onset of the rainy season in this part of the sub-continent. The sights and sounds of the country greeted her, and she describes the first few hours as, follows, when on landing at the new *bunder* (pier) she found *palankeens* waiting to convey them from the shore to the land. The mode of conveyance was described as "litters (the *palankeens)* in which one may either lie down or sit upright, with windows and sliding doors; the modern ones are little carriages, without wheels; those anciently used were of a different form, and consisted of a bed or sofa, over which an arch just high enough to admit of sitting upright; it was decorated with gold or silver bells and fringes, and had a curtain drawn occasionally over the whole. The *palankeen-* bearers are here called *hamauls,* (a word signifying carrier); they for most part wear nothing but a turban, and a cloth wrapped round their loins, a degree of nakedness which

[1] Postans, Marianna, *Cutch* .1.

does not shock one, owing to the dark colour of the skin, which, as it is unusual to the European eyes has the effect of a dress. These people chiefly come from the Maratha country, and are of the *coombee* or agricultural caste. Their wages are seven or eight rupees a month; they are a hardy race and, if trusted, honest, but otherwise they consider theft innocent, if not meritorious. Leaving the *bunder* we crossed the esplanade, which presented a gay and interesting scene, being crowded with people in carriages, on horseback, and on foot. A painter might have studied all the varieties of attitude and motion in the picturesque figures of the *koolies* employed in washing at their appropriate *tanks* or wells which are numerous on the esplanade, each tank being surrounded by broad stones, where groups of men and women are continually employed in beating the linen, while the better sort of native women, in their graceful costume, reminding one of antique sculptures, are employed in drawing, filling, or carrying water from the neighbouring wells. The Hindoo women wear a short bodice with half sleeves, which fastens behind, and is generally made of coloured brocade. The *shali*e, a long piece of coloured silk or cotton, is wrapped round the waist in form of a petticoat, which leaves part of one leg bare, while the other is covered to the ancle with long and graceful folds, gathered up in the front, so as to leave one end of the shalie to cross the breast, and from a drapery, which is sometimes thrown over the head as a veil. The Mussulman and Parsee women have nearly the same clothing, in addition to which they wear long loose trowsers. The hair is drawn back from the face, where the roots are often stained red, and fastened in a knot behind. The hands and feet of the native women are in general delicately shaped, and are covered with rings and *bangles* or bracelets, which sometimes conceal the arm as far as the elbow, and the leg as far as the calf. As the food, lodging, and the dress of the lower class of the natives cost very little, it is common to see both men and women adorned with massy rings and chains of gold and silver, round their necks, arms, waists, and legs, and the toes and fingers decked with fine filigree rings, while the ears and nose are hung with pearls and precious stones. The vanity of parents sometimes leads them to dress their children, even while infants, in this manner, which affords a temptation, not always resisted, to murder these helpless creatures for the sake of their ornaments or *joys*."[1]

Anne Katherine Elwood landed 'at about nine o'clock on the morning of the 29th July' (1825) at the harbor of Bombay. Her initial impressions of Bombay are 'delightful' as "The Island, the fort, the light-house, Colobah, with houses and barracks, intermingled with airy cocoa-nut-trees and lofty palmyras, lay outstretched before us, whilst beyond us was to be seen the Continent of India; and delightful indeed did land appear to us, after so many days tossing on the Indian Ocean."[2] The feel of the firm land below the feet and the familiarity of an English welcome served to reinforce the overwhelming sentiment of delight. "A painted box, denominated a palanquin, but to my mind very much resembling a coffin in appearance was awaiting my arrival. In this I was deposited by the *hamauls*, or bearers, took it up, and the

---

[1] Graham, Maria. *Journal of a Residence in India.* p.1-3.

[2] Elwood, Anne Katherine. *Narrative of a Journey overland from England.* Vol.-I, p.361.

gentlemen being accommodated with other vehicles and conveyances, off we all set to the Government House, the exterior of which is certainly not very superb, and not equal to that of many gentlemen's houses in England. The interior, however, appeared comfortable, and the staircase and drawing-room are handsome; but to the feeling of those just escaped from a little hot cabin, a rolling sea, and the torments of ants, cockroaches, and mosquitoes, the coolness of the air, the freshness and verdure of all around, the spacious hall, surrounded by a nobel verandah the beautiful variety of shrubs in the garden upon which it opened, were positively delightful!........The repast was served up in the Anglo-Indian style, which much resembles our *dejunes a la fourchette*. Different sorts of fish, some of which I had never seen before, and which are, I believe, peculiar to Bombay, ...*kabaubs*, ... the never failing rice and curry, and the many strange and unknown dishes made their appearance; whilst pineapples, pomegranates, shaddocks, mangoes and plantains, and custard-apples, graced the board, and seemed doubly delicious to us, from our having been so long debarred from vegetables and fruits of every kind. In the meantime, the air was fanned and kept fresh and cool by a *punkah* over our head."[1]

Julia Maitland's first impressions about India are filled with pleasure as she landed at Madras on 19th December 1836. "We landed in a great boat with twelve boatmen, all singing a queer kind of howl, and with very small matters of clothes on, but their black skins prevent them from looking so very uncomfortable as Europeans

---

[1] Elwood, Anne Katherine. *Narrative of a Journey overland from England.* Vol.-I, p.362-364.

would in the same *minus* state. The scene in the Madras Roads is the brightest and liveliest possible. The sea is completely studded with ships and boats of every size and shape, and the boats filled with crews even more quaint and picturesque than themselves. But none can compare to the catamarans, and the wonderful people that manage them. Fancy a raft of only three logs of wood, tied together at each end when they go out to sea, and untied and left out to dry on the beach when they come in again. Each catamaran has one, two, or three men to manage it: they sit crouched upon their heels, throwing their paddles about very dexterously, but remarkably unlike rowing." The lure and the anticipation of the exotica was further strengthened, as Julia writes, a week later, on the 27th of December 1836, "I think I shall like Madras very much, and I am greatly amused with all that I see and hear. The heat now is not at all oppressive, this being the cool season. The houses are so airy and large, and the air so light, that one does not feel the heat so much as one would in Italy when the temperature is the same. At present the thermometer is at 78°, but it feels so much cooler, from the draughts they keep up in every room, that I would not believe it to be more than 70°, till I looked with my own eyes. The rooms are as large as chapels, and made up of doors and windows, open day and night. I have seen so many curiosities already, that I do not know which to describe to you first—jugglers, tumblers, snake-charmers, native visitors, &c. &c.; for the last few days we have been in a constant bustle."[1]

While Bombay was 'rendered familiar by the pen and pencil of many an authoress', the first impression

---

[1] Maitland, Julia. *Letters from Madras.* p.29.

of Cutch, a province of Western India, much less visited by the memsahibs, was described by a memsahib, following on the march of her husband's regiment as: "On approaching the Province of Cutch, the coast affords few attractions to the traveller's eye, presenting as it does, a mere sandy outline, slightly diversified by a few patches of stunted vegetation, and straggling palm trees; but on landing at Mandavie, which is the principal sea-port, an appearance of wealth and unusual bustle excites the traveller's attention. A creek, which runs skirting one side of the city for about a mile inland, has its mouth filled with boats, making, mending, receiving, or discharging cargo; whilst carts of a peculiarly rude construction drawn by strong and sturdy bullocks, struggle through the heavy sand laden with goods for the interior. The inhabitants seem a busy, cheerful, and industrious race, and their peculiarly bright and varied costume gives an appearance of gaiety to the place, which is strikingly pleasing, and seldom seen in an Indian town of second rate importance. The population is principally composed of Banyans, Brahmins, and cultivators; many of whom may be seen on the outside of the town, either engaged in their several callings, loitering lazily along, or grouped together in little knots, gossiping with vehement gesticulation, on any trifling subject, of pleasure or profit. Here and there, a retainer of the *Rao* (the reigning prince of Cutch) comes swaggering along, displaying the superior height, aquiline nose, and long moustache of the Rajpoot tribe; his arms are a sword, shield, and matchlock, and his dress and bearing are marked by an air of mingled haughtiness, foppery, and independence. Then are seen swarthy but fine-limbed children, rolling on the soft sand in childish glee, and shouting with joy, as a horseman passes them, circling and passaging with consummate skill, his gaily decorated steed. Near these, a water-carrier urges on his bullock, which, laden with the water bags, slowly saunters forward, whilst his master slowly smokes his hookah, and indulges in a passing chat with the women, who, gracefully bearing their earthen water-vessels on their heads are returning to the well to which he journeys. Lastly, are groups of women, employed in sifting grain from light baskets, in which they display the most graceful attitudes; the passing breeze winnows the corn, as it falls into large heaps, and numerous asses wait leisurely around, to carry it in sacks to the merchants' granaries."[1]

A sentiment, similar to that of Eliza Fay's was echoed in 1837 about the nature of the dress of the women, from the region of Cutch, which was termed as "peculiar, tasteful, and highly picturesque." Going into the details of the dress, it was remarked as consisting "of a satin petticoat, with broad horizontal stripes of red, blue, and yellow, and a bodice tightly covering the bust, and embroidered with various-coloured silks; over the head and shoulder flows the usual *"Saree,"* which, as it gracefully flutters on the breeze, affords a charming effect of grace and softness to the outlines of their elastic figures, whilst the becoming variety of colour selected for their dress, and the brightness of their numerous ornaments, adds gaiety and animation of no common order to the passing scene. On certain holidays, all the women walk together to the sea side in their richest dresses, to render there a votive offering of rice and cocoa-nuts; and on these occasions,

---

[1] Postans, Marianna, *Cutch*. p.10-11.

the grace and beauty of their persons, the richness and variety of their costume, and the barbaric splendor of their jewels, are shown to the greatest advantage."[1]

The British women, arriving in India in regular and large numbers, to set up home, internalized the distinctions between the British and the natives, especially in terms of habitational segregation of their residential areas from the 'native parts of the town', termed the Black Town. The native part of the town of Bombay is thus described, "On entering the Black Town, which is built in a coco-nut wood, I could not help remarking the amazing populousness of this small island; the streets appear so crowded with men, women, children, that it seems impossible for the quiet bullock *hackreys*, or native carriages, to get along without doing mischief; much less the furiously driving coaches of the rich natives, who pride themselves upon the speed of their horses, which are more remarkable for beauty and for swiftness than for strength........The dwellings of the rich natives are surrounded by verandas, equally necessary to guard against the intemperate heat of the sun and the monsoon rains; they are generally painted in flowers and leaves of a green or red colour; those of the Hindoos have usually some of the fables of their mythology represented on their walls. The houses are necessarily of great extent, because, if a man has twenty sons, they all continue to live under the same roof even when married; and uncles, brothers, sons, and grandsons, remain together till the increase of numbers actually forces a part of the family to seek a new dwelling. The lower classes content themselves with small huts, mostly of clay, and roofed with *cadjan*, a mat made of the

[1] Postans, Marianna, *Cutch*. p.17.

leaves of the Palmyra or coco-nut tree, plaited together. Some of these huts are so small, that they only admit a man's sitting upright in them, and barely shelter his feet when he lies down. There is usually a small garden round each house, containing a few herbs and vegetables, a plantain tree and a coco-nut or two."[1]

The disdain for the customs, habits, and life-style of the Indians is evident from the first contact that a memsahib had with India, commencing with the most common mode of transportation in the early years of the nineteenth century, the palanquin. "The motion of the palanquin, is, to a *griffin*, as a person is termed for the first year of his residence in India, somewhat unpleasant, and gives a sensation something similar to sea-sickness, indeed it was long before I quite liked it, and it was still longer before I became perfectly reconciled to its use. There is, at first something quite revolting to the feelings, in seeing your fellow creatures employed like slaves, independent of the apparent effeminacy of this being carried on men's shoulders. "They wanted *me* to get into one of these things," said one of the party to me, as he handed me in; "as if," added he with true English independence, "as if I could not walk." This impression, however, soon wears off, and habit speedily reconciles individuals to this, as well as to other customs, which were, perhaps, at first the most revolting to their natures.[2] These sentiments were acknowledged by other British women; "I can never forget the first impression, on my mind, when witnessing this mode of conveyance (i.e. the palanquin) on my landing at Calcutta, and though I am

[1] Graham, Maria. *Journal of a Residence in India.* p.4-5.

[2] Elwood, Anne Katherine. *Narrative of a Journey overland from England.* Vol.-I p.366.

willing to agree that the measure is one of vast utility in this climate, and to acknowledge with gratitude the benefit I have derived by this personal convenience, yet I never seat myself in the *palankeen* or *thonjaun* with a feeling bordering on self-reproach, as being one amongst the number to perpetuate the degradation of my fellow-beings"[1]

To the British women venturing into the first difficulty they encountered was that of the climate, which affected their lifestyles and attitudes. The earliest indication that the Indian climate would be a major catalyst in the life of the memsahibs was hinted at by Mrs. Kindersley in 1765, when she commented, "It is frequently said, though very unjustly, that this climate never kills the English ladies; and, indeed, it must be allowed, that women do not so often die of violent fevers as men, which is no wonder, as we live more temperately, and expose ourselves less in the heat of the day; and perhaps, the tenderness of our conditions some times prevents the violence of the disorder, and occasions a lingering, instead of a sudden, death."[2]

Arriving at Calcutta in the month of November 1822, Fanny Parks was 'charmed by the climate' as the 'weather was delicious', and also 'delightful'; 'it rendered the country preferable to any place under the sun; could it have continued the same, I should have advised all people to flee unto the East'. However, by March 1823 the initial euphoria about the climate had undergone a dramatic transformation, as Fanny Parks was to write, "I have

---

[1] Mrs. Ali, Meer Hassan. *Observations on the Mussulmauns of India.* Letter XII.

[2] As quoted in Jane Robinson, *Unsuitable for Ladies*; p.242.

now been four months in India, and my idea of climate has altered considerably; the hot winds are blowing; it is very oppressive; if you go out during the day, I can compare it to nothing but the hot blast you would receive in your face, were you suddenly to open the door of an oven". Despite the hot days, "the evenings are cool and refreshing" and "the moonlight evenings at present are beautiful". Julia Maitland records for June 1837, from St. Thomé, "a sort of suburb of Madras, close by the sea-side, and comparatively cool" on the heat, that she could "only compare it to a blast from the furnace, withering one as it passes by. I have a *tatt*, or a thick mat, at my window, which excludes the sun, and men sit outside pouring water on it all day, so that the wind, which is extremely violent, blows always cooled through the water. This keeps the temperature of the room down at 90°, but it is dreadfully feverish, and far more distressing than a higher degree of the thermometer with the sea-breeze."[1]

The dread of the hot months for the memsahibs remained unchanged, even into the next century. The first experiences gained of battling with the weather of India, during these months set the tone and tenor for dealing with the subsequent years of residence in India, as is clear from the following narration. At Delhi, "It was the end of March, and every day the thermometer was rising, till early April it stood at ninety-four degrees, an absurdly high figure for the time of the year. I began to calculate that by June we should have reached the boiling point at the present rate of increase, and mentioned my fears to a lady who was dining with us. "It really ***does*** feel hot here," remarked she, "and we have not yet begun

[1] Maitland, Julia. *Letters from Madras*. p.57.

with the *punkahs*. What time do you shut the house up?" I gazed at her. "We never shut it up. All the doors are open on every side, but for all that, the heat is frightful." A hearty laugh was all the answer I obtained for a minute, in which the whole company joined. It was then explained to me that every day the house should be closed at eight o'clock till sunset, that chinks should all be filled up, and no breath from the outer furnace blast be permitted to enter our dwelling except through the *kus-kus tatties*, which must be fixed in the doorways on the side towards which the wind was blowing, and water poured on them. The following day these directions were carried out, and our house never registered much more than ninety-two degrees in April, though the heat was growing daily."[1]

As the British ladies progressed into their stay in India, another facet of the Indian climate was revealed to them, *its uncertainties.* "The weather is very uncertain; sometimes *very* hot, then suddenly comes a north-wester, blowing open every door in the house, attended by a deluge of heavy rain, falling straight down in immense drops,..". On the rains, it was commented, "as if the windows of heaven were again opened to deluge the earth; the thunder rolls awfully, and the forked lightning is very vivid. I have never heard of such peals of thunder in Europe. No one here appears to think about it; all the houses have conductors, and as the storm cools the air, it is always welcomed with pleasure by those on the shore". Within one year Fanny Parks was writing home, "I have now become acquainted with three seasons in India; the cold weather, the hot winds, and the rains".[2]

---

[1] Bremmer, Christina. *A Month in a Dandi.* p.42-43.

[2] Parks, Fanny. *Wanderings of a pilgrim.* June 1823, p.31,Vol.-I.

Various devices were employed to make the heat bearable, and the chief device was the *pankhas*, the *tatties* made of *khus-khus* [1] (i.e. vetiver grass), and lastly the thermantidotes. "The *pankha* .....is a monstrous fan, a wooden frame covered with cloth, some ten, twenty, thirty, or more feet long, suspended from the ceiling of a room, and moved to and fro by a man outside by means of a rope and pullies, and a hole in the wall through which the rope passes; the invention is a native one; they are the greatest luxuries, and are also handsome, some being painted and gilt, the ropes being covered in silk, and so shaped or scooped, as to admit their vibratory motion without touching the chandeliers, suspended in the same line with the *pankha*, and when at rest occupying the space scooped out."[2] Further, it was acknowledged that, "The *punkah* (fan) is in constant use by day and night, during eight months in the year. In the houses of the Natives, the slaves have ample employment in administering to the several indulgences which their ladies require at their hands; for with them fixed *punkahs* have not been introduced into the zeenahnah[3]: the only *punkah* in their apartments is moved by hand, immediately over or in front of the person for whose use it is designed. In the gentlemen's apartments, however, and in the houses of all Europeans, *punkahs* are suspended from the ceiling, to which a rope is fastened and passed through an aperture in the wall into the verandah, where a man is seated who keeps it constantly waving, by pulling the rope, so that

---

[1] Fanny Parks writes that in 1829, she had employed fourteen men whose sole duty was to throw water on the *tatties*.

[2] Parks, Fanny. *Wanderings of a pilgrim.*, 20th March 1823, p.25,Vol.I

[3] Fixed punkahs were introduced early in the nineteenth century, as per the *Hobson Jobson.*

the largest rooms, even churches, are filled with wind, to the great comfort of all present."[1]

As the summer advanced and the heat became intolerable, the memsahibs yearned for their home country, and this yearning made the string of detachment from India strong and sure. "Oh! how I long for the liberty and freshness of a country life in England— what would I not give for a fine *bracing* air, and the walk by the sea-side, to enable me to shake off this Indian languor, and be myself again! The moon is so hot tonight, I cannot sit on the Terrace; she makes my head ache. A *chatr* (umbrella) is an unnecessary a defense against the rays of the moon at the full, as against the sun".[2] Such sentiments repeated periodically throughout the stay of the memsahibs in India made their alienation with the country complete. "O! Western shore! on which I have passed so many happy days; what would I not give for your breezes, to carry away this vile Indian languor, and rebrace my nerves?" [3]

Inspite of their long years of stay in India the memsahibs were never able to come to terms with the hot season. As late as 1891, the routine remained unaltered, and the only break during these months was 'a drive before dinner', and the memsahibs remarked that 'the burning *loo* (i.e. the hot winds) cracks the lips and dries the skin just as the cold doess in the northern climes'.[4] India's weather was an enemy to European energies, European complexions, and European habits.

---

[1] Mrs. Ali, Meer Hassan. *Observations on the Mussulmauns of India.* Letter XVII.

[2] Parks, Fanny. *Wanderings of a pilgrim.* 21st August 1830, p.146, Vol-I.

[3] Parks, Fanny. *Wanderings of a pilgrim.* 10th May 1833, p.273,Vol.I.

[4] Christina S. Bremer, A month in a Dandi; p.7.

The author of *The Real Life in India*, published shortly before the Mutiny, described what could happen to a woman: "she falls a victim to indolent habits and coarse indulgences—the sylph-like form and delicate features which distinguished the youth of her arrival are rapidly exchanged for an exterior of which obesity and swarthiness are prominent, and the bottle and hookah become frequent and offensive companions".[1]

Once acquainted with the climate, the English adapted their lifestyle to the cyclic changes of weather. The hot weather[2] made them 'as listless as any Indian lady', and this understanding made them more liberal to the fact that what was before 'condemned as indolence and want of energy'[3] was infact the outcome of the hot weather. In what was to be a series of adaptations to the hot climate, the daily life-style was altered. "What would the people at home think of being up at five a.m., and in the church by six o'clock. This is the usual hour for divine service at this time of the year".[4] This was aggravated by the mosquito bites, which were impossible not to scratch and once scratched, they became inflamed, adding to the discomfort.

In such an oppressively hot climate physical activity was impossible, and 'buggy' which was a luxury in England was deemed a 'necessity', to be maintained by 'even the most petty European shopkeeper in Calcutta'. For the British ladies the typical way of spending the

---

[1] MacMillan, Margaret. *Women of the Raj*. p.80.

[2] The weather in the town of Allahabad was so hot that the British gave it the sobriquet of 'chota jahannum' or little hell.

[3] Parks, Fanny. *Wanderings of a pilgrim*. 12th January 1823, p.26, Vol.-I.

[4] Parks, Fanny. *Wanderings of a pilgrim*. 1st April 1832, p.237, Vol.-I.

long afternoons was 'a novel and a sofa' and dream away the long hours, which made life somewhat tolerable. Another device employed to while away the interminable afternoon hours was the game of billiards, as the summer heat also had an impact on the daily routine of the sahibs. Since all outdoor amusements were denied to the men, unless they happened to be before sunrise or after sunset, the military-men spent their time in the house, devoted either to music or drawing, which they preferred to do in the society of women, or else devoted their time to the study of languages, or mostly at the gaming-tables. The young military officers at Cawnpore gambled at exceedingly high stakes—two guinea points at whist, and hundred guineas at rubber.[1] The men in the Civil Services had too much of work, hence kept away from gambling.

Unknowingly the hot summers introduced an essential article of clothing into the fashion of the sahibs and memsahibs alike, and these were the *topis*. In the cold weather one might wear merely the 'double terai', which was made out of two layers of heavy felt, and was the sun-hat. Safer and absolutely essential for the hot weather was the *topi*, which came into general use in the first part of the nineteenth century. Made of layers of pith, it was believed to protect the European complexion against the piercing and vicious heat of the Indian sun. *Topis* came in variety of shapes. In the nineteenth century there was the Meerut version, covered with Pelican skin and feathers, which according to Fanny Parks gave its wearer a "demented air". There was also the helmet shape and the quilted beehive, sold in London to neophytes, and the inverted soup-plate stocked by Simon Artz in Port

---

[1] *Ibid*, 1830, p.140, Vol.-I.

Said. British residents of India preferred styles like the Cawnpore Tent Club (*khaki*-coloured) or the Curzon (a pale grey). There were also the last reminders of retired Governor-Generals, as the Lamington or Minto. The Eurasians, anxious and over eager to prove that they belonged to the ruling race, wore particularly enormous ones. The memsahibs did their best to make the necessity tolerable by covering the *topis* with cotton or silk, piling them with white muslin for riding, adding bits of trim, a few feathers or perhaps lace. One enterprising milliner advertised a feminine model in a "popular sailor shape. With a slight mushroom droop, covered with any colour straw flat velvet, birds, and fancy wool finish". No wonder that one of the reasons women liked going to the Hills was that they could wear proper hats for a change.[1]

The onset of the cold season made a refreshing contrast to the hot summers, when the British become '*per force* most amiable'[2], when the sloth of the summers was shed. "Many a nail is extracted, by this delightful weather, from our coffins. Calcutta opens her palaces, and displays hospitality, after a fashion which far outdoes that of you cold calculating islanders. And there is such a variety in our pastimes, and the season is so short,—about four months, —that we have no time to 'fall asleep in the sameness of splendour'"[3]. The winters marked the beginning of the social season for the British women; the races[4] began, and the theatre was in high force. Fancy-

---

[1] MacMillan, Margaret. *Women of the Raj.* p.69.

[2] Parks, Fanny. *Wanderings of a pilgrim.* September 1824, p.46,Vol.-I.

[3] Parks, Fanny. *Wanderings of a pilgrim.* December 1824, p.49,Vol.I

[4] In 1823 at Calcutta there is the reference to the Derby, the Oaks, and the Riddlesworth.

dress balls and dinner-parties were organized; there were water-parties to the botanical gardens.

The popularity of the temporary transit, in the hot summer months, to the hill-station of Simla can be attributed to that "the temperature of Simla seems peculiarly adapted to the European constitution. "— The scorching ray, Here pierceth not, impregnate with disease."[1] Emily Eden went into spasms of raptures over the climate of Simla, writing, "The climate! No wonder I could not live down below! We never were allowed a scrap of air to breathe—now I come back to the air again I remember all about it. It is a cool sort of stuff, refreshing, sweet, and apparently pleasant to the lungs. We have fires in every room, and the windows are open; red rhododendron trees bloom in every direction, and beautiful walks like English shrubberies cut on all sides of the hills. Good! I see this is to be the best part of India."[2]

Lord Amherst in 1827 had started the practice of moving to Simla; a village in the foothills of the Himalayas, which had been acquired by the British following their victory over the Gurkhas. The advantages of Simla are recommended by Captain Mundy, who wrote in the summer of 1827 that "The salubrity of this little abode of Hygeia is well attested by the presence of no less than sixteen ladies, who gladly embrace the inconveniences attendant upon narrow accommodations and want of equipages (for no carriage has ever been at Simla), for the advantages accruing from the climate to themselves and their children. The cheeks of the latter-quickly exchange their mealy, muffin-like hue –the livery of Bengal—for a

---

[1] Captain Mundy, *The Journal of a Tour*; Vol.-I, p.237.

[2] Eden, Emily. *Up the Country*. Vol.-I, p.178.

good healthy ruddy bronze."[1] Inspite of the difficulties of transport Simla soon became popular, and it came to be popularly regarded as Mount Olympus, the 'Indian Capua', to Rudyard Kipling it was the great and gay summer capital of India.

The hill-station of Simla in the Punjab was a small British enclave surrounded by native States, 7000-8000 feet above sea level; it ran along a narrow, crescent-shaped ridge five miles long, bounded to the west by Observatory Hill and to the east by the higher Jacko Hill. The town itself, stretching for about a mile along the saddle of the ridge, consisted of a main street, the Mall, ending at the church (Christchurch, consecrated in 1857), and, on a lower level, a native bazaar. A thatched wooden cottage was the first to be put up by Lieutenant Ross, Assistant Political Agent for the Hill States, in 1819. His successor, Captain Kennedy built the first house in Simla in 1822. As time passed, the place was dotted with elegant villas like Swiss chalets standing amid flower gardens with their English names on the gateways. There were 30 houses in 1830, and by 1841 there number was 100, rising to 290 by 1866. By 1880, there were as many as1000 houses. When the Eden sisters visited Simla in 1838, on their arrival, they found it 'really worth the trouble-such a beautiful place'. During their residence there they tried to give their house the look of an English house by, ".....I have got a native painter into the house, and cut out patterns in paper, which he then paints in borders all round the doors and windows and it makes up for the want of cornices and breaks the eternal white

---

[1] Captain Mundy, *The Journal of a Tour*; Vol.-I, p.237.

walls of these houses. Altogether it is very like a middle-sized English country house and extremely enjoyable".[1]

Privileged as the Eden sisters were, being the sisters of the Governor-General, they were able to visit another hill-station, that is Mussoriee. The scenic beauty of the place, the hint of Englishness in the setting, all created an ambience of home and happiness. For the foothills of the Himalayas, at Dhera, it was written, "Nothing can be more beautiful than the country with its line of mountains. For seven months in the year the climate seems to be perfect too and when the hot winds set in, a ten miles' drive will take them up to the hills to a real cold bracing climate. Today in the tents it is hot from the sun beating on them; tomorrow we shall be at Colonel Young's house at Mussoriee in fur shoes and cloaks—the thermometer in the rooms where fires are burning, at 55 degrees. Our tents are filled with English flowers of every description they have sent us from their gardens...."[2] And, on the very next day Fanny Eden describes in glowing words the hill-station of Mussoriee, "How it never entered human creatures' heads to settle here I cannot imagine, but having done it nothing can be more beautiful—hills above and hills below and the snowy mountains within reach. There seems to be literally not an inch of level ground. The foundations of most of the houses are poles stuck in the side of the hill. People's houses which look within a quarter-of-a-mile turn out to be three or four miles off because of the deep ravines between. Of course no carriage can come here, but we were carried part of the way in *jonpauns*, sort of open sedan chairs..........

---

[1] Eden, Emily. *Up the Country*. Vol-I, p.183.

[2] Fanny, Eden, March 16th 1838; The Second Journal; p.150.

There is a large hotel just built on the hill here, and slate billiard tables in it.......The rhododendron trees are splendid—long timber trees, one mass of the deep crimson blossoms...............There is a want of water in these mountains, but it is impossible to imagine grander or more awful looking scenery. As a little child said the other day, looking at the snowy range which towers above all others: 'We seem to have got upon the steps which are leading to heaven.'"[1]

By 1863 Simla had became the summer-capital of the Supreme Government, a number of shops appeared on the Mall. There were also a number of hotels, a club library, a bank, a town-hall, a post-office, assembly rooms for concerts, a theatre for amateur theatricals and a hall for the popular sport of 'rinking' (roller-skating). Government House was then an ordinary country house called Peterhof, rented from the Raja of Simur, on hill-top to the west of the town near the beginning of the *tonga* road. Lady Curzon's first opinion of Simla echoes that of her predecessors. She wrote to her father on 8th March 1899, from the Viceregal Lodge, Simla to her father that, "Simla is a funny place and so hilly & such narrow roads that only three carriages are allowed & those belong to us, the Lt.-Gov. of Punjab and the Comm.-in–Chief. Everyone else goes in a rickshaw pulled up by men & when they come to Simla in carriages they have to leave their carriages before reaching Simla & either walk, ride or go in rickshaws. You never saw such mountains; they go for miles in all directions & you see nothing but the tops as our house is sitting on a mountain 6000 feet high. All the little houses in Simla are clinging to the sides &

---

[1] Eden, Fanny, March 17th 1838; The Second Journal; p.150.

while the back of every house is flat against the hillside the front is supported by tall poles; it is impossible to imagine a quainter spot. All the government buildings are slipping & slithering down mountains—the hill men pull the rickshaws very fast, two go in front & and two push behind you & you think every minute you must go head over heels as you spin down the hill like lightning."[1] Like the Eden sisters, Edith Lytton was delighted with the house which she described as like an old English rectory except for the wide verandahs, whose rent was £ 2,000 a year (in addition to £ 400 spent each year on repairs).[2] According to Edith, the furniture was 'hideous stuff but old English shapes'. Mary Curzon wrote in March 1899,about the Viceregal Lodge that, "This house is like a big American country house, but not so well planned as there are no servants' rooms at all. My maid & the nurses are in the best guest rooms & Betty &Daisy's maid will have to be hung up on hooks!"

The Delhi Sketch Book, a sort of Indian *Punch*, commenting on why so many women really went to Simla wrote about the typical residents. "Good motherly Mrs. A- because her children's health requires it, and the little flirtatious Mrs. B-who had no children, because of her own did. Mrs. C-certainly lived at the dullest outstations and everybody knew its weather half-killed her.....Miss O- went up because she was Miss O- and did not wish to be so any longer- while Mrs. L-was determined that

---

[1] Bradley John (ed.). *Lady Curzon's India*. p. 36.

[2] The reason for this being the ravages of the phenomenon which were the periodical rains termed the *chota bursat* (little rains), which set in the first week of June, and by the beginning of July the *burra bursat* (great rains), after which the rainy season set in, in real earnest.

her daughters should not be long in the plains, so took them up the first season". The presence of so many grass widows and husband hunters around made Simla popular with the bachelors. It acquired a reputation as a resort for philandering and frivolity, becoming the haunt of the gallant, the match-maker, the chivalrous and the flirt. Dr. Hoffmeister who accompanied Prince Waldemar to Simla in 1845 wrote that 'kind and thoughtful relatives at Simla never fail to bring up from the plains everything in the shape of young and marriageable nieces and cousins; and where so many agreeable officers are stationed for pleasure's sake alone, many a youthful pair are thrown together, and many a match is made".[1]

Before the Lyttons infused glamour into the social life at Simla, the life of the English inhabitants were rather staid. "Our mode of life during the six months of our residence at Simla was somewhat monotonous; enlivened, however, occasionally by little excursions, in the form of *pic-nics*, and diversified, now and then, by the novelties that are always to be found by an inquiring sojourner in a strange country. Of sporting we have very little; for though there are several beautiful species of pheasants in the hills, black partridges in the ravines, and quails in the little patches of cultivation, game is on the whole is so scarce as not to repay the great fatigue by which it must be attained."[2] For the want of any good entertainment to occupy the leisure hours the officers at "were employed in building their houses, and afterwards in enlarging and beautifying them. Lord Combermere amused himself, and benefitted the public, by superintending the formation

[1] Neville, Pran. *Rare Glimpses of the Raj.* p.48.

[2] Captain Mundy. *The Journal of a Tour*; Vol.-I, p.238.

of a fine, broad, level road round the Mount Jacko, about three miles in length.......Across a deep ravine, a quarter of a mile from the town, his Lordship erected a neat *Sangah,* or mountain-bridge of pines; and under it a capacious stone tank was constructed, to obviate the great scarcity of water."[1]

Down in South India, where the temperatures were all year round on the warmer side, the city of Bangalore was the chosen destination for retreat by the British. The city is thus described by Julia Maitland in 1839, "There are fire-places in most of the houses, and no *punkahs* in any of them. It is altogether very pleasant, but a queer place—a sort of cross-breed between the watering places of every country in the world. Ladies going about dressed every pitch of distraction they can invent, with long curls which the heat would not allow for an hour elsewhere, and warm close bonnets with flowers hanging in and out of them like queens of May; black niggers, naked or not, as suits their taste; an English church, a Heathen pagoda, botanical garden, public ball-rooms, Dissenting meeting-house, circulating library, English shops, and Parsee merchants, all within sight of each other; elephants and horses walking together in pleasant company over a great green plain in front of our house, where the soldiers exercise; European soldiers and Sepoys meeting at every step; an evening promenade, where people take brisk walks at English pace, and chirp like English sparrows, while a band of blackies play "God save the Queen" and call it the "General Salute."[2]

---

[1] Captain Mundy, *The Journal of a Tour*; Vol.-I, p.241.

[2] Maitland, Julia. *Letters from Madras.* 16th October 1839; p.191-192.

Of the social life at Bangalore it was said; "The Europeans here are chiefly military, and the ladies are different from any I have seen yet. The climate does not tempt them to the dawdling kind of idleness, so they ride about in habits made according to the uniform of their husbands' regiments, and do various spirited things of that sort. Then there is another set—good -natured, housekeeper-like bodies, who talk only of ayahs and amahs, and bad nights and babies, and the advantages of Hodgson's ale while they are nursing, and that sort of thing; seeming, in short, devoted to "suckling fools and chronicling small beer!" However, there are some of a very superior class—almost always ladies of the colonels or principal officers of the European regiments. They never seem to become Indianized, and have the power of being exceedingly useful. Some of them keep up schools for the English soldiers' children, girls specially—superintend them, watch over them, watch over the soldiers' wives, try to keep and encourage them in good ways, and are quite a blessing to their poor countrywomen."[1]

To the memsahibs, living away from the mother-country, any recollection of home; be it in the flowers; the fruits; or the geographical terrain; were triggers to an instant outburst of nostalgia. Emily Eden experienced such an emotion when she visited Seetakund, a hot water spring, near the town of Monghyr.[2] "The drive there was real refreshment; it was for the first time in two years I felt the carriage going *up hill* at all, and this was not a simple slope but a good regular hill. Then we came to some genuine rocks—great, bleak, grey stones, with

---

[1] *Ibid.* 1st November 1839; p.195.

[2] Eden, Emily. *Up the Country*. Vol.-I p.14-15.

weeds growing between them, and purple hills in the distance. I felt better directly. We all sketched away, and did not come back till it was dusk. Altogether, it was a nice scrambling, home-like expedition." These bouts of nostalgia strengthened the felling of banishment from their homeland, straining on the slim threads and tenuous attachment that the memsahibs could build up for India.

The attitudes of the memsahibs towards India, in the eighteenth century, and by the beginning of the nineteenth century were a study in contrast. In the preceding century, the small number of English women in alien surroundings, residing away from the umbilical comfort of their gender compatriots, i.e. family and friends, tentatively recorded their impressions about India. The parameters of this intercourse revolved around the problems of setting house in India in adverse climatic conditions; unfamiliarity with local religious customs and social groupings; and the efforts at regaining the affections of their sahibs who had been ensnared by the *bibis*. By the beginning of the nineteenth century as the East India Company moved away from the original charter of a 'mercantile company trading in the East Indies', and donned the character of a 'nabob' having vested administrative and military interests, the British women began arriving in India in large numbers, 'the fishing-fleet' for the prize of 'three hundred dead or alive'. These women coming from England brought their prejudices with them, and were to a great deal successful in creating 'islands' of insularity of English life in India, thus gradually weakening the close contact the sahibs had with the natives of the land they governed .

Chapter V

Memsahibs: Into her Preoccupations

The daily life, its routine and chores for the memsahibs, whether they resided in the Presidency towns or the 'mofussils', was unvaryingly similar. In the eighteenth century, the English were either engaged in commerce, or were Residents in the courts of native Indian kings, who were still responsible for the administration of the country. As the nineteenth century unfolded, the British through the East India Company administered over half of India. This phenomenon gave rise to the '*mofussil*' (inland towns) as distinct entities from native Indian cities. From the early nineteenth century onwards few women lingered long in the ports, they dispersed to join one of the British enclaves that were spreading across India with the growing power of the Raj.

For the British ladies in India, life in the *mofussil* was no different from any other place of residence in India. While the gentlemen went out on early morning rides, the ladies began their day more quietly. A long day ahead, it was good to take one's ease, to recline in a long basket-chair while the ayah brushed one's hair endlessly—it was pleasantly soothing that brushing. It was the *ayah's* duty to provide all the gossip of the station. It was particularly important to know what was eaten or said at dinner-parties at which one had not been present. There were some houses which, owing to distinction of rank it was impossible to visit; but it was all the more important to know if the scandalous stories one had heard of Mrs. X could be true, and whether Mrs. Y really got all those flashy dresses from Europe as she pretended—and if so, how could her husband afford it, for one knew what his pay was?—and if not true, as one had all along suspected, she had fashion-plates copied by the bazaar dressmaker? All these things the *ayah* was expected to find out. She also had to flatter her lady, exclaim with clasped hands and upturned eyes over a new dress or water-colour sketch of the military cemetery with its shady trees and crowded tombs. When at last she was dressed the lady of the house would review the provision-cupboards to forestall the servants' pilfering, would inspect the pencil-strokes she had dawn on her husband's bottles after dinner to mark last night's level of brandy, would visit the various rooms of the bungalow to see that they were dusted, the silver cleaned, the paper, pencils, pens ready on the drawing-room table for her morning letters to her friends in England—those immense long letters with long accounts of local feuds, of Hindu customs and Indian plant-life, of the sickness of pets and the daily perils from snakes, of the recent conversions and the wickedness of the Government in not supporting the missionaries more strongly.[1]

Even for the ladies in the Governor-General's household, the routine did not differ much in terms of activity or variety. Emily Eden, the sister of Lord Auckland describes her day: "We had breakfast at nine..........I throw a great deal of sentiment into my eating, always having watercress for breakfast, because they are so English........ We dawdle about the hall for a quarter of an hour, reading the papers, and doing a little civility to the household; then Fanny and I go to the drawing-room and work and write till twelve, when I go up to my own room, and read and write till two. Fanny stays downstairs, as she likes it better than her own rooms. I do my shopping too at this hour: the natives come with work, and silks, and anything they have a chance of selling, and sometimes one picks up a tempting article in the way of work. At two we all meet for luncheon and George (Lord Auckland) brings with him anybody who may happen to be doing business with him at the time. Then I go up to my room. and have three hours and a half comfortably by myself. I draw a great amount, and was making a lovely set of costumes, but my own pursuits have been cut in upon by other people. One person wants a picture of a sister she had lost touched up, and in fact renewed, as the damp has utterly destroyed it. There are no professional artists in Calcutta, except one who paints a second-rate sort of sign-post, and though I cannot make much of all these likenesses, yet it feels like a duty to help anybody to a likeness of a friend at home, and it is one of the very few good-natured things it is possible to do here, so I have been very busy the last

[1] Kincaid, Dennis. *British Social Life in India, 1608-1937.* p.179-180.

ten days making copies of these pictures. To finish our day: at six we go out. George and I ride every day now; Fanny about once in three days. At 7:30 we dress; dine at night, and at ten we go off to bed".

The ladies generally did their shopping in the mornings. For Bombay, the memsahibs frequented the large number of Parsi provision shops and grocers' stores. Of these the most favoured was Jangerjee Nasserawanjee; and there were few things you could not buy there. As Mrs. Postans discovered, "The walls were surrounded with glass cases, filled with fine French china, bijouterie, gold lace, sauces, brandied fruits, riding whips.........A central avenue is flanked with cases containing jewellery, French clocks, and all description of knicknackery. On the floor have subsided Cheshire and Gruyere cheeses, hams, cases of sardine, salmon and other edibles; and from the ceiling depend bird cages, lamps, and coloured French lithographs in handsome frames". If there was no shopping to be done, one could always call on the Governor's Lady between eleven and two 'on days advertises for reception'. Government House was at Parrel, and after a long drive the visitors arrived too exhausted for much animation. They sat in a circle and made languid conversation. Lady Falkland[1] (in the forties) complained that the talk "was not lively" among the ladies during an official reception. "Our topic was dusty roads, cool houses, the reviving climate of the Deccan, healthy and unhealthy stations, and the coming monsoons."[2]

---

[1] Lady Falkland was the daughter of William IV and Mrs. Jordan, the Irish actress. She came to Bombay in 1848, as the wife of the Governor.

[2] Kincaid, Dennis. *British Social Life in India, 1608-1937*. p.161.

While the men went to work, the married women either visited each other, or lacking other occupation, settled down and amused themselves, by writing to each other endless '*chits*', in which they excused themselves for not calling in person but the heat or a headache made rest essential for the day. Mr. Stoequeler noted that these *chits* were "neatly written, neatly folded, on pretty paper, and either sealed with all discretion of Donna Julia's own or else so cunningly implicated into cocked hats, twists and other sacred involutions, that to make wax itself *render up its trust* would be far less trouble than the unfolding of such missives by unpracticed hands".

The preoccupation of the memsahibs with this form of entertainment to while away the afternoon hours was acknowledged. "I really believe the Madras ladies spend all their time in writing notes—"*chits*", as they are called. I do not know ten people now, and yet there never passes a day without my having one or two "*chits*" to answer—what with writing them , composing them, finding my pen-knife, mending my pen, hunting for proper note-paper, which is always hidden in some scribbled foolscap beginnings of tracts, or such-like, all my morning is hindered;--and their *chits* are generally only to say "how sorry they have not been able to call lately, and that I must have wondered at it, and *thought*," & c., &c. Now, I never *think* about it,—"*les absens*", & c.,—and I would always rather they did not call, because I must sit all day with my hair dressed and my best clothes on, waiting for them; and remember the thermometer is at 92. I am going tomorrow to Mrs. W—E—. I have not been able to call on her yet, because we live so far off that I quite dread going out for a *morning* visit according to this horrid Madras fashion. If I see her I shall say that I cannot come in the morning, and beg her to come to me in the evening; but for the first visit there is no help:— just now the weather is cloudy; so I shall take advantage of it before it clears up."[1] It was further conceded; "You can scarcely imagine such a life of life inanity. A thorough Madras lady, in the course of a day, goes about a good deal to shops and auctions; buys a great many things she does not want, without inquiring the price; has plenty of books, but seldom reads—it is too hot, or she has not time—*liking to "have her time her own"*, I suppose, like old Lady Q—; receives a number of morning visitors; takes up a little worsted work; goes to tiffin with Mrs. C., unless Miss D. comes to tiffin with her; and writes some dozen of "*chits*." Every inquiry after an acquaintance must be made in writing, as the servants can never understand or deliver a message, and would turn every "politesse" into an insult. These incessant "*chits*" are an immense trouble and interruption; but the ladies seem to like them, and sit at their desks with more zeal and perseverance than their husbands in their *cutcherries*. But when it comes to any really interesting occupation, it is pitiable to see torpor: their minds seem to evaporate under this Indian sun, never to be condensed or concentrated again. The seven-year' sleep of the Beauty in the fairy-tale was nothing to the seven-years' lethargy of a beauty's residence in Madras, for the fairy lady awoke to her former energies, which I think they never can."[2]

By the third decade of the nineteenth century, the 'memsahib culture' was gradually being formulated. As

[1] Maitland, Julia. *Letters from Madras.* 14th March 1839; p.186-187.

[2] *Ibid*, 24th September 1839; p.189-190.

it was noted that, "The real Indian ladies lie on a sofa, and, if they dropped their handkerchief, they just lower their voices and say, "Boy!" in a very gentle tone, and then creeps in, perhaps some wizened, skinny brownie, looking like a superannuated thread-paper, who twiddles after them for a little while, and then creeps out again as softly as a black cat, and sits down cross-legged in the verandah till "Mistress please to call again."[1] This is further expounded: "In fact, one has less time at one's command here than at home, although the very early rising seems to give way to so many hours. But we are obliged to go out in the early morning; it is indispensible to lie down for some time in the middle of the day; we go out again in the cool of the evening, and come home again tired to employ ourselves much at night. One's time seems to be spent in tiring and resting."[2]

Despite the widespread languor which was characteristic of these ladies, when desirable or on the occasions of duty, these women were physically hardy, and as indifferent to discomfort and danger. Honoria Lawrence accompanied her husband Henry Lawrence on his most trying journeys. As Revenue Surveyor he had once visited "a dense jungle at the foothills of the Nepaul hills, intersected with belts of forest trees—a famous tiger tract. The dews were so heavy, that my bed under a small tent was wet through. Fires were constantly kept lighted to keep off the tigers and wild elephants, which gave an unmistakable indication of their proximity, and it was not till eleven or twelve o'clock that the fog cleared sufficiently to permit our laying a theodolite. It was in

---

[1] *Ibid*, 27th December 1836; p.30-31.

[2] *Ibid*, 15th August 1837; p.71.

such a tract that, after three or four days, we[1] connected our survey, and when we met, to my surprise I found Mrs. Lawrence with him. She was seated on the bank of nullah, her feet overhanging the den of some wild animal. While she, with a portfolio in her lap, was writing overland letters, her husband, at no distance, was laying his theodolite".

It was only in the evenings that the ladies seemed to revive and to show signs of animation, either at some dance in which 'the floor was covered with a white cloth stretched tight over the boards and rubbed with a kind of steatite or French chalk' or at one of the formal dinners which had superseded the light -hearted suppers of thirty years before. These dinner-parties had developed a formidable ritual. First came an invitation written by the daughter of the house on dainty rose-or violet-coloured paper, with an appropriate motto—"*qui me néglige me perd*" for instance—on the back of the envelope. The nature of entertainment would be indicated and the *soirées musica es* were coming into favour. After the musical acts were performed, refreshments would be brought by the ladies of the house; these included sandwiches and 'asidulous drinks' for the ladies, cakes and negus for the gentlemen. The party would break up before eleven.[2] The parties at Bombay were labeled as the "most dull and uncomfortable meetings one can imagine" by Maria Graham in October 1809. At these parties etiquette was adhered to with due seriousness by the

---

[1] The story is told by an unnamed fellow-Surveyor of Lawrence's quoted in Kaye's *Lives of Indian Officers*, reported from Margaret Mac Millian.

[2] Kincaid, Dennis. *British Social Life in India, 1608-1937*. p.161-162.

memsahibs, which subsequently grew elaborate, strict, and non-breachable, called the 'demon of precedence'.

The British Government of India had published the Warrant of Precedence.[1] This was intended to be a guide to the position the Government servants on official occasions. The memsahibs, perhaps because they managed the social life, took this official text with great seriousness, and, by the middle of the nineteenth century, this had become the Bible for every hostess. For the memsahibs, precedence determined the order in which you went in to dinner, where you sat, and the order in which you left at the end of the evening. In the ladies side of the Club, the best sofa was reserved by unspoken agreement for the senior memsahibs. In badminton, it was considered polite to serve the first shuttlecock to the senior lady on the other side of the net. A humorous anecdote of the society governed by etiquette and The Warrant of Precedence was, that for all official hospitality, undertaken by the government, it required that invitations should be sent to all who qualified for them, even if this included a divorced women, her co-respondent, her former husband and his new wife. Alfred Lyall, as Lieutenant-Governor was tickled by a peculiar situation, when at Nainital, he wondered if he should extend an invitation to 'a lady who ran away from her husband, was divorced, and then married her husband again. He did so, concluding that 'her husband knew the best.'

---

[1] The Order of Precedence in India was fixed by the warrant of the Prince Regent dated 31st May 1814. The next modified version was the Royal Warrant of Precedence of 18th October 1876, subject to modifications in 1905 and there afterwards.

Even the Vicerine was subject to the order of precedence, as Lady Curzon was initiated early into the official procedure and conduct. For an official banquet, at Calcutta she noted, "At 8:15 the two ADC's-in-waiting come and fetch us and walk ahead of us to the drawing-room where the dinner guests are arranged in a kind of horse-shoe. George goes first and shakes hand with them all, and I come after him. I should say that as we come to the door one ADC says, 'Their Excellencies' and all the guests bow. After shaking hands all round and getting back to the door through which we entered George takes his lady into dinner and I go in with my man. .... After dinner I have to walk out of the room alone, preceded by an ADC, the ladies coming behind. The men smoke, and when George comes into the drawing-room we all get up and stand till he sits down, and have to jump up every time he does. We each sit and talk to guests, ADC's bringing up relays." The fact that it was this learning process was not easy and fraught with difficulties is clear from this passage. "On Sunday we went to the Cathedral which was rather an ordeal as the Viceroy's seat is an odd box with two large Gothic chairs in full view of the whole congregation, and as every single creature spent his time gazing at us it was pretty trying, and as the service consisted of long anthems and every sort of elaborate music we got tired, and I was glad to get out that I nearly committed the awful crime of climbing into the carriage before George. It is difficult to remember always to allow him to go through a door first, and he never thinks of it, but I manage usually. The custom is for the Viceroy and his wife to walk side by side, but when we march through big crowded rooms I think he should go first.........."[1]

[1] Bradley, John (ed.). *Lady Curzon's India*. p. 23

Referring to another drawing-room at Calcutta on 17th January 1899 Lady Curzon recorded, "Last Thursday we held a drawing-room—at 9:30 we were escorted to 'God save the Queen' into the throne room—where all the high officials were grouped either side of the throne—the throne was covered with a perfectly *magnificent* solid gold carpet which was laid over it, the ends coming far out on carpet of the room—on the dais were two immense chairs, one of silver with gold tigers behind G. A smaller one for me. We stood in front of them and all the entrée ladies filed past making two curtseys—they then took their places to the left of the throne besides their husbands who were already there –as each lady came up her name on a card was given to the ADC who handed it to the Military Secretary & he called out her name—she then proceeded to curtsey to G. who bowed solemnly & then another curtsey to me & I bowed & smiled. We did not shake hands with anyone-just bowed-the ladies were beautifully dressed and did their bows[1] far better than I should have done them—trains and feathers are optional, but *many* wore them. After all the entrée ladies had passed the public entrée were admitted, all the ladies looked very well dressed and it took the private & public entrée just an hour to pass; after they all had passed we marched upstairs to the Great ball-room preceded by the staff and followed by the private entrée who had remained throughout the drawing-room in the throne room. The rooms were crowded as all the husbands of the ladies had joined them upstairs and there ensued a kind of evening party, we were sitting in big chairs which

---

[1] It was only during the time of Lord Minto's Viceroyalty (1905-10) that curtseying to the Viceroy was introduced.

were arranged in a semi-circle & in about three-quarters of an hour ADC's bringing up a steady stream of people for G. & me to talk to. When the time came to go we were marched out of the room & retired to well earned bed". [1]

The hierarchical ordering of internal social grading among the memsahibs, with the passage of time acquired complexity, and manouevring among its ranks required great dexterity, as was discovered by Christina Bremmer, at Kasauli, at the close of the nineteenth century. She wrote, "The relations of the ladies at the station is a delicate topic which should be touched with fear and trembling. 'There are eleven ladies at our station,' said a cheerful little doctor's wife to me at Simla, 'and five of them are cuts.' For a moment I wondered how a lady with a fine south England accent could possibly descend to so vulgar a comparison, but the explanation was soon offered that they did not know each other at the club or on the road, and that for a hostess to get up a dinner party, a necessary preliminary was to submit the list of guests to the invited ones. To invite B and C when they were "cuts," or to omit to invite one of them after they have made it up would be invidious, and argue a shocking want of tact on the part of the hostess. 'You need to know the ropes here,' said one who did; but even she occasionally found that she had pulled the wrong ones, though she devoted a naturally fine intelligence to her study. 'It would not do to invite Mrs. D.; her husband is a ranker.' My artless simplicity made me think she would be related to the Howards or Nevilles. "She would look upon herself as a Sévres vase among clay pots?" I queried. A pitying reply was the first smile. 'I mean D rose from the ranks to his

[1] Bradley, John (ed.). *Lady Curzon's India.* p. 25-26.

present position of captain, and the other men don't like it. That's why he has more friends among the civilians than among the military.' "[1]

Within the contours of the British society, a distinction between the civilian and military memsahibs was discernable. Julia Maitland[2], who published her Letters from Madras anonymously, wrote, "... the officers' ladies are curiously different from the civilians. The civil ladies are generally quiet, rather languid, speaking almost in a whisper, simply dressed, almost always lady-like and *comme-il-faut*, not pretty, but pleasant and nice-looking, rather dull, and give one very hard work in pumping for conversation. They talk of 'the Governor', 'the Presidency', the 'Overland', and 'girls' school at home'[3], and have always daughters of about thirteen at home. The military ladies, on the contrary, are always quite young, pretty, noisy, affected, showily dressed, with a great many ornaments, *mauvis ton*, chatter incessantly from the moment they enter the house, twist their curls, shake their bustles, and are altogether what you may call 'Low Toss'. While they are alone with me after dinner, they talk about suckling their babies, the disadvantages of scandal, 'the Officers', and 'the Regiment'; and when the gentlemen come into the drawing-room, they invariably flirt with them most furiously." The divide between the civil and military wings of the English society in India was so well defined that it could lead to some unwelcome

---

[1] Bremmer, Christina, *A month in a Dandi*; p.18-19.

[2] Maitland, Julia. *Letters from Madras.* 16th February 1838; p.120-121.

[3] Kaye, M.M.; *The Golden Calm*, p.24. Emily and Georgie, the daughters of Sir Thomas Metcalfe were sent to England at the young age of seven and five respectively, in 1836.

moments. Julia Maitland further recounts, "The military and civilians do not generally get on well together. There is a great deal of very foolish envy and jealousy between them, and they are often downright ill-bred to each other, though in general the civilians behave much the best of the two. One day an officer who was dining here said to me, "Now I know very well, Mrs. --, you despise us all from the bottom of your heart; and you think no one worth speaking to in reality but the Civil Service. Whatever people may really be, you just class them all as civil and military—civil and military; and you know no other distinction. Is it not so?" I could not resist saying, "No; I sometimes class them as civil and uncivil." He has made no rude speeches to me since." The feeling of the great divide between the civil and the military was finely delineated with passage into the second half of the nineteenth century, and a memsahib to such divisions recorded, " It is commonly reported that the civilians and military will not mingle at some stations, each looking down at on the other with lofty contempt. "There is no doubt that the man who rules India is Tommy Atkins; the blessed thing is he does not know it." As the speaker was himself a Colonel, the inference is quite plain; at any rate, it was evident in his bearing. The civilian sees the immense administrative machine revolving from one single centre. From centre to circumference, every spoke measures twelve feet of bright and burnished steel. Its throbbing is the same at Calcutta as at Tinnevelly, and at each thud he mutters: "Tis exceedingly good." ....The differences between civilians and military men are not the only ones that exist. It is a fact related by one of themselves that in

1857 officers of the Queen's Regiments declined to mess with Company officers. Noble fellows!"[1]

Meanwhile, back to Maria Graham, who in the first decade of the nineteenth century, warily talks of the demon of precedence, wrote, "Forty or fifty persons assemble at seven o'clock, and stare at one another till dinner is announced, when the ladies are handed to the table, according to the strictest rules of precedency, by a gentleman of a rank corresponding to their own. At the table there can be no general conversation, but the different couples who have been paired off, and who, on account of their rank, invariably sit together at every great dinner, amuse themselves with remarks on the company, as satirical as their wit will allow; and woe be to the stranger, whose ears are certain of being regaled with the catalogue of his supposed imperfections and misfortunes, who has the chance of learning more of his own history than in all probability he ever knew before. After dinner the same topics continue to occupy the ladies, with the addition of lace, jewels, intrigues, and the latest fashions; or if there be any newly-arrived young women, the making and breaking matches for them to furnish employment for the ladies of the colony till the arrival of the next cargo. Such is the company at an English Bombay feast. The repast is as costly as possible, and in such profusion that no part of the table-cloth remains uncovered. But the dinner is scarcely touched, as every person eats a hearty meal called tiffin, at two o'clock, at home. Each guest brings his own servant, sometimes two or three; these are either Parsees or Mussulmans. It appears singular to a stranger to see behind every white

[1] Bremmer, Christina. *A Month in a Dandi*; p.25-26.

man's chair a dark, long bearded, turbaned gentleman, who usually stands so close to his master, as to make no trifling addition to the heat of the apartment; indeed, were it not for the *punka*, (a large frame of wood covered with cloth), which is suspended over every table, and kept constantly swinging, in order to freshen the air, it would scarcely be possible to sit out the melancholy ceremony of an Indian dinner."[1]

Similar to Bombay, the dinner hosted at Madras during the 1800-1850's is described as follows; "We have been to one or two large dinner-parties, rather grand, dull, and silent. The company are generally tired out with the heat and the office-work all day before they assemble at seven o'clock, and the houses are greatly infested by musquitos, which are generally in themselves enough to lower one's spirits and stop conversation. People talk a little in a very low voice to those next to them, but one scarcely ever hears any topic of general interest started except steam navigation. To be sure, "few changes can be rung on few bells"; but these good folks do ring on the "the changes in service", till I cannot help sometimes wishing all their appointments were permanent. At an Indian dinner all the guests bring their own servants to wait upon them, so there is a turbaned sultan-like creature behind every chair. A great fan is going over our heads the whole time, and every window and door open; so that, notwithstanding the number of people in the room, it is in reality cooler than an English dining-room. What would grandmamma say to the wastefulness of an Indian dinner? Everybody dines at luncheon, or, as it is here called, *tiffin*-time, so that there is next to nothing eaten, but about four

---

[1] Graham, Maria. *Journal of a Residence in India.* p.29-30.

times as much food upon the table as would serve for an English party. Geese and turkey, joints of mutton for side-dishes, and everything else in proportion. All the fruit in India is not worth one visit to your strawberry-beds. The ingenious French at Pondicherry have contrived to cultivate vines; but the English nothing will grow, and they remain content to waste their substance and their stomach-aches on spongy shaddocks and sour oranges, unless they send to Pondicherry for grapes, which the French are so obliging as to sell at a rupee a bunch. After dinner the company all sit round in the middle of the great gallery-like rooms, talk in whispers, and scratch their mosquito-bites. Sometimes there is a little music, as languid as everything else. Concerning the company themselves, the ladies are all young and wizen, and the gentlemen are old and wizen. Somebody says France is the paradise of married women, and England of girls: I am sure India is the paradise of middle-aged gentlemen. While they are young, they are thought nothing of—just supposed to be making or marring their fortunes, as the case may be; but at about forty, when they are "high in the service", rather yellow, and somewhat grey, they begin to be taken notice of, and are called "young men". These respectable persons do all the flirtation too in a solemn sort of way, while the young ones sit by, looking on, and listening to the elderly gentlefolks discussing their livers instead of their hearts."[1]

Life in the first decade of the nineteenth century Madras was no different from that of other Presidency towns for the British women. "It was the fashion of all gentlemen and ladies of Madras to repair, in their gayest

[1] Maitland, Julia. *Letters from Madras.* 11th January 1837, p.36-37.

equipages, to the Mount Road (that lead from Fort-George to St. Thomas Mount), and after driving furiously along, they loiter round and round the cenotaph (to the memory of Lord Cornwallis) for a hour, partly for exercise, and partly for the opportunity of flirting and displaying their fine clothes, after which they go home, to meet again every day of the year. But the greatest lounge at Madras is during the visiting hours, from nine o'clock till eleven, when young men go from house to house to retail the news, ask commissions to town for the ladies, bring a bauble that has been newly set, or one the lady has obliquely hinted, at a shopping party the day before, she would willingly purchase, but that her husband does not like her to spend so much, and which she thus obtains from young man, one quarter whose monthly salary is probably sacrificed to his gallantry. When all the visitors who have any business are gone to their offices, another troop of idlers appears, still more frivolous than the former, and remains till *tiffin*, at two o'clock when the real dinner is eaten, and wines and strong beer from England are freely drunk. The ladies then retire, and for most part undress, and lye down with a novel in their hands, over which they generally sleep. [1]About five o'clock the master of the family returns from his office; the lady dresses

[1] Quoted in Michael Maclagan, 'Clemency' Canning p.57, as Lieutenant-Colonel Lord Dunkellin, the Military Staff with Lord Canning, told Lady Clanricarde, "It appears that in the old times Indian ladies were in the habit after 'tiffin' of loosing themselves (I mean their garments) and rolling upon their beds in search of sleep to work off the heavy meal which they had just gorged themselves, and tho' modish dames are not now quite greedy or quite comatose in their nature, still it is considered proper to give them an opportunity of becoming so in case they should feel so disposed.

herself for the Mount Road; returns, dresses, dines, and goes from the table to the bed, unless there be a ball, when she dresses again, and dances all night; and this I assure you, is a fair, very fair, account of the usual life of a Madras lady."[1] Gentlemen paying informal calls were supposed to visit in the mornings, but they had to content themselves with conversation, for it was "considered an act of glaring impropriety in a lady to invite any gentleman to stay and partake of *tiffin* who is not either a relative or an intimate friend of the family".

For the British women entertainment included picnics, but picnics required 'arranging', as servants had to be sent ahead with tents and provisions; and the weather might suddenly turn hot, making riding fatiguing. So the ladies more often spent the early evenings in their gardens. Or if the afternoon wind died down, as it often did in the hot weather in Bombay, at the approach of evening, the garden was too warm for comfort and it was better to recline in a long chair on the veranda.

If the late evening were cooler the ladies would venture out for a drive. In the early nineteenth century palanquins were still used, but very few people kept their own; they were hired by the hour. The palanquin-bearers had a bad reputation for insubordination, and for their continual strikes for higher wages. They would put the palanquin down in the middle of the road and would scamper off, or crowd round their anxious 'fare' shouting and gesticulating. Palanquins were ousted by the buggies only in the sixties; and the buggy-drivers inherited all the blackmailing practices of their predecessors. The carriages which succeeded the palanquins in popular favour

[1] Graham, Maria. *Journal of a Residence in India.* p.130-131

were known for their variety as chariots, shigrampos, curricles, sociables, britzkas and clearances; if one could not buy them they could be hired for £ 20 a month and in them the ladies, reclining under coloured parasols and gentlemen in dark blue or bottle-green coats drove down the Esplanade. Mrs. Postans wrote in 1838 that, "There may be seen the English landau fresh from Long-acre; the smart dennet of the military aspirant marked by its high cushions; the roomy buggy of the mercantile Parsee, adorned with gold and green; the richly gilt chariot of a high cast Hindoo, with its silken reins and emblazoned panels".[1]

Dancing as a form of entertainment had become well established in the nineteenth century, in the form of 'balls'. Emily Eden notes that 'some ladies came sixty miles to these balls.' And in the organizing of these balls a great deal of energy was expounded, and these were organized with a degree of difficulty as the number of British women in comparison to men was small. It was further recorded for the station of Ghazeepore (Ghazipur); "There was a great deal of doubt whether a ball could be made out, as the want of ladies in the Moufussil makes dancing rather difficult. However, we took a large party, and the ladies we had seen in the morning all assembled and had raised two or three extras. The mess-room was very prettily illuminated, with G's arms painted on the floor, and they gave us a grand supper, so it all did very well. I wish you could have seen the dancers. A Mrs.___, something like Mrs. Glover the actress, only much fatter, with a gown two inches shorter than her petticoat, *bounding* through every quadrille, with her three grown-up sons dancing

---

[1] Kincaid, Dennis. *British Social Life in India, 1608-1937*. p.155-156.

around her. She is an exemplary mother, and has been a widow many years, and a grandmother many more, but she never misses a dance!"[1]

By the third decade of the nineteenth century, the memsahibs had acquired a novel avenue for their entertainment, and this was the acquisition of proficiency in drawing and painting. There was no longer an excuse for ignorance, as in 1822 Signor Constantine Augusto had set up a School of Art for Ladies in Bombay, and the proprietor advertised himself as "well versed in the doctrine of the angles of animo-anatomic proportion, and peculiarly correct in his treatment of landscape with chaste colouring and perspective". And every lady wanted to paint a landscape, a sketch which included a quiet river with high banks lined with casuarinas: the jagged and pleasant *ghats*; a temple embowered in a mango-grove. And India provided the most impressive canvas. Lady Falkland was charmed by what she saw and commented, "What bits to sketch! What effects here! What colouring there!" Maria Graham refers to her friend a Mr. A (i.e. Ashburner)—who had inherited a considerable estate in the Island of Salsette, and owned a distillery at Bhandoop, and it was Mrs. A—whose drawing were admired as 'that of an artist'. The artistic talent of Mrs. Ashburner is endorsed by another contemporary traveler, albeit a male[2], who refers to her, during a ten day trip to the island of Elephanta, as "Mr. Erskrine's first assistant was *a lady of high qualification and an artist;* not a mere fashionable screen-sketcher and a murderer of the picturesque, but

---

[1] Eden, Emily. *Up the Country.* Vol.-I, p.29-30.

[2] The individual was Captain Basil Hall, who has referred to Mrs. Ashburner.

a regular painter, trained by long study, and under the influence of good taste". Mrs. Ashburner's sketches were used as illustrations in Mr. Erskrine's paper on Elephanta Caves in the "*Transactions of the Literary Society*".

Before the middle of the nineteenth century, sports had been exclusively for men, but by the end of the nineteenth century, British women in India, like their counterparts at Home, were busy with archery, badminton, and later, with tennis and golf.

Chapter VI

Memsahibs: Coexistence with the Domestics'

Flora Annie Steel wrote that one of the greatest tests faced by the memsahibs was the management of the house. "The end and object is not merely personal comfort but the formation of a home—that unit of civilization where the father and the children, master and servant, employer and employed, can learn their several duties. When all is said and done also herein lies the natural outlet for most of the talent peculiar to women." For the memsahibs the home was the Empire in miniature, which had to be governed peacefully, with dignity and prestige.[1]

The number of servants considered indispensable for a moderate establishment in Presidency towns of Bombay and Madras were nearly the same as in Calcutta. The system of domestic service was well organized with different departments of the establishment under the charge of professional experts. At the top of the list

[1] MacMillan, Margaret. *Women of the Raj*. p.142.

was the *sircar* (in Calcutta)[1] or *dubash* (in Madras), who helped the newcomers to settle down; found them a house and servants. The *sircar* controlled the financial side of the household, as he arranged loans for the master of the house, and for these services rendered he took no salary but 5 per cent commission on the total turnover of all payments. Next was the *khansaman*, the butler, who controlled the under-kitchen servants, usually selecting and appointing them. An expert cook, his wages varying from eight to twenty-five rupees, depending on his experience and calibre. He also made the daily purchases from the bazaar, for which he received a modest *dustoorie* (commission). The duty of the *khidmatgar* was to bring food to the table in an orderly manner and be in attendance. Among the well-to-do families, there was a *khidmatgar* for each member and sometimes even two, but generally the usual domestic complement was two or three. The *khidmatgar* was in turn followed by the *bawurchee* or cook who was a Muslim, a Portuguese, a Mug[2], or a Hindu of a low caste. The cook was assisted by a *mushalchee*, literally a torch-bearer, for his real work was carrying a torch when travelling with the master, but in the household, he was the dish-washer. The *sirdar* was the head-bearer, who was assisted by house-bearers or under-bearers. The *durwan* was an imposing figure guarding the access to the house. Other servants included the *mali* (gardener), *syce* (groom for every horse),

[1] According to Fanny Parks, 'a useful but expensive person in the establishment, who came every morning early to receive orders, obtaining a percentage on all the purchases he made for the family, termed 'dustoorie'.

[2] Mugs were from the borders of Burma, and were regarded as heaven-born cooks.

ghaskot (grass-cutter), *bhisty* (water-carrier), *mehtar* (sweeper), the *punkahwala*, the *chowkidar* (watchman). If the master possessed a boat, he would also employ a *manjy* (steersman), *goleeah* (bowman), and a number of *dandys* (rowers). A number of occasional or part-time servants attached to the household included the *dhobi* (washerman), the *darzi* (tailor), and the *hajaam* (barber). Among the servants the darzi was of the greatest importance in the life of the memsahib, as 'a great many ladies always have tailors to work in their drawing-rooms—and their chief occupation seems to be to watch them".[1] Then there were the *hookahburdar*, who attended to the sahib's *hookah*, blew on the charcoal and renewed the rose-water. Another special servant was the *abdar*, responsible for cooling the water, wines, beer and other table delicacies. Other functionaries were the *chuprasee, hurkarah, piyada;* all appellations for the peon. The *jemadar,* was a domestic overseer and general confidential assistant who acted on ceremonial occasions as gentleman usher. The memsahibs were attended by the *ayah*, who acted as the lady's maid, and looked after the *baba-logue* or children. For breast-feeding of the infants, *amahs* or wet-nurses were employed. On the large number of servants it was said that "so necessary are these servants to the domestic economy of sojourners in the East, that, their merits as a people must be a continual theme of praise; for I know not how an English establishment could be concluded with any degree of comfort without these most useful domestics."[2]

---

[1] Eden, Fanny. The Second Journal; entry of 15th March 1838.

[2] Mrs. Ali, Meer Hassan. *Observations on the Mussulmauns of India.* Letter XII.

Immediately on her landing at Calcutta in November 1822, Fanny Parks was struck by the bewildering array of servants needed to be employed in the household, which was 'surprising to a person fresh from Europe' as 'it appeared the commencement of ruin. Their wages were not high, [1]and they find themselves in food; nevertheless, from their number, the expense is very great." It was acknowledged that "It is *impossible* to do with a few servants, you *must* have many; their customs and prejudices are inviolable, a servant will do such and such things, and nothing more"[2]. And, in 1830, while stationed at the city of Cawnpore, her servants were "only fifty-four". She also provides us with a list of servants required in a private family along with their wages per month (in rupees) for the year 1828, which was as follows:

1. *Khansaman*, or head man;
   a Mussalman servant who purchases
   the provisions, makes the confectionary,
   and superintends the table.............. Rs.12.
2. *Abadar*, or water-cooler; cools the water,
   ices the wines, and attends with them at
   the table................................Rs.8.
3. Head *khidmatgar*; he takes charge of the
   plate-chest, and waits at the table ....Rs.7.
4. A second *khidmatgar*, who waits
   the table ....Rs.6.
5. A *bawarchi*, or cook..................... Rs.12.
6. Mate *bawarchi*..........................Rs.4.

[1] Helen C. Ford noted in February 1889, at Suri, that wages were not very high and E—d's head gardener receives only six rupees a month.

[2] Parks, Fanny. *Wanderings of a pilgrim.* 12th January 1823, p.26, Vol.-I.

7. *Mashalchi*; dish-washer and torch bearer .... Rs.4.8.
8. *Dhobee*, or washerman .... Rs.8.
9. *Istreewala*, washerman for ironing .... Rs.8.
10. A *darzee* or tailor .... Rs.8.
11. A second tailor .... Rs.6.
12. An *ayha*, or lady's maid .... Rs.10.
13. An under-woman .... Rs.6.
14. A *doriya*; a sweeper, who also attends to the dogs .... Rs.4.
15. *Sirdar*-bearer, an Hindoo servant, the head of the bearers, and the keeper of the sahib's wardrobe; the keys of which are always carried in his *kamarband*, the folds of the cloth around his waist .... Rs.8.
16. The mate-bearer; assists as valet, and attends to the lamps .... Rs.6.
22. Six bearers to pull the *pankhas*, and dust the furniture, & c .... Rs.24.
23. A *gwala*, or cowherd .... Rs.4.
24. A *bher-i-wala*, or shepherd .... Rs.5.
25. A *murgh-i-wala*, to take care of the fowls, wild-ducks, quail, rabbits, guinea-fowls, and pigeons .... Rs.4.
26. A *malee*, or gardener .... Rs.5.
27. A mate, -do- .... Rs.3.
28. Another mate or a *cooly* .... Rs.2.
29. A gram-grinder, generally a woman who grinds the *chana* for the horses ...... Rs..2.
30. A coachman .... Rs.10.

38. Eight *sa'ises*, or grooms, at five rupees each, for eight horses Rs.40
46. Eight grass-cutters, at three rupees each, for the above.............................. Rs.24.
47. A *bihishti*, or water-carrier ....Rs.5.
48. A mate *bihisti* ....Rs.4.
49. A *Barha'I mistree*, a carpenter ....Rs.8.
50. Another carpenter ....Rs.7.
52. Two *coolies*, to throw water on the tatties. . Rs.4.
54. Two chaukidars, or watchmen.............Rs.8.
55. A *durwan*, or gate-keeper ....Rs.4.
57. Two *chaprasis*, or running footmen, to carry notes, and be in attendance in the verandah .... Rs.10.

The combined wages of these 57 servants amounted to 290 rupees per month.

It was remarked another memsahib that "Servants are expensive altogether, though cheap individually; but we are obliged to have such a number of them that their pay mounts up. We keep fewer than many people, because we wish to be economical. Here is our establishment: one butler, one dress-boy (i.e. valet), one *matee*, (cleans plates, washes china, and lights candles), two *ayahs*, one *amah* (wet-nurse), one cook, one tunnicutchy (housemaid), two gardeners, six bearers, one water-carrier, two horse-keepers, two grass-cutters, one dog-boy, one poultry-man, one washerman, one tailor, one hunter, and one *amah's* cook—altogether twenty-seven: and this is reckoned few; and it is as much as ever they can do to get through their little work in their lazy dawdling ways."[1] The *ayah* held

[1] Maitland, Julia. *Letters from Madras.* 3rd October 1837; p.78.

a special bond of affection in the memsahibs' heart. Mrs. Sherwood said of her meeting with her son's old ayah on the banks of the river Ganges, "There are moments of intense feeling, in which all distinctions disappear, and in their place there only remains between two human beings, one abiding sense of human nature."[1]

It was also added that additional workforce could be employed, which included, " during the hot winds, a number of extra *coolies*, twelve or fourteen, are necessary, if you keep it going all night as well as during the day; these men, as well as an extra *bihishti*, are discharged when the rains set in........ We, as quiet people, find these servants necessary. Some gentlemen for state add an *assa burdar*, the bearer of a long silver staff; and a *sonta burdar*, or *chob-dar*, who carries a silver club, with a grim head on the top of it. The business of these people is to announce the arrival of company."[2] "If anybody comes to dinner, the cook sits down and cries for a cook's *maty* or helper, and I am obliged to hire one for him."[3]

Fifty years down the line the number of servants required to be employed in a British household continued to be large, but their requirement was more "on the Bengal side than here (i.e. Bombay)",[4] but the reasons behind such a statement are not given. In Bombay of 1889, it was recorded that "the butler and the cook here are Goanese (Roman Catholics, descendants of those converted by the Portuguese, and in some cases having Portuguese blood them in their veins)".

---

[1] As quoted in Margaret Mac Millian, p.64.

[2] Parks, Fanny. *Wanderings of a pilgrim*. 1828, p.210. Vol.- I.

[3] Maitland, Julia. *Letters from Madras*. 3rd October 1837; p.78.

[4] Ford, Helen C. *Notes of a tour in India and Ceylon*; p.25.

Arriving in December 19th 1836, Julia Maitland quickly grasped the intricacies of setting up a house hold in India, and the first gendered understanding of the domestic culture was concerning servants. She records, "There is one great convenience in visiting a Indian house, viz.-every visitor keeps his own establishment of servants, so as to give no trouble to those of the house. The servants provide for themselves in a most curious way. They seem to sleep nowhere, and eat nothing, -- that is to say, in our houses, of our goods. They have mats on the steps, and live upon rice. But they do very little, and everyone has their separate work. I have an *ayah* (or lady's maid), and a tailor (for the *ayahs* cannot work); and A—has a boy: also two muddles-one to sweep my room, and another to bring water. There is one man to lay the cloth, another to bring in dinner, another to light the candles, and others to wait upon the table. Every horse has a man and a maid to himself—the maid cuts grass for him; and every dog has a boy. I enquired whether the cat had any servants, but I found that she was allowed to wait upon herself; and, as she seemed to be the only person in the establishment capable of so doing, I respected her accordingly. Besides all these acknowledged and ostensible attendants, each servant has a kind of muddle or double of his own, who does all the work that can be put off upon him without being found out by the master and mistress. Notwithstanding their numbers, they are dreadfully slow. I often tire myself with doing things myself rather than wait for their dawdling; but Mrs. Staunton laughs at me, and calls me a "griffin", and says I must learn to have patience and save my strength. "[1]

---

[1] Maitland, Julia. *Letters from Madras.* 27th December 1836; p.30.

As a result of the feminine pre-occupation with dressing themselves the *darzee* occupied a special status, which could never be ignored by the memsahibs; as dressing well, in fashions approximating Home, was almost a duty owed to the prestige of the Raj. The memsahibs' couture was a visible symbol that they were not going native. Although the dresses might not be convenient and were certainly not comfortable, the memsahibs kept firmly to their corsets well into the twentieth century even after they had passed out of fashion at Home. In the nineteenth century they had insisted on crinolines and bustles.[1] The memsahibs subscribed to magazines, had patterns sent out by their families, dissected the appearance and apparel of the latest export from Home, and made heroic efforts to keep up with the European fashion, while in exile in India. In these efforts' the memsahibs were valiantly assisted by the Indian tailors, the *durzis*. "The *derdjees*, or taylors, in Bombay, are Hindoos of a respectable caste, who wear the *zenaar*. My *derdjee*, a tall good-looking young man, wears a fine worked muslin gown, and a red or purple turban bordered with gold. He works and cuts out beautifully, making as much use of his toes as his fingers in the last operation; his wages are fourteen rupees a-month, for which he works eight hours a-day; inferior workmen receive from eight to twelve rupees."[2] "A *darzee* works beautifully, as strongly and as finely as French milliners: they have great patience as they are paid by the month and not by the piece."[3] In a short span of fifty years these good *darzees* were snapped up by the commercial

[1] Mac Millan, *M. Women of the Raj. p.69.*

[2] Graham, Maria. *Journal of a Residence in India*. p.30-31.

[3] Parks, Fanny. *Wanderings of a pilgrim*. Vol.-I, p.141.

establishments, (i.e. the shops) and those employed in the households "worked rather slowly", but they continued "making ladies clothes" and charged "about twelve *annas* a day" in the city of Bombay.[1] Despite the good work of these milliners, the Indian tailors were open to the oft-repeated charge of procrastination and laziness, as any other Indian servant. "I scold him (the tailor) from the "best of motives", and here are my reasons: he is hired by the month, and is paid a great deal more than he is worth, - dawdle that he is!-but it is the only way of getting the needlework done at all here. He often asks for a day's leave of absence, and often takes it without asking. I used to be compassionate with him at first, believing his excuses; but when I repeated them to Mrs. Staunton, she said they were all lies. One day he told me that his mother was sick, and that she would soon be dead, and he would "put her out of the way"; but Mrs. Staunton said that his mother had already died three times to her knowledge, and that I must forbid her ever being sick again without my permission; so I gave my orders accordingly, and she (the tailor's mother) has been quite well ever since. Sometimes he sits on his mat crying, and saying he is "plenty sick" himself, so then I send him away for half a day, with orders to come back quite well the next morning, or I shall get another tailor; and this always cures him."[2]

All servants came with their set of emotions. While the memsahibs concentrated largely on the tailor, their litany of woes with the other servants was no less. "The *amah* is a caste woman, and her whims are the plague

---

[1] Ford, Helen C. *Notes of a tour in India and Ceylon*; p.36.

[2] Maitland, Julia. *Letters from Madras.* 16th May 1837; p.56.

of my life: I am obliged to keep a cook on purpose for her, because her food must be dressed by a person of her caste; and even then she will sometimes starve all day rather than eat it: she has a house built of cocoa-nut leaves in the compound, on purpose to cook her food in. I am also obliged to keep a separate nurse for her baby, and see after it regularly myself, because they are so careless about their own children when they are nursing other people's, that she and her own husband would let the poor little creature die from neglect, and then curse us as the cause of it."[1]

The memsahibs were at loggerhead with the 'indolence' of these servants, which was termed as 'excessive'. Fanny Parks writes, "My *ayha* will dress me, after which she will go to her house, eat her dinner, and then returning, will sleep in one corner of my room on the floor for the whole day. The bearers also do nothing but eat and sleep, when they are not pulling the *pankhas*". The Indian servants were characterized as a "lazy race".[2] "I (Julia Maitland) have been trying to entomologize, as there are abundance of curious insects..........so I employed beggar-boys, who at first liked the amusement and brought me a great many, but they gradually grew tired of it, and are now too lazy to find me any more at all. I raised my price, but in vain. These naked imps prefer sitting on the grass all day with nothing to do, crumpled up and looking like tadpoles, and will not give themselves the trouble even to put out their paws to take an insect if he crosses their path. They are indeed a lazy race. The servants lie on their mats, strewing the floor like cats

---

[1] Maitland, Julia, Letters from Madras. 3rd October 1837; p.78-79.

[2] *Ibid*, 16th May 1837; p.54.

and dogs, and begin to puff and whine whenever one gives them any employment. The truest account of their occupation was given to me in her blundering English by my muddle. I said, "Ellen, what you are doing, I say?" "Ma'am, I never do", meaning, "I am doing nothing."

The refrain about the indolence of the Indian servants was a never ending story, which was recorded by the memsahibs in great detail. On her journey from Bombay to Cutch in 1837 by boat, Marianna Postans recorded, "the crew of these boats are usually half Hindu, and half Mahomedan; they are a satisfied and slothful race, who lie scattered about the poop, or on the rafters of the bows during the noontide heat, with the exception of the helmsman, alternately sleeping and smoking until sunset, when they assemble round a large platter of rice, curry, and coarse grain cakes, which after the prefatory measure of pouring a little water over their hands, they rapidly despatch—sitting round in a circle, and gathering up the rice between their fingers, each dipping into the same dish..........A boat's crew can imagine no state of existence half so desirable as one of rest; they consequently display a total apathy as to their amount of daily progress. If a foul wind set in, they immediately anchor; and if at night a fair breeze should spring up, they never set sail again, but remain very quietly until the following morning: thus they can have no sympathy with their unhappy passenger, whose every sense furnishes him with fresh avenues for disgust and suffering. Remonstrance is vain; but daily does he groan in spirit, as the approach of evening sees him little advanced on his weary way, and the crew again prepare, even under a fair wind, and a refreshing breeze, to drop anchor, and wait the morning tide."[1]

Another habit of the Indian servants which was frowned upon by the memsahibs was 'drunkenness'. "Drunkenness is very common among the servants, they drink a good deal at night, and are stupefied in the morning, and people say it is generally a mistake to give orders before eleven o'clock in the morning as until that time they have not worked off the effects of the opium or drink they have taken".[2]

On the issue of the treatment of the servants by the English, it was held that "their servility is disagreeable, but the rudeness and the contempt with which the English treat them are quite painful to witness. Civility to servants especially seems a complete characteristic of *griffin-age*. One day I said to my *ayah* (a very elegant lady in white muslin), "Ayah, bring me a glass of toast-and-water, if you please." She crept to the door, and then came back again, looking extremely perplexed, and whined out, "What Mistress tell? I don't know." "I told you to bring me some toast-and-water." "Toast-water I know very well, but mistress tell 'if you please'." I believe the phrase had never been addressed to her. Everything seems to be done by means of constantly finding fault: if one lets the people suppose they have given a moment's satisfaction, they begin to reason, "Master tell very good; try a little more than worse; perhaps Master like plenty as well." One day I gave some embroidery to be done by a Moorman recommended by my tailor: the Moorman did not bring his work home on time; I asked Mrs. Staunton

---

[1] Postans, Marianna. *Cutch*; p.5-7.

[2] Ford, Helen C. *Notes of a tour in India and Ceylon*; p.45.

what was to be done. "Oh," she said, "of course stop the tailor's pay." "But it is no fault of the poor tailor's." "Oh, never mind that: he is the Moorman's particular friend, and he will go and beat him every day till he brings the work home."[1]

An equally large number of helpers were required if one travelled by some form of water-transport. Fanny Parks in December 1834 commenced on a journey from Allahabad to Agra, in a pinnace, the '*Sea Gull*', and her crew consisted of twenty-two members. The list of those employed was: one *sarang*, who commands the vessel; four *khalasis*, who held the next rank; one *gal'haiya* (from *galahai* or forecastle) the forecastle man; fourteen *dandees* or sailors; one cook and his mate; all Musalmans.

Servants in India were an undeniable part of the life of any British household, but their numbers became even larger if the memsahib was a member of the Governor-General's family. Fanny Eden, the sister of Lord Auckland, talks about the entourage which was to accompany her when she was going on a tiger-shooting to the Rajmahal hills in 1836, with her cousin William, and, her friend and her husband for company. The number of servants who were to accompany them was to be 'limited', as they were 'travelling in the marching fashion'. On this journey Emily Eden wrote that Fanny was to be accompanied by her servants, as "everybody in India has their own set of servants, who are no more trouble travelling than living at home. They find their own way from station to station, cook for themselves, sleep on the ground, and, in short, are quite unlike the fussy lady's maid and valet who dispute every inch of the imperial and expect tea,

[1] Maitland, Julia. *Letters from Madras.* 27th December 1836; p.32.

beer, and feather beds, etc., at every bad inn on the road. But then, to be sure, it takes about fourteen natives to do the work of one English servant. I suppose William and Fanny could not march without thirty servants of their own, besides guards, elephants, etc."[1] While still on the number of servants who were to go on this hunting trip, William advised Fanny had she had better take Jones(her English maid), in case she should fall ill; and the *ayah*, Myra (Fanny's Indian maid), to be the companion for the English maid, apart from Fanny's own sixteen bearers, she would require ten to twelve more to carry her things, apart from her *kitmutgar* who was to wait on her at dinner, and peons to pitch her tents and the *jemadar* to go after all these underlings. And in these preparations one had to take along the washerman and the tailor, and lastly the elephants, who would require only a guard of twenty. These few, with their own tail of servants would do very well. When Fanny Eden ventured to suggest that she would not require the tailor for three to four weeks, William retorted that tailors were always useful, as his tailor had saved his elephants life by sewing up his trunk when a tiger had nearly clawed his mount, in a previous expedition. The reality of the insidious presence of the servants was revealed strongly to Fanny Eden when on the tiger shoot she decided to go sketching. She had her *jemadar* Dulhoo, and there was one servant to carry her book, another carried her pencils, a third carried the armchair, a fourth the footstool and the fifth an umbrella. Emily Eden, the elder sister of Fanny, recorded in her letter of 26th October 1837, the complaint of Major J.- as she accompanied her brother, the Governor-General,

[1] Emily Eden's letter of 29th December 1836.

Lord Auckland, across the Northern provinces. "Major J. observed in a gentle, ill-used voice: 'I think Captain K. behaved very ill to us; he said that between both the steamers and the flat he could lodge all the servants that were indispensably and absolutely necessary to us, so I only brought one hundred and forty, and now he says there is room not even for them."[1]

Emily Eden too was bewildered by the number of servants attached to her. She wrote: "An astonishingly agreeable *khidmatgar* and four others glide behind me whenever I move from one room to another." A similar sentiment was echoed by Helen C. Ford, while she was in India for barely three months in1888-89, "all the servants go about bare-footed and one does not hear them come into the room". The usefulness of the servants is evident in the fact that, "In their white garments and bare feet, they noiselessly minister his (the master or the mistress's) wants, not even remarking that it is hot. I often felt grateful to a black-handed bearer who incited the *punkah-coolie* to renewed exertions, warned the *bhisti* to pour more water on the *kus-kus tattie*, and silently placed an iced drink near my hand without bothering me with questions, when the afternoon sun grew unendurable."[2]

Realizing that the servants were an undeniable necessity for a British family's survival in India, the East India Company provided a few to their employees. Julia Maitland recounted that in 1837, at Madras "the "John Company" allows us nine Peons, to look grand with. Their business is to stand about, go on messages, walk after us (which, by the bye, we cannot endure), do odd

---

[1] Eden, Emily. *Up the Country*. Vol-I. p.7.

[2] Bremmer, Christina. *A Month in a Dandi*; p.43.

jobs, and help "help Bill" in various ways. The other day I sent the baby and nurse out for a walk in our garden, not supposing that she required any escort, but a great Peon immediately stepped forward to march after her. She crowed at his dagger and red belt, and much approved of his attendance. A—has given me two of the Peons for my particular service: I have nothing on earth for them to do, so I mean to set them collecting the pebbles found in the river here, which are very beautiful onyxes and agates. When they have got over their surprise, and are a little broken in to the *"Dooresany's"* (lady's) ways, I mean to set them catching insects; but I must wait a little first, for fear they should think me mad."[1]

The luxury of having a large number of servants in attendance on oneself was perceived as a sign of high rank, and while Julia Maitland is unable to appreciate this value. She writes, "Some Anglo-Indians think themselves too grand to walk in their gardens without servants behind them; and one may really see them, skinny and straw-coloured, and withered like old stubble, creeping along their gravel walks, with a couple of beautiful barefooted peons, with handsome turbans, strutting behind them, and looking like bronze casts of the Apollo in attendance upon Frank's caricature of our old dancing-master."[2]

Lady Curzon, spouse of the Governor-General, akin to experiences of the ordinary memsahibs, talks with bated breath about the number and quality of Indian hired helps. She writes to her mother on 9th February 1900, from the Government House at Barrackpore: "We are getting used to the Indian customs and peculiarities.

---

[1] Maitland, Julia. *Letters from Madras.* 11th August 1837; p.65-66.

[2] *Ibid,* 11th January 1837; p.37-38.

Everything is wonderfully peaceful and tranquil and no one is ever in a hurry. Everyone has a quantity of attendants and each of these has his special occupation and his caste only permits him to do that *one*. One man heats your bathwater, another one brings it & a third pours it into a tub—a fourth empties it and he being the low caste does the objectionable things which no drains necessitate—quite a different lot wait on you at breakfast and there is a waiter for every person at the table. The result is that the waiting is admirably done—and they all glide about in red livery & bare feet and a dinner of a 100- or one of 8- are wonderfully smooth and perfect, and the immense number of native servants in the house are all under the head English steward named Hiller who came out with Lord Lansdowne[1], he literally does everything—he is steward, butler, and housekeeper and an invaluable man. George and I each have a high caste attendant who sits outside our doors & attends us wherever we go. My swell's name is Ramdas, and whenever we drive out he sits up in the rumple behind the Great barouche & behind him stands a *Syce*—two postillions in front two outriders, eight body guards & one officer & a policeman so it takes eighteen people besides an ADC *in* the carriage to take a Viceroy out. Irene and Cynthia (her daughters) have quite an army and everyone does nothing, but it is part of the magnificence."[2]

Inspite of the large number of servants employed in the average British household, the memsahib was ever busy superintending and managing her army of servants.

---

[1] The fifth Marquess of Lansdowne, who was Viceroy of India from 1888-94.

[2] Bradley, John (ed.). *Lady Curzon's India*. p. 58.

The activities of the memsahibs were as commonplace as that of any women arranging for the house, and it's smooth and efficient running, whether it entailed care of food items, or the procurement of potable water for drinking purposes. The efficient housewife in 1830 is as concerned about the care for meat in the rainy season, where it is good for not 'more than twenty-four hours', while roasted meat 'will keep until the next day'. The provisions for water entailed greater worry for the memsahib as it was recorded that, "In Calcutta, the tank water being unwholesome to drink, it is necessary to catch rain-water, and preserve it in great jars; sixty jars will last a full year in our family. It is purified with alum, and a heated iron is put into it. Here (Cawnpore) we drink the Ganges water, reckoned the most wholesome in India; it is purified in jars in the same manner. The water of the Jamuna is considered unwholesome, and in some parts, my old *abdar* declares, it is absolutely poisonous".[1]

"You in England imagine a lady in India has nothing to do. For myself, I superintend the household, and find it difficult at times even to write letters, there is which is so much necessary to attend. At this moment I would willingly be quite, but am continually interrupted. The coachman, making his salaam, "Memsahiba, Atlas is very ill, I cannot wait for the sahib's return; I have brought the horse to the door, will you give your orders?" The *durwan* (gate-keeper), "Memsahiba, the deer have jumped over the wall, and have run away." The *sirdar*-bearer, "Memsahiba, will you advance me some rupees to make a great feast? My wife is dead." The mate-bearer

[1] Parks, Fanny. *Wanderings of a pilgrim* . 16th July 1830, p.143,Vol.I.

then presented his petition, "Will the memsahiba give me a plaister? The rats have gnawed my fingers and toes" [1].

The memsahibs during their regular interaction with the servants to communicate their commands and instructions evolved language which had its with its own unique grammar and syntax, and what was humorously referred to as "John Company's English".[2] Such a language to a new memsahib appeared to be "silly and childish" and "gibberish", which they contemptuously abjured. However, as the memsahibs settled down to a long residence in India, the formality of the King's English was soon forgotten in the desire and need to have their instructions understood.

The memsahibs indulged in a constant war of attrition with their servants; they did acknowledge that "with all their badness, and all their laziness, there is some good in them. If their master or mistress is in distress or difficulty, they do not grudge any trouble or fatigue to help them." [3] This trait of the Indian servant is substantiated by Julia Maitland by the following incident. "Last Saturday I was in a great fright: A—did not come, as I expected, and I had not heard from him for two days. There is no regular post to this remote place, so we have messengers of our own to carry letters and parcels, and we send each other a note every day to say that all is well; for in a country like this, where all attacks of illness are so frightfully rapid, we could not be easy without hearing from day to day. But on Saturday evening, as he neither came nor sent, I was frightened, and thought he must

---

[1] *Ibid*, 9th May 1825, p.51,Vol.I.

[2] Maitland, Julia. *Letters from Madras.* 27th December 1836; p.32-33

[3] Ibid, 9th July 1838; p.139-140.

certainly have the cholera and be too ill to write, and that I must go and see after him immediately. Accordingly I dispatched messengers to post bearers for me all along the road, bade Moonshee write me a letter every day about the baby, and in the evening I set out in a great bustle for Rajahmundry, attended for some miles by all inhabitants of the nearest villages, all shouting. I took the Peon with me, and told him that he was to go half-way, and then stop, and send a change village Peon on with me the other half; thinking twenty-five miles quite enough for a man to run in one night; but he said that he would rather go all the fifty miles himself; for that he did not mind being tired, and should not be happy in trusting the Mistress to the care of a strange Peon. However, after I had gone about nine miles, I met the messengers with A—'s letters, which had only been delayed by the very common occurrence of the postman being lazy—they were fast asleep by the river-side when I met them: so, as A—was quite well, and only detained by some unfortunate visitor, I returned home again. The bearers, Peons, people whom I had scuffled half out of their lives to get ready in time, all laughed very heartily; but I was glad enough that it was only a laughing matter, and laughed myself as they shouted with redoubled vigour all the way home."

The faith reposed by Julia Maitland in her Indian servants was not a solitary example, but was reflective of the immense faith that the British had in their Indian servants. This faith was revealed, curiously in the travel patterns in India, when the sahibs let their women and children travel great distances on their own, with only their Indian servants for company and protection. Emily Eden, while she was travelling in India with Lord

Auckland, the Governor-General of India from 1835-1842, she came across the real incident recounted by Mr. T., who had looked after three little children, a little girl nine years old and her two younger brothers who were being sent to their school in Mussoorie alone, without even their names written down; being passed from one set of bearers to another.[1] In another instance, when Henry and Honoria Lawrence were travelling together across the Northern Indian plain barely three weeks after she had given birth to their first child, Henry Lawrence often rode miles ahead leaving Honoria to be carried in her litter. On one occasion the baby was sick, and she feared that she herself was dying; she tried to send a message to her husband ahead. When Henry Lawrence did return, it was to find her by the roadside, clutching the baby in despair. Yet in later years Honoria Lawrence with her small son covered hundreds of miles from Kurnaul, north of Delhi, to Gorakhpur, in the east without trouble at all. She wrote for the benefit of her friends in England, that it was quite commonplace for a memsahib to find herself "travelling with twenty men or upwards at night through a country where for hours no habitation is seen, she very unlikely to speak a sentence of Hindustani intelligently...." All this too "on the very ground where *thugs* are slaying scores, hundreds of travelers, strangling a man for half a crown's worth of silver ornaments he may happen to have, or not unfrequently, without any purpose of plunder, merely to keep their hands in".[2] In another instance it was recorded, that "the safety with which the female foreigners travel *daak* (post) in their *palankeens*, from one point of the

---

[1] Eden, Emily. *Up the Country* . Vol.-I p.146-147.

[2] Extracted from MacMillian, M. p.75.

Indian continent to another, without the knowledge of five words of the Hindoostaunie tongue, and with no other servant but the *daak*-bearers, who carry them at the rate of four miles an hour, travelling day and night successively."[1]

To the memsahibs in India motherhood was a paradox, as it was marked with the parting from their infant children. The children born to the British in India were regarded as the "outposts of the Empire". Children were a sign that the British were established in India, and that the community was 'sound' and propagating. This is especially to be seen against the backdrop that the presence of white children indicated that the British men had abjured the bad old practice of keeping *bibis*. And the consciousness that they were the ruling race, and that their rule would endure, was demonstrated by their offsprings who would carry their task forward. These young children were thus the 'outposts of the Empire' who had to be protected, to be trained to shoulder their share of the burden of carrying the Raj forward. The 'tender mother' was a phrase widely used as a commemorative phrase on the tombstones of the memsahibs, but bringing up children was not an easy task in India.[2]

The English children brought up in India cherished their memories, but the memsahibs were unhappy with the "native system" of bringing up their children and one of the reasons for removing them from India was to ensure immunity from the ill-effects of the "native system". "Baby is very well and very intelligent. Every now and

---

[1] Mrs. Ali, Meer Hassan. *Observations on the Mussulmauns of India*. Letter XII.

[2] MacMillan, Margaret. *Women of the Raj*. p.125.

then she learns to pronounce some new word, which she thinks is very clever; but I intend, as much as possible, to prevent her from learning the native languages; though it is very difficult—most English children do learn them, and all sorts of mischief with them, and grow like little Hindoos. If my child were to stay long in the country, it would be worthwhile to send for an English nurse; but, as it is, I hope to bring her home before it becomes of any consequence, and meanwhile I keep her as much as possible with me. The native "system" of managing a child is to make it cry for everything. If "Missy", as they call her, asks for anything, Ayah is too lazy to give it, but argues, and tries to persuade her to do without it: then Missy whines—Ayah does not care for that, she whines too: then Missy roars—then, whether right or wrong, good or bad, Ayah gives her whatever she wants. She has nothing to do but roar long enough and loud enough, and she is sure to get her own way—anything may be done by means of naughtiness."[1]

The moral dangers that the mothers feared were greater than the physical discomfort. Since most of the children spoke Indian languages before they spoke English, there was the serious danger that they would pick up the native ways of thought, hence the children had to be sent Home. "At Home, the children born into the Raj, were sent to schools where India was to be driven out of their systems and Britain drummed in."

Children who went Home were in a minority but an élite one; if they returned to India, they would take their places in the upper levels of the Raj. Whenever it was possible, the mothers went Home with them;

[1] Maitland, Julia. *Letters from Madras*. 9th January 1839; p.160.

otherwise the children were consigned to relatives or foster-parents. The lower levels of the British society in India—the smaller merchants, planters, and perhaps the subordinate civil servants—could not afford the luxury of sending their children Home. Instead they sent them to the Hills, to schools like St. Paul's in Darjeeling or Bishop Cotton's in Simla, with solidly British curriculum. Their mothers faced the same dilemma as the upper-class mothers did. Should they go to the Hills with their children, or stay in the Plains with their husbands? The one consolation being, that at least the periods of separation were not extended, as there was one school term from March to November, and, as winter set in the children came home for their holidays.

British children growing up in India grew up accustomed to having their whims obeyed, and it was the bane of all mothers to prevent their children from growing up to become 'proverbially captious, disobedient, and easily thrown out of gear'. Hence, these children had to be trained, and there was no better school than Home. By the end of the eighteenth century, some wealthy families had started to send their children Home. In the nineteenth century, as communications improved, this practice received a fillip. And children, as tender as five years, were shipped back home. While the boys were sent Home early, the girls could stay a few years more with their parents in India.

For Emily, the daughter of Sir Thomas Metcalfe, who was sent to England at the age of seven, India remained the magical country, whose treasures were to remind her and her sister of their home in India. "Oh! How Georgie and I treasured some Indian coins—gold *mohurs* and rupees—one of each, given to each of us in Calcutta. We looked at them on particular days during our childhood with reverence and love as part of our Indian belongings."[1]

The practice of sending away children to be brought up in England was termed the "grand Indian sorrow—the necessity of parting with one's children"[2] for the purpose of sustaining the Raj, and more especially before they fell victims to attack of the "Indian fever." For the Metcalfe sisters, who had been born in India but educated at Home, the return journey was marked by a sudden sense of the rush of familiarity, the rush of recollections that had faded during the long cold years away in England. The homecoming for the Metcalfe sisters, in 1847 was no less rapturous. "The brightness of those first days in India threw a glow over all my Indian experience. The brilliant climate, the beautiful flowers, the gay plumage of the birds, the novelty of all the scenes I witnessed every hour and the lavish hospitality which was then such a marked feature of Indian life, were all new and delightful experiences to me, a simple girl fresh from a very retired home in England."[3] Furthermore, "The happiness I experienced on my first arrival threw a halo over all my residence in India, especially over my life in Delhi, and the letters that awaited me in Calcutta from my dear Father were so full of tender love and eager anticipation of our reunion, that they made me intensely happy, and I was most anxious to get to my home as quickly as possible."[4]

---

[1] Kaye, M.M. *The Golden Calm*. p.27.

[2] Maitland, Julia. *Letters from Madras*. 24th September 1839; p.189.

[3] Kaye, M.M. *The Golden Calm*. p.115.

[4] *Ibid*, p.115-116.

Chapter VII

Memsahibs: Into the Gendered Interface with their Indian Counterparts

To the memsahibs arriving in India, after the initial days of settling down into their households, and getting acquainted with the picturesque, the area which naturally attracted their attention was the status of their kindred Indian counterparts, generically termed 'the native women'. The memsahibs interaction with the Indian women took place at three levels, in the form of the nautch-women; the women who committed sati; and the women in the seclusion of the zenana. And it was on all three issues that the memsahibs recorded their views and opinions prolifically. A fourth issue also evinced the memsahibs that, which was their perspective on the *bibis*, but this topic was referred to obliquely, and that too in private conversations amongst themselves.

The British memsahib to furnish the first account of her impressions about the '*nautch*' was Mrs. Kindersley, who was in India from 1765 to 1768. The *nautch* was a predominantly male pastime, as the *nawabs, rajas* and the nobility maintained their own set of *nautch*-girls and musicians. Mrs. Meer Hassan Ali recounts that, "The *nautchunies* (i.e. the nautch-girls) are entirely excluded from the female apartments of the better sort of people; no respectable Mussulman would allow these impudent women to perform before their wives and daughters."[1] All new arrivals to India were introduced to this popular entertainment where even the ladies were invited, though it was essentially intended for a male audience. In a description of a *nautch*-party in Calcutta, Mrs. Kindersley recorded that the performance consisted chiefly of repetitive movements of hands and feet in unison with music. She further wrote that, "It is their languishing glances and attitudes not consistent with decency which are so much admired and who so much admired and whoever excels most in these is the finest dancer". As for the songs, were "both Persian or Hindostanee", Mrs. Kindersley found them really pleasing to the ear. She further observed that a beauty much esteemed in the *nautch*-girls was "the long cut eye and long eyebrows".

The *nautch*-girls captivated the hearts of the English sahib by her song and dance, enthralled the more sophisticated by her conversation and wit, so much so that in 1803 the Anglican chaplain W. Tennant did not object to the *nautch* as a form of entertainment. Capt. Williamson wrote in his *Costumes and Customs of Modern India* (1813) that between the years 1778 and 1785, the prime sets of dancing girls moved from

[1] Mrs. Ali, Meer Hassan. *Observations on the Mussulmauns of India.* Letter VIII.

their native quarters to several cantonments where they received considerable encouragement. According to him, the celebrated *nautch* girl, Kaunum, was at the zenith of her glory and held in thrall many young British officers. The Bengali *nawabs* and *rajas* organized fabulous *nautch*-parties in Calcutta during Durga Puja to entertain European guests. James Forbes in his *Oriental Memoirs* (1813) noted the *nautch* girls were dedicated from their infancy to this profession, for preserving 'a decency and modesty in their demeanour, which is more likely to allure than the shameless effrontery of similar characters in other countries'. Lt. Thomas Bacon in his journal (1837) has given a detailed description of the *nautch* performances. "The movements of the dance are extremely graceful, and we have nothing in England to which I can compare them. At first, the action is quiet and the expression of soft delight, then as the dance proceeds, the music rises in tone, and the countenance and gesture grow more animated, suggesting love, then adoration, then alternatively, or in accordance with the humour of the song, fear, homage, affection, hatred and other ardent feelings, until both music and song, ascending in force and sentiment, inspire the dancers with the most passionate gesticulation, speaking the language of fervent love and sometimes even of despair, and this I have more than once seen depicted with a truth we could hardly expect from them".[1]

The adverse reaction of the British men to the Indian forms of entertainment, especially the '*nautch*' exhibited their prejudices, and these became formalized once the British women started coming to India in large numbers.

---

[1] As quoted in Pran Neville, *Rare Glimpses from the Raj*.p.18.

A typical reaction of their impression is illustrated in the following verse:[1]

"The Rajah he bowed and he bowed and he bowed,
Shaking hands as they came with the whole of the crowd;
And he led to a couch the Commissioner's wife,
And said 'twas the happiest hour of his life.
Then suddenly sounded a loud-clanging gong'
And there burst on the eyes of the wondering throng
A bevy of girls
Dressed in bangles and pearls
And other rich gems,
With fat podgy limbs.......
And sang a wild air
Which affected your hair
While behind them a circle of men and boys,
With tomtoms and pipes, made a terrible noise".

The Indians likewise, were not able to appreciate the intricacies of the European dance forms, and once the British guests departed from the entertainment organised by the Indian hosts at their residences, there followed an entertainment of which few British guests were aware. The doors would shut on the British and the dancing-girls, dressed in English costumes would execute an Orientalised version of the English dances, those minuets and country-dances, which appeared so innocent to the English eyes, were utterly scandalous to the Indian eyes. The dancing–girls would give an imitation of the bored guests who had just left, and the uncomfortable tension

[1] Kincaid, Dennis. *British Social Life in India, 1608-1937.* p.116.

of the previous hours would vanish in bursts of laughter. Maria Graham commented on this caricaturized version of the European dances, as she records that, "Sorry I could not go to the *nautch* the next night, where I hear there was a masquerade with several Pariahs appeared as Europeans and imitated our dances, music and manners". Maria Graham's attitude was a restrained version of the contempt with which the British looked down upon the Indian customs, and typical reaction to this mime is that of Flora Annie Steel, "Two white-masked figures, clasped waist to waist, were waltzing about tipsily. One had a curled waxen wig, a muslin dress distended by an all-too-visible crinoline giving full play to a pair of prancing brown legs. The other wore an old staff uniform, cocked hat and feather complete.........It was a vile travesty".

In another instance quoted of December 1827, suggests that the British women were not permitted to indulge in dancing in the presence of Indians. The incident relates to the time when Lord Combermere, the commander-in-chief was visiting Lucknow, and he invited the Nawab of Oudh for dinner at the Residency. "That night his majesty (the Nawab) dined at the residency, and took his departure at ten p.m., when quadrilles immediately commenced. The ladies were not allowed to dance while his majesty was present, as, on one occasion, he had said, "That will do, let them leave off," thinking the ladies were quadrilling for his amusement, like *nach* women. Describing the reaction of an average India at the station-ball of Dinapore, Emily Eden wrote, "At the ball there were some rajahs in splendid dresses; such magnificient jewels, and some of them had never seen an English ball before. They think the ladies who dance are utterly good for nothing, but seemed rather pleased to see so much vice." Describing India of approximately the same decades, the lack of appreciation of the European dance forms was justified on the grounds that, "Amateur performers are very rare amongst the Mussulmauns; indeed, it is considered indecorous in either sex to practice music, singing, or dancing; and such is the prejudice in their minds against this happy resource amongst happy people of other climates, that they can never reconcile themselves to the propriety of 'The Sahib-Logue', – a term in general use for the English people visiting India, – figuring away in a quadrille or country dance. The nobles and gentlemen are frequently invited to witness a 'station-ball'; they look with surprise at the dancers, and I have been often asked why I did not persuade my countrywomen that they were doing wrong. "Why do people fatigue themselves, who can so well afford to hire dancers for their amusement?" Such is the difference between people of opposite views in their modes of pleasing themselves: a Native gentlemen would consider himself disgraced or insulted by the simple inquiry, "Can you dance, sing, or play?"[1]

Mary Martha Sherwood, who was in India from 1805 to 1815, was disturbed by the British infatuation with nautch, and lamented upon those who came within the influence of the nautch girls. "It steals upon those who come within its charmed circle in a way not unlike that of an intoxicating drug, being the more dangerous for young Europeans because they seldom fear it". Yet she however was much impressed by Indian music and considered

[1] Mrs. Ali, Meer Hassan. *Observations on the Mussulmauns of India.* Letter VIII.

it not only "sweet and melancholy but wonderfully melodious".

Fanny Parks in May 1823 attended a *nautch* organized by 'Ram Mohun Roy, a rich Bengallee *baboo*'. In her first-hand account of this account she wrote, "In various rooms of the house *nach* girls were dancing and singing. They wear a petticoat measuring, on dit, one hundred yards in width, of fine white or coloured muslin, trimmed with deep borders of gold and silver; full satin trousers cover the feet; the *douputta,* or large veil is worn over the head, and the various ornaments of native jewellery adorn the person. They dance or rather move in a circle, attitudinizing and making the small brass bells fastened to their ankles sound in unison with their movements. Several men attended to the women, playing on divers curiously shaped native instruments. The style of singing was curious; at times their tones proceeded finely from their noses; some of the airs were very pretty".

Mrs. Elwood in her *Narrative of Journey* (1830) describes the novelty and splendor of the *nautch*. For her the *nautch* was so perfectly new and so completely oriental that she wished that she had Sir Walter Scott's power of description to capture the beauty of this graceful form of entertainment. "It is surprising that a regular set of *nautch* girls have never been imported for the English stage.......the novelty and splendor of a *nautch* would recommend them for a season at least". Mrs. S. C. Belnos, a reputed artist who lived in Calcutta in the early nineteenth century, says in her explanatory notes to her paintings of the *nautch* girls that she was so "enchanted by the whole atmosphere of a *nautch* party with its raining of rose-water, flower garlands and musical airs," that she felt herself "transported to some enchanted region and the whole scene .... a fairy vision". Watching a *nautch* at a party given by the Rajah of Benaras in 1837, Emily Eden, the sister of the Governor-General, Lord Auckland, she was entranced by the Flower Dance by the two *nautch* girls. One of them, she writes, was "the prettiest creature I ever saw and the most graceful". It was further said, " She and another girl danced slowly round with their full draperies floating around them, without stopping, for a quarter of an hour, during all the time they were making flowers out of some coloured scarfs they wore, and when they finished a bunch they came and presented it to us with such graceful Eastern genuflexions. The whole thing was like a dream, it was so curious and unnatural." [1] Her sister Fanny records that she 'never grew tired of looking at her' and the whole scene of the *nautch* and fireworks made it look 'like the Arabian Nights put to life'.

There were other memsahibs who were disappointed and disillusioned with the *nautch*. Maria Graham (1810) who was otherwise impressed with Indian culture, as was Fanny Parks (1820's), belonged to this group. Maria Graham when invited to a *nautch* by Maharajah Rajhissen Bahadur, on the occasion of Durga Pooja, at Calcutta in October 1810 records that "though they were pretty, and their motions rather graceful, I was disappointed, after hearing so much of the *nautch*-girls of India." Mrs. Fenton, an army wife (1820's) found the *nautch* girls she saw "an odious specimen of oriental beauty making frightful contractions with her arms, hands, head and eyes". Mrs. Meer Hassan Ali, too felt an "utter dislike both to the amusement and the performers." Julia Maitland, a judge's

---

[1] Eden, Emily. *Up the Country*. Vol.-I p.40.

wife in South India in the 1830's found the *nautch* boring enough to "send one to sleep and the singing nothing better than a fearful noise"; a sentiment echoed by Fanny Eden in 1838, when a *nautch* party was hosted in honour of Ranjeet Singh of Punjab, where she remarked that the '*nautch* girls' singing generally runs to screaming', though appreciating their beauty, and thought best to have it replaced by their 'own band play'. Ranjeet Singh, however, requested that the *nautch* girls' resume their singing. Flora Annie Steel regarded the *nautch* as one of the "deadliest of dull and decorous entertainments." Fanny Eden's further exposure to *nautch* strengthened her opinion about this art form, when she was invited to one by James Skinner at Delhi in February 1838, she maintained that as usual 'the *nautch* girls' dresses were splendid and their dancing very graceful, but there was a sameness to it', but their singing sounded 'positively frightful'. A similar sentiment was recorded earlier in Madras in January 1837. "...and the Nabob's dancing girls came in: most graceful creatures, walking, or rather sailing about, like queens, with long muslin robes from their throats to their feet. They were covered with gold and jewels, earrings, nose-rings, bracelets, armlets, bands round their heads, sévignés, and rings on all their fingers and all their toes. Their dancing consisted of sailing about, and bending from side to side: there were neither steps nor figure, as far as I could make out. The prettiest of their performances was their beautiful swan-like march. Then they sang, bawling like bad street-singers—a very fearful noise, and no tune."[1] The same narrative continues, "Then we had a Hindoo dancing-

---

[1] Maitland, Julia. *Letters from Madras.* 31st January 1837, p.42-43.

girl, with the most magnificent jewellery I ever saw: her dancing was very much like that of the Mahometans, only a little more difficult. There was a good deal of running backwards and forwards upon her heels, and shaking her silver bangles or armlets, which jingled like bells: then glissading up to me, waving her pretty little hands, and making a number of graceful, unmeaning antics, with her eyes fixed on mine in a strange unnatural stare, like animal magnetism. I think those magnetic actings and starings must first have been imitated from some Indian dancing-girl, and in fact the effect is much the same; for I defy any one to have watched this girl's dull, unvarying dance long, without going to sleep."

All accounts and views about the *nautch* were more or less unanimous that there was nothing indecent or obscene in either the costumes of the *nautch* girls or their performance. "The dress of the Indian dancing-girl is infinitely more decent than that of our French or Italian figurantes, the long silken trousers descending quite over the feet. The upper portions of the costume, however, I am bound to say is not always so quite impervious to sight as a bodice of more opaque texture than muslin might render it". [1] Even during the anti-*nautch* campaign by the Indian reformers and Christian missionaries at the end of the nineteenth century, Lord Lansdowne, the Viceroy, from 1888 to 1893, in reply to their memorandum, said that he "was not inclined to surrender to these intolerant gentlemen as he had not seen any impropriety in the *nautches*".

In the context of the *nautch* it would be appropriate to mention the "*Domenie,* who are singers and dancers

---

[1] Captain Mundy, *The Journal of a Tour.* Vol.-I p.91.

admitted within the pale of the zeenahnah life; these, on the contrary, are women of good character, and their songs are of a most chaste description, chiefly in the Hindoostanie tongue. They are instructed in the Native music and play on the instruments in common use with good taste,-- as the *saattarah* (i.e. the sitar), with three wire strings; the *surringhee* (i.e. the sarangi), a rude shaped violin; the *dhome* or *dholle* (i.e. the drum), in many varieties, beaten with the fingers, never with sticks. The harmony produced is melancholy and not unpleasing, but at best all who form the several classes of professors in Native societies are indifferent musicians."[1]

In the early decades of the nineteenth century, the British followed an ardent 'hands-off' policy in social legislation in India, as is evident from the Despatch from the Court of Directors, dated 7th September 1808 to Lord Minto (1807-1813), on the subject of Christian missionaries. The despatch insisted that, "It will be your bounden duty, vigilantly to guard the public tranquility from interruption and to impress upon the minds of all inhabitants of India, that the British faith, upon which they rely for the exercise of their religion, will be inviolably maintained."

This assurance to the Court of Directors was coming under severe strain, and the memsahibs too played a role in fraying the edges of religious tolerance. The sentiment of intolerance, found expression in their writings, in the diaries and journals they maintained. "To-day's *Gazette* brings word that Government have just issued their orders that "*no salutes to idols be discontinued*, but that all respect

---

[1] Mrs. Ali, Meer Hassan. *Observations on the Mussulmauns of India.* Letter VIII.

be paid to the native religions as heretofore." Is this not disgraceful? A fortnight ago, at a Mohammedan festival at Trichinopoly, the European troops—Artillery men—were kept exposed to the sun for nine hours, firing salutes, and "showing respect" to Mohammed. The Government lately presented a shawl to a Hindoo idol, and the Government officer, Mr. D., with whom we are acquainted, was ordered to superintend the delivery of it. He does not pretend to be a religious man—a mere commonplace, hunting, card-playing dandy: but even *he* was disgusted as having such an office to perform; so he went with the shawl in his *tonjon*, and told the Bramins they might come and take it, for that he would not touch it with his own fingers, to present it to a Swamy. At the same place the Swamy was making a progress in its car, and the officiating Bramin came and told Mr. D. that it had stopped at a certain point for want of sufficient offerings; so Mr. D. went to see about it, and found that they had stuck a wedge under the wheel, which prevented it from going on. He had the wedge knocked out, and gave orders that the Swamy must arrive at his destination without delay, before all the poor officers were ruined, or the cholera broke out, as generally happens at these horrible feasts, from the concourse of people, dirt, & c. In consequence of all this, Mr. D. was much blamed and reprehended at Madras, for having caused the feast to be hurried over more quickly than the Bramins liked. The cars are drawn by men and very often these men are unwilling to leave their work for the service, and the Bramins cannot catch as many as they want; so the Government order the Collector to take any unwilling men by force, and *make* them drag the car. I believe that, if idolatry were merely tolerated and protected, the idol services would fall almost to nothing, from the indifference of the mass of the people; but our Christian Government not only support and encourage it, but force it down the people's throats. They have made a law that a Heathen Sepoy may not be flogged, but Christian Sepoy may. If a Sepoy turns Christian, he is subject to a punishment which they are pleased to say would degrade a Heathen or a Mohammedan."[1] And it is further said at another point; "Here is another disgraceful story of English ungodliness. When Shah Soojah arrived at his capital, Candahar, he and all his Mussulmans went directly to pay their devotions to a rag of Mohammad's shirt, which is kept there as a precious relic. Of course, all Mussulmans had a right to do so, and no one would think of preventing them; but think of our Envoy and the British troops and authorities all accompanying him in state on such an errand! I could scarcely believe it, but it is really true."[2]

The memsahibs when they expressed antagonism towards Indian customs, rituals and religious practices, were only reflecting a debate which was raging in the British political circles, on the stand to be adopted by the East India Company vis-à-vis social legislation in India. In this scenario, the two contending parties were; on the one hand the 'non-interventionists' also called the 'preservationists'; they were pitted against the Utilitarianists, receiving support from the Evangelists. During the early years of the nineteenth century, in the administration of India, there flourished some of the most remarkable men Britain ever exported to India—

[1] Maitland, Julia. *Letters from Madras*. 8th March 1838; p.128-129.
[2] *Ibid*, 9th August 1839; p.185.

Mountstuart Elphinstone in the Deccan, Colonel Tod in Rajputana, and Thomas Munro in Madras, John Malcolm (Bombay and Deccan), Charles Metcalfe in the North and Deccan, and the Governor-Generals'; Lord Minto and Lord Moira. They were men who knew India as a reality, not as an administrative or geographical fiction, and they felt a genuine responsibility for the people they governed. They believed that Britain's role in India was not only to govern justly but to educate their subjects so that one day they would be able to govern themselves. Thomas Munro, John Malcolm, Mountstuart Elphinstone and Charles Metcalfe were preservationists, at times derided as 'sloppy sentimentalists' who wished to preserve and conserve the traditional institutions. Their common aim was, not to engage in some vast operation designed to transform the Indian sub-continent into a vague simulacrum of British society, but to conserve traditional institutions. Thomas Munro told the Directors of the East India Company that, "You are not here to turn India into England or Scotland. Work through, not inspite of, native systems and native ways, with a prejudice in their favour rather than against them; and when in fullness of time your subjects can frame and maintain a worthy Government for themselves, and get out and take away the glory of the achievement and the sense of having done your duty, as the chief reward of your exertions."[1]

Thomas Munro in his Minutes '*On the State of the Country*' of 31st December 1824 wrote, "The ruling vice of our government is innovation........it is time that we should learn that neither the face of the country, its property, nor its society, are things that can suddenly be

[1] Moon, P. *The British Conquest.* p.426-428.

improved by any contrivance of ours, though they may be greatly injured by what we mean for their good." This romantic school of British administrator in the first half of the nineteenth century was fearful of violent change. John Malcolm wrote, "The most important of the lessons we can derive from our past experience is to be slow and cautious in every procedure which has a tendency to collision with the habits and prejudices of our native subjects. We may be compelled by the character of our government to frame some institutions, different from those we found established, but we shall adopt all we can of the latter into our system...........Our internal government............should be administered on a principle of humility not pride. We must divest our mind of all arrogant pretensions arising from the presumed superiority of our own knowledge, and seek the accomplishment of the great end we have in view by the means which are best suited to the peculiar nature of the objects." Malcolm further expounded, "All that Government can do is, by maintaining the internal peace of the country, and by adapting its principles to the various feelings, habits, and the character of its inhabitants, to give time for the slow and silent operation of the desired improvement, with a constant impression that every attempt to accelerate this end will be attended with the danger of its defeat."[1]

The views of men like Thomas Munro, were soon to be challenged by a group whose intellectual orientation had been foreshadowed in the writings of Charles Grant in1792. A former adviser of Cornwallis in India, and later the Chairman of the Court of Directors of the East India Company, Grant's views provided the proposed activity

[1] Malcolm, John. *Political History.* Vol-II, p.142.

for Christianity in the colony. "In considering the affairs of the world as under the control of the Supreme Disposer, and those distant territories (i.e. India) providentially put into our hands.........is it not necessary to conclude that they were given to us, not merely that we might draw an annual profit from them, but that we might diffuse among her inhabitants, long sunk in darkness, vice and misery, the light and benign influence of the truth, the blessings of well-regulated society, the improvements and comforts of active industry?........In every progressive step of this work, we shall also serve the original design with which we visited India, the design still so important to this country—the extension of our commerce." Charles Grant argued with vehemence the need to open up Indian society which was in desperate need for reform, on the basis of the firm conviction that, "We cannot avoid recognizing in the people of Hindostan, a race of men lamentably degenerate and base; retaining but a feeble sense of moral obligation; yet obstinate in their disregard of what they know to be right, governed by malevolent and licentious passions, strongly exemplifying the effects produced on society by a great and general corruption of manners." James Mill, had never visited India, but on the basis of second-hand references wrote, comparing India with China, that, "both nations are, to nearly an equal degree, tainted with vices of insincerity; dissembling, treacherous, mendacious, to an excess which surpasses even the usual measure of uncultivated society. Both are disposed to excessive exaggeration with regard to everything relating to themselves. Both are cowardly and unfeeling. Both are in the highest degree conceited of themselves, and full of affected contempt for others. Both are, in the physical sense, disgustingly unclean in their persons and in their houses."[1]

By the 1820's the evangelical Christians too had decided that Hinduism was too benighted to reform—or even to tolerate—and must give away to Christianity. William Wilberforce, the indefatigable opponent of slavery, believed that the conversion of India was still more important than the abolition of the slave trade. William Wilberforce wrote in July 1813, "Let us endeavour to strike our roots into the soil by the gradual introduction and establishment of our own principles and opinions; of our laws, institutions, and manners; above all, as the source of every other improvement, of our religion, and consequently of our morals." In an unlikely alliance with the new spirit of Utilitarianism, the Evangelicals did indeed try to turn India as far as possible into England. While the Evangelists attacked the "heathenism", the Utilitarians went as far as possible for the suppression of the 'heathen' customs—'sati' or widow burning; human sacrifice; female infanticide; and the 'thuggee' combination of theft and ritual murder by 'thugs' devoted to the cult of the Goddess Kali. As one historian has pointed out, the two groups complemented each other. "Utilitarians hoped to improve the morals by reforming society; Evangelicals hoped to improve society by reforming morals".[2]

And, despite the best efforts of the Utilitarian's and the Evangelists, there were very few converts, a fact attested from the personal accounts of the memsahibs. "There are times when a sickening feeling comes over

---

[1] Mill, James. *History of British India*. Vol.-II, p.195.

[2] Hutchins, *The Illusion of Permanence*; p. 10.

me at being in 'a heathen land'—at Delhi when towards sunset voices from the great mosque were calling the people to prayer, and sometimes in small temples where there is noisy worship of some grinning idol—and still from time to time horrible facts come out about human sacrifices. I suppose at this moment when the rage for education is very great and the mussulman chiefs no longer oppose it, there is more hope of converts being made, but considering the time the Europeans have been in the country it seems quite extraordinary that with a very few individual exceptions not one native seems to have adopted a single European custom."[1] Mrs. Meer Hassan Ali, after residing for twelve long years with her husband's Muslim family wrote, "It may be regretted, with all my influence that I have not been the humble instrument of conversion. None can I lament more than myself that I was not deemed worthy to convince them of the necessity, or the efficacy of the great Atonement on which my great hopes are founded."[2]

The streams of Utilitarian and Evangelical thought find expression in context of the records of the memsahibs, in their deep seated desire to ameliorate the depressed social and intellectual position of women in the east. After her visit to the Ranees of the Rao of Bhuj, Marianna Postans writes, "I was pleased with their (i.e. the Ranees) amiability, but felt sincere commiseration for their degraded, useless, and demoralizing condition. These poor girls are permitted the free association of numerous beings of their own sex, all equally ignorant,

---

[1] Eden, Fanny. The Second Journal: March 6th 1838; p.142.

[2] Mrs. Ali, Meer. Hassan. *Observations on the Mussulmauns of India.* Letter XXVII.

and many of them far more evil in their nature: they are themselves the slaves of a web of circumstances, woven round their lives by a long and systematic practice of jealous tyranny, and a series of debasing customs, from the social injustice of which the mind of every liberal observer must recoil, when he reflects that the same beings whose moral and rational qualities are thus restricted have, notwithstanding, displayed an energy of mind, determination of purpose, and a cunning aptitude for political intrigue, which, originating in the recesses of the harem, has spread anarchy over kingdoms and deluged them with blood. If, in a state of real ignorance, and apparently habitual apathy, the women of the East display at times so much natural capacity, and mental energy, why, it may be reasonably asked, should they not be equally capable of receiving intellectual culture, and by the consequent development of their faculties and feelings, be prepared for, and permitted to take the part of real usefulness and responsibility in social life, which nature designed in the creation of women?.......... The emancipation of Eastern women from their present mental and personal imprisonment, would require that the prejudices of their forefathers should be laid low, and that the great spirit of change should move over their political, moral, and religious institutions, sweeping away the dust of ages, and erecting toleration as the emblem of awakening truth, over the fallen fanes of heathen worship. To effect this, a series of renovating circumstances must produce opinions very far in advance of those which now bow down to the intellects of the benighted people; and whether it be consistent with the objects of the British power in India, to introduce wise means conducive to such improvement, I leave to the conscientious consideration of those, whose information, talents, and position afford them peculiar advantage for forming a just estimate of the probable gain, but the certain risk, of any attempt to raise the people of India from beneath the yoke of their prejudices, by cultivating their faculties, imbuing them with knowledge, and softening their hearts with all the nameless graces of civilization."[1]

The evangelicals found support from the liberal Utilitarians, who went beyond the universalisation of free trade. They firmly believed that the industrial revolution which had invested Britain with the commercial leadership of the world resulted from a superior civilization, and the passing on of its benefits was not only good business but a heaven-ordained duty. The only way this could be carried out was by spreading English institutions and English education. Essentially this denoted a *mission civilisatrice* rather than a philosophy of conquest.

Contemporary writings of the memsahibs in India dealt with this overwhelming sentiment of the time, at length in their works. "In most cases, the hand of the conqueror has scattered the seed of improvement, and civilization has followed the track of his chariot-wheel; but it must be remembered, that the love of liberty is the twin-sister to the love of knowledge; and both will unfold themselves together, in the minds of those whom the introduction of truth may awaken to seek redress "For India's injured realm." Here rests the question; and it should be fairly investigated, without subterfuge, and without delay: Will our interests permit us to civilize the Hindus? Shall India wear her plumed and jeweled turban

---

[1] Postans, Marianna. *Cutch* p.56-58.

with an air of peace? Or are her civil warfare, and her darkened policy, necessary to our wealth and safety? We are the conquerors, and in our power it rests. We know we cannot convert them to Christianity, as a people—we know we cannot throw them down the barrier of castes—without *first* supplying them with intellectual and moral truth. Experience continues to teach us this, and reflection must convince us that her teaching is just. Can we hope then, that learning, wisdom, change of opinion, and the conviction of power so gained, will attach these people to us by the social band of gratitude and reverence? Or may we not rather fear, that the desire of liberty may rise so warmly in their hearts, that, they may spurn our control, trample on our government, and at length expel us from their rich and glowing land? It would be well to consider this: the riches of India, which first attracted us to her shores, are rapidly diminishing, from the want of knowledge, and of self-interest of sufficient power to stimulate the natives to industry. Her plains, rich and fertile as they might be made, lie desert and uncultivated; her mines are unworked, her manufactures unimproved; and where individual interest commands that the land should yield her increase, it is obtained only by a waste of human labour, grievous to behold. Such is the effect of the system we have long acted upon in India; but the present is not the time calculated to support its continuance. A new description of European society has lately been introduced in her capitals, and will rapidly increase, and spread over the country. Ere many years elapse, we shall have middle and working class of Anglo-Indians; and from their examples, a power will be acquired by the native population, highly prejudicial to our interests, unless some means are taken to anticipate the effect of this supposed introduction of general, mechanical, and agricultural improvement. Thus, at this particular epoch in history of our Indian possessions, the question of native improvement appears to carry with it considerations of a very high political importance. Our policy is liberal, our founded on benevolence and justice, our native lands yields to none in her energetic efforts to deliver the oppressed from him that is too strong for him, and to diffuse knowledge and tolerance among her people. Let, then, the conquered of her colonies share the influence of her civilizing power, that so wisdom, religion, and peace shall "circulate through every vein of her empire;" or at least, let the question be entertained, if only on the ground of political security."Britain! thy voice can bid the dawn ascend!

On thee alone, the eye of Asia bend!
High arbitress! to thee her hopes are given,
Sole pledge of bliss, and delegate of Heaven.
In thy dark mantle all her fate repose,
Or bright with blessings, or o'ercast with woes;
And future ages shall thy mandate keep,
Smile at thy touch, or at thy bidding weep."[1]

The views of the Evangelicals represented a challenge to the East India Company's avowed religious policy of non-interference in social customs and religious practices of the masses in India, as any attempt to convert Indians to Christianity promised to subvert the foundations of civil peace by offending the most deeply entrenched religious sentiments. In the meantime, the charter of the East India

[1] Postans, Marianna. *Cutch* p.112-115.

Company had come up for renewal in 1813. Flora Annie Steel[1] notes that, when the Charter came up for review in 1813 before the British Parliament, "there were two additional clauses in the bill which, though grafted in upon it during the lengthy passage through Parliament, were of more gravity than some of the original import. One was the forming of a regular Church Establishment in India—a formal declaration, as it were, of the creed of the new master; the other the inclusion of missionaries as persons to whom a license to pursue their trade might be given. Taken together, these two clauses went far towards an admission that it was the duty of England to uphold her own faith." The East India Company was permitted to rule India for another twenty years, its trading monopoly with India was abolished, but its monopoly with China was continued. The Act was the first triumph for the evangelicals, as by this charter the East India Company was forced to appoint a bishop with his headquarters at Calcutta and his See the whole of the British dominions of India; to open up India to Christian missionaries; and to appropriate an annual sum for education, the last clause read as , "......it shall be lawful for the Governor-General-in Council to direct that......a sum of not less than one lakh of rupees in each year shall be set apart and applied to the revival and improvement of literature and the encouragement of the learned natives of India, and for the introduction and promotion of a knowledge of the sciences among the inhabitants of the British territories in India." In the context of these decisions it was the personal opinion of Marianna Postans, to introduce the merits of English education, coming from the mouth of

[1] Steel, Flora Annie. *India through the Ages*. p.326.

the Orientalist, and, in their own vernacular language, as the recipe for the success of the upliftment of the heathen Indians. "It is true, that, in the Presidencies of Bombay and Calcutta, colleges are endowed, which, supplied by able professors, afford the native population great facilities for the acquirement of learning; but these advantages are circumscribed, and inefficient to the purpose of general improvement. The natives, so educated, obtain lucrative appointments, which establish in large stations, whilst the great mass of the people remain in darkest ignorance. If grants of lands could be cultivated by English colonists—if elementary works on agriculture, the useful arts, and the first principles of natural philosophy, were to be translated into, and published in, the native languages, and intelligent native teachers directed to explain and read them to the people—I believe much general good might be effected. The reasoning faculties of the natives once exercised, and curiosity and interest awakened, their own intelligence would work the rest; and in this way do I think that the barriers of caste can be lowered in India, the Brahminical power be abolished, or the country its sources of wealth and consideration."[1]

The fear that missionaries could become unsettling led Sir Thomas Munro to protest in 1821 that he could not share faith "in the modern doctrine of the rapid improvement of the Hindoos, or of any other people. The character of the Hindoos is probably much the same as when Vasco da Gama first visited India, and it is not likely that it will be much better a century hence. When I read, as I sometimes do, of a measure by which a large province had been suddenly improved, or a race of semi-

---

[1] Postans, Marianna. *Cutch*; p.258-259.

barbarians civilized almost to Quakerism, I throw away the book." Sentiments as these constituted but a miniscule minority, and the Company's servants conscious of their 'Christian duty' was reflected in the increasing number of social legislation introduced in India, as by the Bengal Regulation (XXI) of 1795, the practice of female infanticide was declared to be murder, and the application of this Act was extended to other territories by 1804.

A perception that the object of conversion of the 'heathen Indians' would not be an easy task, as predicted by the evangelicals, was indicated to by Maria Graham (1814), who said that it would not be easy to dislodge an ancient creed, which was liberal and humane in its approach. She further predicts that mere verbal discourse on the greatness of the Christian faith was a poor approach, and for success in their mission, the missionaries must strike at the very root of the Indian faith, by learning its doctrines and then systemically decimating them. "Our missionaries.............in order to place our religion in the brightest light,.......they lay claim exclusively to all sublime maxims of morality, and tell those they wish to convert, that their books contain nothing but abominations, the belief of which they must abandon to receive the purer doctrine of Christianity. Mistaken men! could they desire a better opening to their hopes than to find already established that morality which says, it is enjoined to man even at the moment of destruction to wish to benefit his foes, *"as the sandal tree in the instant of its overthrow sheds perfume on the axe that fells it"*. How happy would it be instead of fighting with the air as these good men persist in doing, they were employed in the teaching the rudiments of knowledge, in searching for, and compiling such moral passages from the ancient Hindu books, as, taught to the young Indians, might improve them, and render them still further advantages, an improvement they would be far from refusing, as it would accord with their prejudices, and being founded on the wisdom of their forefathers would carry with it the authority of religion and the attractions of affection".[1] She further adds, "I am not as you know, among those who either extravagantly praise or extravagantly condemn the Hindus or their religion. It is enough that the latter is false, to wish it exchanged for a better; but the Hindus are men, and moved by human emotions and by human passions, and never, never will conversion be wrought among them by the present system of missionaries. They must be bad judges indeed of human nature, who can suppose, that millions of men are, without a miracle, to be converted by a few hundreds of preachers, who go among them, ignorant of their language and philosophy, and even the religion they combat. Moses, the Lawgiver of the Jews, was learned in the wisdom of the Egyptians, and consequently would sooth or elude the prejudices of the people who were born on the land Misraim. St. Paul, the Apostle of the Gentiles, was versed in the philosophy of Rome and of Athens, and wielded against their superstitions, the very doctrines and forms of their own sages."[2]

Some seventy-five years later, a similar sentiment was voiced in words not very different, and this time emanating from a newspaper report, which raised questions about the perceived failure of the Christian

---

[1] Graham, Maria. *Letters*. p.86-87.

[2] *Ibid*. p.284.

missionaries with Hinduism, the latter, a religion which the missionaries could not comprehend. This report generated the same expostulation which had been made in the first quarter of the nineteenth century. "It would appear they (i.e. the missionaries) lack the necessary subtlety of intelligence to grasp the meaning of religion they wish to overthrow. Many missionaries can be heard to say they know nothing about Hinduism and mean to know nothing. They will even quote Scripture in support of their mental indolence: *"I am determined not to know anything among them, save Jesus Christ, and him crucified."* They are thus in the position of one who has an excellent remedy but knows not whether it will suit the patient's malady..........Meantime educated Hindus calmly tell us they look with extreme coldness on appeals to their emotions such as that Christ died to save them, and tell us that they see in their Vedas as much regenerative power as in our Bible. "The Vedas," says a native paper "are the store-house of all that was the truest, noblest, and purest in humanity. They contain the highest thoughts, the most ideal system of religious aspiration, a perfect code of morals, and faultless constitution of society, such as that the world had not seen for many a century. All the reforms in the Hindu social system which are now necessary for Hindu progress—adult marriage, the higher education of women, maritime enterprise, why, these are as laws authoritatively laid down in the Vedas. What a foreign and unsympathetic government effect by tons of legislation, the Vedas can do for Hindu society by their simple but divine authority."[1] The newspaper report reflected the increasing sentiments of the social

---

[1] Bremer, Christina. *A month in a Dandi.* p.133-134.

reform movements of the nineteenth century unleashed by the Indians themselves, the British lady sentiments were symptomatic of the failure of the missionaries to counter Hinduism with its own fallacies, leading to the expression of the sentiment, "A singular hallucination, bred of deepest ignorance, that we can do away with the power and affection of the Vedas, when we know absolutely nothing about them. From presumptuous sin and blind ignorance do Thou, Good Lord, deliver us."

By 1833 mission work had begun almost all over India, and the years into the third decade of the century, were marked by greatly increased efforts in proselytizing of the Indians. One cause for this was the shortening of the ocean passage to India by the adoption of the Red Sea route.

The perception of the Indians towards the missionary activities was characterized by indifference, as they regarded it as merely 'a job' done by the British for pecuniary gains, and conversions were undertaken/accepted by the Indians for the same motivation. An illustration of the duality of the sentiments is apparent from the personal encounter that Fanny Parks had with a Hindu at the Magha Mela of Allahabad in January 1833[1]; and, the second incident occurred on the 4th of November 1838[2]. The first incident is narrated as follows: "On the platforms raised of mud and sand, some ten or twelve missionaries were preaching; everyman had his platform to himself, and a crowd of natives surrounded each orator. Seeing one of my own servants, an Hindoo, apparently an attentive listener, I asked the man what he

---

[1] Parks, Fanny. *Wanderings of a pilgrim*. p.262, Vol.- I.

[2] *Ibid.* p.288-89, Vol.- I.

had heard. "How can I tell?" said he, "the English padre is talking." I explained to him the subject of the discourse, and received for an answer, "Very well; it is their business to preach, they get paisa for so doing; what more is to be said?" As regards the second incident, it was recorded, "The clergyman at Allahabad converted a Hindu to the Christian faith; consequently, the man became an outcaste, --he could neither eat, drink nor smoke with his own family; he complained to the clergyman, and was taken into service. His attendance at church was constant. His patron died: the man was afterwards not seen at Divine Service. The newly appointed clergyman inquired the reason, and this answer was returned:--"I received eight rupees a month from your predecessor; if you give me the same I will go to church every Sunday!" –So little did the man comprehend his adopted religion, or the kindness that induced the Clergyman to support him!" Fanny Parks further laments, that the Hindoos converting to the Christian faith were not sincere in their efforts, and "(Christian) religion is often used as a cloak by the greatest schemers after good appointments. Religious meetings are held continuously in Calcutta, frequented by people to pray themselves into high salaries, who never thought of praying before."

The spreading of the glory of the Christian gospel was the great desire of the memsahibs, who made every effort to assist in the Evangelical movement, but, they were perturbed by the unedifying lack of understanding among the uncivilized 'natives'. "Those ladies, who are kind enough to support and educate the native children of natives, are startled at times by the curious occurrences. A lady at this station (Allahabad) lately married one of her orphans to a drummer in the 72nd regiment, and gave twenty rupees as a portion; the man was drunk for about a week; in a fortnight he made over his wife to another drummer, and in a month came to the lady saying, "If you please, Ma'am I should like to marry again." When turned down, the drummer told his officers that he had been 'very ill-used', and the lady dismissed the drummer and his wife as beyond redemption as "the man was a half-caste Christian, the girl a converted native'.[1]

The numbers of Christian converts was not only small, but also the genuineness of their conversion was under doubt, and the realization among the memsahibs was one of resigned acceptance, and not of undisguised approval. "There are very few natives who are even nominal Christians, and still fewer whom we can reasonably believe to be anything but what is here called "curry and rice Christians." And the lack of success of the evangelical mission was attributed to the absence of a policy adopted by the British government. "In England, I think they have a very false impression of what is done in India. That is not the fault of the Missionaries, who write the real truth home; but the Committees seem to publish all the good and none of the bad, for the fear of discouraging people. In fact, it is unreasonable to expect more to be done without more efficient means. Suppose thirty clergymen to the whole of England,--what could they do? And that is about the proportion of the Missionaries in Madras, and they have to work amongst the Heathens. Perhaps about half of them know the language well, and the rest speak it like school-French. The chaplains are not Missionaries: their duties lie almost completely among Europeans

[1] *Ibid*. 27th November 1838, p.293, Vol.-II.

as if they had remained at home. Mr. C., for instance, is a very excellent, useful clergyman, with large English and half-caste congregation, but no more a Missionary to your Heathen than your vicar. There are thousands needed where one or two come; and schoolmasters are wanted as much as preachers. There is a great difference of opinion as to the class of men most wanted, and most likely to be useful as Missionaries. Some people have an idea that it is scarcely necessary to have persons of birth and education of our English clergymen, but that a larger number of rather inferior men might be employed at a smaller salary, and be quite as efficient. Of course any Christian really working among the Heathen is likely to do some good; but I believe that the more educated and the more of a gentleman he is, the more influence he will have among the Hindoos. They are themselves more excellent judges of manners and standing in society, and invariably know a gentleman, and respect him accordingly. Their own priests are of the highest caste, and it lowers our religion in their eyes if they see that our *Padres*, as they call the Missionaries, are what they consider the low caste."[1]

In their desire to help in augmenting the adherents to the Christian credo, to the memsahibs, even in a calamity there lay an opportunity. The famine in the north-west provinces of 1838 became an opportunity to spread the Christian faith by linking assistance with conversion. The opportunity was provided by the occasion when the Indians were selling off their children in the face of extreme starvation, aggravated by a scarcity of food. The

---

[1] Maitland, Julia. *Letters from Madras.* 21st December 1837; p.103-104.

parents were resigned to the hard reality that the sale of their children would bring some financial assistance, however meager and temporary it might be. Against this backdrop it was recorded; "A most excellent and religious lady at the station (Allahabad) proposed sending to the up-country, where the famine raged the most severely, and purchasing ten young girls; these girls she undertook to bring up in the Christian religion, to teach them reading, writing, and needlework, and on their attaining a suitable age, to put them into the service as *ayahs* to European ladies. The ladies at the station entered into her plans, and I agreed to buy and support two girls as my share..................my friend wrote to a clergyman up the country, who purchased for us ten girls, all under eleven years of age, and sent them down; the market for children was looking up; he charged us the enormous price of ten rupees apiece. They were placed in a comfortable house, with a school mistress to instruct them; every care was taken of them, and the ladies of the station attended the school, and superintended their morals. It certainly flourished to a very great degree; they studied the commandment, "increase and multiply and replenish the earth," with so much assiduity, that in a short time all the little girls were in a fair way of becoming mammas;--a circumstance perfectly inexplicable."[1]

The failure of so noble an experiment rankled very much, that stories on this failure were exchanged, with the satisfying outcome that the Indians could never realize the benefits of the Christian faith due to their heathen ways. Fanny Parks in the epilogue on the above efforts

---

[1] Parks, Fanny. *Wanderings of a pilgrim*. 4th November 1838, p.294-295, Vol.-II.

recorded, "It was an annoying failure, that experimental school of ours. Speaking to an officer in the 16th Lancers, of the care that had been taken of these girls, of the religious instruction that had been bestowed upon them, and the disheartening finale of our charitable labours, he said, "In that dreadful famine hordes of wretched famished Bundelas flocked into Cawnpore, and very liberal subscriptions were collected to feed them; great numbers, however, perished from hunger, and mothers offered their children for sale for one rupee each: several were bought by very well-intentioned persons, to be educated, and converted to Christianity. Some little time after the Bundelas had disappeared from the station, I happened to be dining with an old friend, who, in the evening asked, if I could accompany her in her drive to the bungalow where the children were being educated to form ladies' maids, as she had a favour to ask of me, that I would that evening stand god-father to twenty-two of these children; I declined the honour, and some months afterwards heard that these children would shortly require god-fathers and god-mothers for their own offspring, should they bring them up as Christians."

By the close of the nineteenth century it was apparent that the Christian missionaries operating in India were not a monolithic block, but open to internal segmentation among themselves. Christina Bremer, while on her tour to the Himalayas in 1891, visited the British station of Kotegurh. She stayed for a few days in the mission of the German, Herr Beuteland and his wife, and was a witness to their simple life and charitable acts, amidst the natives of the region. She was forced to acknowledge the veracity of the report that "in India the Germans and Americans make much better missionaries than the English, for they lay themselves out not only to preach Christianity, but to live among the people in a simple way, coming near to them in their everyday life, and teaching them spinning, weaving, house-building and the many other arts after the European fashion. They thus gain a hold on the people, and themselves acquire the gift of gifts needed by a missionary, knowledge of the people, of their ways of living and thinking, and of the best ways of applying the principles of a civilization higher than the Indian in some respects, but by no means in all."[1]

An apt summary of the missionary activities of these fifty years is provided by Flora Annie Steel, a memsahib herself. She wrote in 1919, "The changes inaugurated by the inclusion of the "introduction of religious and moral improvement" as a licensable trade had borne much fruit. One only has to read missionary reports to find out how enormously organized efforts to convert the people of India had increased since 1813, and still more from1833. In the year 1840 Dr. Duff's Christian College at Calcutta numbered over six hundred pupils, and in 1845 came the added interest to the cause of the Missions brought by the great Evangelical movement, not only in the Church of England, but throughout all Europe. This wave of religiosity left no Christian sect untouched, and part of its result was the introduction into India of a race of Church-Militant officials, admirable in character, in work, who, despite their faithful performance of duties to Caesar which demanded absolute impartiality, could not divest themselves absolutely of their other duty (as they held it) to God; that is to say, to influence the natives for good—

[1] Bremer, Christina. *A month in a Dandi.* p.99-100.

in other words, to Christianity. Without attempting to praise or blame, it is impossible to deny that the example of such strong and militant Christians as Lawrences, as Havelock, as half a hundred other well-known names, to say nothing of the hundreds of lesser-known ones who in civil stations and cantonments were encouraging mission work with all their might and main, must inevitably have attracted the attention of *pundits* and *moulvies*, whose profession, whose bare living, was bound up in so-called heathendom."[1]

In the wider context of the desirability of introducing social legislation in India, an Indian custom, which was perceived as the tour-de-force of the argument was the need to abolish the custom of *sati,* which would be instrumental in securing the human-rights of the feminine gender of India. *Sati;* the practice of widow burning themselves with their dead husbands, was an issue of morbid interest, scorn and acrid comments, in various measures by the memsahibs. The word '*sati*' is of Anglo-Indian origin, derived from the word implying 'virtuous women.' The Sanskrit word for act was sahagamana (keeping company) or *sahamarana* (dying together). The practice was one by which the virtuous widow usually died by self-immolation, on the funeral pyre, along with her dead husband. The earliest historical account of sati is found in Diodorus Siculus's account in 317 B.C. This practice is mentioned as firsthand accounts in the works of Alberuni (eleventh century), Marco Polo (thirteenth century), Ibn Batuta (1348 A.D.), Nicolo de Conti (1430 A.D.), Tavernier (1648 A.D.), and by Bernier (1667 A.D.), among others. The practice of *sati* was not prevalent all

[1] Steel, Flora Annie. *India through the Ages.* p.346.

over the country, but was confined to the Indo- Gangetic belt, especially in Bengal, among the high-caste Brahmins and in the states of Rajputana. Colonel Todd records that 84 women committed *sati* with the Raja of Bundi, and 64 with Maharaja Ajit Singh of Bundi. The custom of *sati* was not popular in Punjab as the Adi Granth, the holy scripture of the Sikhs frowned upon this practice, yet there was the case of 300 women burning to death when Suchet Singh of Kashmir was cremated. It is also a historical fact that the wives and seven concubines of Maharaja Ranjit Singh entered the funeral pyre with him. In western India the cases of *sati* were rare, while to the south of Deccan it was almost unknown. Wherever the practice of *sati* prevailed in South India, it was directly introduced by the Brahmins, as in Vijaynagar. In Madura, only the wives and concubines of the princes were supposed to perform sati. The practice of *sati* later on spread among the Marathas. Sir John Malcolm recorded that Ahilya Bai Holkar in 1795 was unable to prevent her daughter from committing sati. F.B. Solvyns, in his work *Les Hindous* (1810) has left a detailed account of different kinds of sati that were practiced.[1]

Eliza Fay admitted to the fact that she 'never had the opportunity of witnessing the various incidental ceremonies' nor did she know of 'any European who was present at them'. This practice of *sati,* was criticized by her as this act was not symptomatic of the affection that a wife held for her husband but was a means of enslavement of the female gender by the men. Her argument goes thus:" I cannot suppose that the usage originates in the superior tenderness and ardent attachment of the Indian

[1] Neville, Pran. *Rare Glimpses of the Raj.* p.113-115.

wives towards their spouses, since the same tenderness and ardour would doubtless extend to his offspring, and prevent them from exposing the innocent survivours to the miseries attendant on an orphan state, and they would see clearly that to live and cherish these pledges of affection would be the most rational and natural way of showing regard for both husband and children. I apprehend that personal fondness can have no part here at all,--since all matches are made between the parents of the parties, who are betrothed to each other at too early a period for choice to be consulted,--this practice is entirely a political scheme, intended to insure the care and good offices of wives to their husbands, who have not failed in most countries to invent a sufficient number of rules to render the weaker sex totally subservient to their authority".[1] And in condemning the practice of *sati* Eliza Fay places the English womanhood as superior to her Indian counterpart, by especially highlighting the heroic efforts of women, like herself, who are to be found in her homeland. Her arguments are that, "I cannot avoid smiling when I hear gentlemen bring forward the conduct of Hindoo women as a test of superior character, since I am well aware that, so much are we the slaves of habit *everywhere*, that were it necessary for a women's reputation to burn herself in England, many a one who has *accepted* a husband merely for the sake of establishment, who has lived with him without affection, perhaps thwarted his views, dissipated his fortune, and rendered his life uncomfortable to its close, would yet mount the funeral pyre with all the imaginable decency,

---

[1] Fay, Eliza. *Original Letters from India.* 5th September 1781. p.160-161.

and die with heroic fortitude. The most specious sacrifices are not always the greatest. She who wages war with a naturally petulant temper, who practices a rigid self-denial, endures without complaining the unkindness, infidelity, extravagance, meanness, or scorn of the man to whom she has given a tender and confiding heart, and for whose happiness and well-being in life all the powers of her mind are engaged—is ten times more of a heroine than the slave of a bigotry and superstition, who affects to scorn the life demanded of her by the laws of her country or at least the country's custom. Many such we have in England, and I doubt not in India likewise: so indeed we ought: have we not a religion more pure than that of India."

In 1826 Fanny Parks noted the practice of maintaining '*sati* grounds', as her attention was drawn to one at Nobutpoor; "............there are seven *suttee* mounds of raised earth, one of which is kept in good repair, and there are several more in the mango tope to the left. The people said, no *suttee* had taken place there for twenty years, but the family who owned the large mound kept it in repair, and were very proud of the glory reflected on their house by one of the females having become *suttee*."[1] At Alopee Bagh in Allahabad, in the midst of a large mango plantation was a small temple dedicated to goddess Bhawani. There were small buildings on the right which contained the ashes of the *suttee*. "There are seven *suttee*-graves of masonry on this, and six of earth on the other side, near the temple, in the mango tope. The largest *suttee*-tomb contains the ashes of a woman who

[1] Parks, Fanny. *Wanderings of a pilgrim*. 23rd December 1826, p.65, Vol.- I.

was burnt in 1825, i.e. six years ago. The ashes are always buried near a temple sacred to Bhawani, and *never* by any other. Families too poor to raise a tomb of masonry in memory of the burnt-sacrifice, are contended to raise a mound of earth, and place a *kulsa* of red earthenware to mark the spot."[1]

As early as 1803, Lord Wellesley had proposed the abolition of *sati* in the territories of the East India Company, but he had first referred the idea to the Supreme Court at Calcutta. Then, in-tune with the Court of Directors policy of non-interference, it was suggested that the government was to be guided by 'the religious opinions and prejudices of the natives.' Following this advise the officials were advised in 1812 to permit the rite of *sati* in cases where it was 'countenanced by their (the Hindu) religion and to prevent it in others in which it is, by the same authority prohibited.' This meant that *sati* undertaken by a widow of above sixteen years of age and who was not pregnant was legally permissible. However, the police were to ensure that the act of *sati* was being undertaken voluntarily, and that the women were neither drugged nor were forcibly consigned to the flames.

This ambivalence on the part of the British were comprehended by the natives as a kind of governmental sanction to this practice, hence the number of officially recorded cases of *sati* rose from 378 in 1785 to 839 in 1818. W. H. Carey has given the number of widows as 'burnt' in Calcutta Presidency as follows; in 1816,442;in 1817, 707; in 1818, 839; in 1819, 650; in 1820, 597; in 1821, 654; in 1822, 513; and in 1823, 575, making a

---

[1] *Ibid*, November 1828, p.96, Vol.- I.

gross total in nine years of 5425. And if the numbers of widows burned at Madras and Bombay were added, the figures would be over 6000. In *The Adventures of Qui Hi* (1816), the author lampoons the government legislation when he writes,

'Twas here Qui Hi saw first with horror,
The burning system in its terror
Here British mercy shut her eyes,
Nor will she hear her victims' cries,
Because a fee anytime
can make a sacrifice sublime.'

Under the above proviso, an episode of *sati* is recorded, dating to the first week of November 1828 from Allahabad, recounted by a memsahib, whose husband as an officer was a witness to the proceedings. A rich Hindu *baniya* had died, leaving behind a widow between twenty-twenty five years of age, who was determined to perform *sati*. The site selected for sati was a holy spot, as it lay on the bank of the Ganges, under the Bund between the Fort and the Raj Ghat. "The magistrate sent for the woman, used every argument to dissuade her, and offered her money. Her only answer was, dashing her head on the floor, and saying, "If you do not let me burn with my husband, I will hang myself in your court of justice." The *shastras* say, "The prayers and imprecations of a *suttee* are never uttered in vain; the great gods themselves cannot listen to them unmoved." If a widow touches either food or water from the time her husband expires until she ascends the pile, she cannot, by Hindoo law, be burned with the body; therefore the magistrate kept the corpse forty-eight hours, in the hope that hunger would compel the women to eat. Guards were set over her, but she never touched anything. My husband accompanied the magistrate to see the *suttee*: about 5000 people were collected together on the banks of the Ganges: the pile was then built, and the putrid body placed upon it; the magistrate stationed guards to prevent the people from approaching it. After having bathed in the river, the widow lighted a brand, walked round the pile, set it on fire, then mounted cheerfully: the flame caught and blazed up instantly; she sat down, placing the head of the corpse on her lap, and repeated several times the usual form: "*Ram. Ram, suttee; Ram, Ram, suttee;*" i.e. "God, God, I am chaste." As the wind drove the fierce fire upon her, she shook her arms and limbs as if in agony; at length she started up and approached the side to escape. An Hindoo, one of the police who had been placed near the pile to see she had fair play, and should not be burnt by force, raised his sword to strike her, and the poor wretch shrank back into the flames. The magistrate seized and committed him to prison. The women again approached the side of the blazing pile, sprang fairly out, and ran into the Ganges, which was within a few yards. When the crowd and the brothers of the dead man saw this, they called out, "Cut her down, knock her on the head with a bamboo; tie her hands and feet; and throw her in again;" and rushed down to execute their murderous intentions, when the gentlemen and police drove them back. The women drank some water, and having extinguished the fire on her red garment, said she would mount the pile again and be burned. The magistrate placed his hand on her shoulder (which rendered her impure), and said, "By your own law, having once quitted the pile you cannot ascend it again; I forbid it. You are now an outcaste from the Hindoos, but I will take charge of you, and you will never want food or clothing". He then sent her, in a palanquin, under a guard, to the hospital. The crowd made way, shrinking from her with signs of horror, but returned peaceably to their homes; the Hindoos annoyed at her escape, and the Mussalmans saying, "It was better that she should escape, but it was a pity we should have lost the *tamasha* (amusement)of seeing her burnt to death."[1]

The public act of sati always drew large crowds for its value as a spectacle. For the British it was an opportunity and the novelty of witnessing a 'barbaric custom', and for the Indian spectators it was afforded a sense of participation in a sacred act of supreme sacrifice, and for such an event, there was never a shortage of spectators. Soon after the above, aborted attempt, Fanny Parks was requested by her friends that in the event of another incident of *sati*; they should be informed well in time. She writes, "Five days afterwards, I was informed that a *ranee* was to be burned. Accordingly I sent word to all my friends. Eight thousand people were assembled on the *suttee*-ground, who waited from mid-day to sun-set: then a cry arose—"The memsahiba sent us here! see, the sun has set, there can now be no *suttee*!" The people dispersed. My informant told me what he himself believed, and I mystified 8000 people most unintentionally."

Combined with the increasing tide of evangelism, and the outcry against the government's passive support for this heinous act, recommendations for the prohibition of this practice poured from all over the country. Sati was

[1] *Ibid.* November 1828, p.91-92, Vol.-I.

adopted by the women primarily due to the hardships of a widow's life in India, with its attendant humiliations and privations. The belief of enjoying a better after-life with her husband in the next life, and that she would be revered as a holy women and goddess by her family and society added a charm, by mitigating the perils of a torturous death by burning. These were brought out in one such report in 1818, which had been submitted by Mr. Ewer, Superintendent of Police in Lower Bengal. "There are very many reasons for thinking that such an event as a voluntary *suttee* rarely occurs; few widows would think of sacrificing themselves unless overpowered by force of persuasion, very little of either being sufficient to overcome the physical and mental powers of the majority of Hindu females. A widow, who would turn with natural instinctive horror from the first hint of sharing her husband's pile, will be at length gradually brought to pronounce a reluctant consent because, distracted with grief at the event, without one friend to advise or protect her, she is little prepared to oppose the surrounding crowd of hungry Brahmins and interested relations......... In this state of confusion a few hours quickly pass, and the widow is burnt before she has had time to think of the subject. Should utter indifference for her husband, and superior sense, enable her to preserve her judgment, and to resist the arguments of those about her, it will avail her little—the people will not be disappointed of their show; and the entire population of the village will turn out to assist in dragging her to the bank of the river, and in keeping her on the pile."[1]

---

[1] Pegg, J. *India Cries to British Humanity.* p.14.

Faced with the general disgust of the public at home, and that of the civil and military servants in India, the Court of Directors and the government of India were forced into action. On 17th June 1823 the Court of Directors wrote to the Governor-General in India, "You are aware that the attention of parliament and the public has lately been called to the subject (of suttee). It appears that the practice varies very much in different parts of India both to the extent to which it prevails and the enthusiasm by which it is upheld....... It is upon intelligible grounds that you have adopted the rules which permit the sacrifice when clearly voluntary and conformable to the Hindu religion. But to us it appears very doubtful (and we are confirmed in this doubt by responsible authorities), whether the measures which have been taken in pursuance of this principle have not tended to increase rather than diminish this practice. It is moreover with much reluctance that we consent to make the British Government, by specific permission of suttee, an ostensible party to the sacrifice; we are also averse to the practice of making British courts expounders and vindicators of the Hindu religion when it leads to acts which not less as legislators than as Christians we abominate." The Directors however left it to the Governor-General's discretion to do whatever his 'superior means of estimating consequences may suggest.'[1]

Lord Amherst, the Governor-General, was convinced that it was the appropriate time for the abolition of *sati* by legislative action. Amherst was faced with the situation, where on the one hand, he was petitioned by the supporters of *sati*, while on the other progressive Hindus

[1] Parliamentary Papers, 1824, XXIII; p.44-45.

as Raja Ram Mohun Roy, strongly opposed this social custom. Lord Amherst succumbed to a wait-and-watch policy, hoping that 'the more general dissemination of knowledge among the better informed Hindus themselves might...... prepare gradually the minds of the natives in such a manner."[1]

As regards the attitude towards legislation on *sati*, the Court of Directors had reiterated their earlier opinion to Lord Amherst's successor, Lord Bentinck. Bentinck's own temperament was inclined towards instant reform. On 4th December 1829, *sati* was declared illegal in Bengal Presidency by the Regulation XVII. By this Regulation, anyone assisting a voluntary sacrifice was held guilty of culpable homicide, and anyone using violence to force a widow to burn herself was liable to be given death sentence. This was followed by a similar resolution in Madras on 2nd February 1830, and also made effective in Bombay.

The abolition of sati aroused much indignation, leading to agitation in Bengal and a petition was submitted to Bentinck appealing against the Regulation, and the proponents of *sati* also appealed to the Privy Council in London in January 1830. The Court of Directors presented an overwhelming case against *sati* thereby favouring its abolition, which in turn received support from Raja Ram Mohun Roy who took to England a petition in favour of abolition of *sati*, which he presented himself to Parliament. The appeal for revocation of the Regulation was dismissed.

---

[1] Parliamentary Papers, 1825, XXIV; p.153-154.

Gladstone, the Prime Minister of England, composed a poem, paying tribute to Bentinck's bold step on the abolition of sati.

"Bentinck: 'Twas thine the bloodless crown to win,
Proud victor over deeds of death and sin,
Spirit of England's fame, no longer dim,
A voice of thunder thou didst speak to him,
Echoed the glad command from shore to shore
And martyr's ghastly flame ascends no more."

Though the practice of sati was abolished in the provinces of British India, however it lingered on for some time in the princely states of Rajputana and Punjab, the last case being recorded in 1861 from Udaipur. The practice of sati was forbidden in British provinces, but it was lamented, "Alas! too frequently (acts of sati) occurs, where the native power is most influential." This is supported by a record of 1837, by Marianna Postans of the "circumstances connected with a Suttee which lately took place in Cutch: the province being under Native Government, its people acted in perfect independence of our control."[1] The episode in great detail is described as follows,[2] "The woman whose sacrifice I am about to describe was of high caste, the only wife of Bhoojray, a man possessing some power and much wealth in the province, and an intimate and confidential friend of the Rao (of Bhuj). During the latter days of his life, his wife declared her intention of performing suttee at his death, which being made known to the British Resident, he immediately requested the Rao to use his influence with the woman, when she became a widow, to prevent the

[1] Postans, Marianna. *Cutch.* p.62-63.

[2] *Ibid.* p.63 ff.

completion of her design. When the time arrived, his Highness sent for the woman, expostulated with her, and offered her protection both in his own name, and in that of the British Government, but found her intention unalterable; and the widow left the palace, to prepare by prayer and purification for the intended sacrifice...... News of the widow's intentions having spread, a great concourse of people of both sexes, the women clad in their gala costumes, assembled round the pyre. In a short time after their arrival, the fated victim appeared, accompanied by the Brahmins, her relatives, and the body of the deceased. The spectators showered chaplets of *mogree* on her head, and greeted her appearance with laudatory exclamations at her constancy and virtue. The women especially pressed forward to touch her garments; an act which is considered meritorious, and highly desirable for absolution, and protection from the Evil Eye. The widow was a remarkably handsome woman, apparently about thirty, and most superbly attired. Her manner was marked by great apathy to all around her, and by a complete indifference to the preparations which for the first time met her eye: from this circumstance an impression was given that she could be under the influence of opium; and in conformity with the declared intention of the European officers present to interfere, should any coercive measures be adopted by the Brahmins, or relatives, two medical officers were requested to give their opinion on the subject. They both agreed that she was quite free from any influence calculated to induce torpor or intoxication. Captain Burnes (the Assistant Resident in Cutch) then addressed the woman, desiring to know whether the act she was about to perform were voluntary, or enforced; and assuring her that, should she entertain the slightest reluctance to the fulfillment of her vow, he, on the part of the British Government, would guaranty the protection of her life and property. Her answer was calm, heroic, and constant to her purpose: "I die of my own free will; give me back my husband, and I will consent to live; if I die not with him, the souls of seven husbands will condemn." Having said this with placid manner, which nothing appeared likely, appeared likely to change, further expostulation was deemed useless; but, as a message had been dispatched to the Rao, requesting his interference, an hour's delay was demanded. It was also insisted, that the crowd should withdraw to a short distance from the spot, leaving the widow alone with her relations; and the hope was great, that during this pause from the exciting influences of the scene, the tenderness of her nature might shake her resolution at the approach of her death, and yet avail to save her. Before the full expiration of the hour, the Rao returned a message, declaring the inefficiency of his power to arrest the ceremony. Ere the renewal of the horrid ceremonies of death were permitted, again the voice of mercy, of expostulation, and even of entreaty, was heard; but the manner with which the woman still declared her determination unalterable, chilled and startled the most courageous. Physical pangs evidently excited no fears in her: her singular creed, the customs of her country, and her sense of conjugal duty, excluded from her mind the natural emotions of personal dread; and never did martyr to a true cause go to the stake with more constancy and firmness, than did this delicate and gentle woman prepare to become the victim of a deliberate sacrifice to the demoniacal tenets of her heathen creed...........All further interference being useless, the ceremony proceeded...........Thorns and grass were piled over the door (of the funeral pyre); and again it was insisted, that free space should be left, as it was hoped the poor victim might relent, and rush from her fiery prison to the protection so freely offered. The command was readily obeyed, the strength of a child would have sufficed to burst the frail barrier which confined her, and a breathless pause succeeded; but the woman's constancy was faithful to the last; not a sigh broke the death-like silence of the crowd, until a slight smoke, curling from the summit of the pyre, and then a tongue of flame darting with bright and lightning-like rapidity into the clear blue sky, told us that the sacrifice was completed. Fearlessly had this courageous woman fired the pile, and not a groan had betrayed to us the moment when her spirit fled. The sight of the flame, a fiendish shout of exultation rent the air; the tom-toms sounded, the people clapped their hands with delight, as the evidence of their murderous work burst on their view; whilst the English spectators of this sad scene withdrew, bearing deep compassion in their hearts, to philosophise as best as they might, on a custom so fraught with horror, so incompatible with reason, and so revolting to human sympathy. The pile continued to burn for three hours; but, from its form, it is supposed that almost immediate suffocation must have terminated the sufferings of the unhappy victim..........By the order of the Rao, a tomb has since been erected on the spot. It is usual in all parts of Cutch to set up a large block of stone where a Suttee has been performed, and an upright hand and arm are carved on them as the emblem, and daubed with the pigment of red ochre. The Rao's conduct in this matter is considered highly blamable, as notwithstanding the superstitions of his people, and the strong feeling of caste which connects itself in their minds with this time-consecrated sacrifice, his Highness's command would have sufficed to prevent it. There is, however, reason to fear, that his Highness, debased as his otherwise amiable character is by the tenets of Hinduism, secretly favoured and approved the Brahmin's proceedings; and so determined were the parties concerned not to admit a chance of our interference, until their arrangements were far advanced, that the intention of celebrating the funeral obsequies of Bhoojray was absolutely unknown to the British Resident, until their preparations for the tragedy were completed. The whole of the Rao's people were present, from his prime minister to the lowest wrestler of his court; and this, at least, seemed like the tacit countenance of a deed, which, on his inauguration, he had pledged himself to use his highest influence to prevent. The Bombay Government have expressed their disapprobation on the subject, and have notified to his Highness, that a repetition of the act will not be overlooked; it is hoped therefore, that the Cutch will not be made the theatre of another scene, so full of horror, and which even at a distance off time, it is impossible to recall, without feelings of mingled compassion and disgust; disgust which not even the purest benevolence can allay."

The fact that an act of sati took place, in the Indian provinces having widespread support of the local population, and the tacit approval of the ruling chief, despite being lawfully banned in British provinces, Marianna Postans wrote that despite the efforts of the British to raise the Indians out of the "darkest institutions of heathenism (that) shall vanish at the bright day-spring of improvement" many more years would be required. Marianna Postans who recorded the above incident was forced to record further, "till then, the poor Hindu women must be content to remain, during life, the debased slave of her master's will, and at his death, be doomed, in accordance with immemorial usage, to yield her life by cruel torture, a sacrifice to the fanatic faith of her country, and the rapacious wickedness of Brahminical priesthood;--who will thus continue to deceive their miserable votaries,

> "With gay religions, full of pomp and gold,
> And devils to adore for deities."[1]

The memsahibs recorded with shock and horror as episodes of sati came to light from the native states. Julia Maitland wrote, "Have you heard in England of the horrors that took place at the funeral of that wretched old Runjeet Singh? *Four* wives and *seven* slave-girls were burnt with him; not a word even of remonstrance from the British Government! J—says there cannot be a doubt that a word of disapprobation from the British Resident would have stopped it at once, for the whole power of the Punjab depends on our will, and they profess to follow our wishes in everything. Is it not shocking? The four Ranees burnt themselves at their own desire, from pride of family and caste; but the poor slave-girls could have had no such motives, and must have been burnt by

[1] Postans, Marianna. *Cutch.* p.58.

the wretches around them. One Grandee *man* pretended he meant to burn himself too, and could scarcely be persuaded against it; but I believe his was all sham: he knew very well they would not let him, because he was too useful to the county."[1] The letter of Hon. W. Osborne, dated July 12th 1839, from Simla, records the details of the funeral obsequies of Ranjit Singh.

A great deal of curiosity centered around the women within the zenana and its internal dynamics , as this mysterious world remained veiled from the prying masculine, for no male, who was not a close relatives of the inmates of the zenana could secure an entry. The memsahibs, on an expedition of discovery of India, set out to unveil the mysterious details and intricacies which prevailed within the walls of the zenana. And, in order to unravel these details, for their personal quest of gendered spaces, and to present and convey these very same details to their sisters in Europe, the memsahibs prevailed upon their acquaintances to secure them an entry into this mysterious world of the zenana. Maria Graham secured one such invitation in Bombay, when, "My sister and I paid a visit to Shahab o'dien's harem, but could by no means prevail on the *cazy* to admit any of the gentlemen of our family...............We ascended the women's apartment by a ladder, which is removed when not in immediate use, to prevent the ladies from escaping, and were received by the *cazy's* wife's mother, a fine old women dressed in white, and without ornaments, as becomes a widow. Shahab o'dien's mother, and the rest of his father's widows, were first presented, then Fatima his wife to whom our visit was paid, and afterwards his

[1] Maitland, Julia. *Letters from Madras.* 9th August 1839,184-185.

sisters, some of them fine lively women. They all crowded round us to examine our dress, and the materials of which they were composed. They were surprised at our wearing so few ornaments, but we told them it was the custom in our country, and they replied that it was good. I was not sorry that they so openly expressed their curiosity, as it gave us a better opportunity of gratifying our own. The apartment in which we were received was about twenty feet square, and rather low; round it were smaller rooms, most of them crowded with small beds, with white muslin curtains; these were not particularly clean, and the whole suite seemed close and disagreeable. Most of the women were becomingly dressed. Fatima's arms, legs and neck, were covered with rings and chains; her fingers and toes were loaded with rings; her head was surrounded by a fillet of pearls, some strings of which crossed it several ways, and confined the hair, which was knotted up behind. On her forehead hung a cluster of coloured stones, from which depended a large pearl, and round her face small strings of pearl hung at equal distances. Her ear-ring were very beautiful; but I do not like the custom of boring the hem of the ear, and studding it all round with joys, nor could Fatima's beautiful face reconcile me to the nose-jewel. Her large black eyes, the *cheshme-ahoo* of the eastern poets, were rendered more striking by the black streaks with which they were adorned and lengthened out at the corners, and the palms of her hands, the soles of her feet, and her nails, were stained with *hinna*, a plant, the juice of whose seeds is of a deep red colour. Fatima's manner is modest, gentle, and indolent; before her husband she neither lifts her eyes, nor speaks, and hardly moves without permission from the elder ladies of the harem. She presented us with perfumed sherbet, fruits, and sweetmeats, chiefly made of ghee, poppy seeds, and sugar; some of them were tolerably good, but it required all my good manners to swallow others. Prepared as I was to expect very little from the Mussulman ladies, I could not help being shocked to see them so totally devoid of cultivation as I found them. They mutter their prayers, and some of them read the Koran, but not one in thousand understands it. Still fewer can read their own language, or write it at all, and the only work they do is little embroidery. They thread beads, plait coloured threads, sleep, quarrel, make pastry, and chew betel, in the same daily round; and it is only at death, a birth, or a marriage, that the monotony of their lives is ever interrupted. When I took leave, I was presented with flowers and *paung*, (*chunam* and betel-nut wrapped in the leaf of an aromatic plant) and sprinkled with rose-water. As visits in the East are matters of ceremony, not of kindness, they are considered as a burden on the visitor, from which the person visited relieves him, as soon he is satisfied with his company, by ordering refreshments, or offering the paung, which is a signal to depart. The highest affront one can offer to an Oriental is to refuse his betel. Bernier tells of a story of a young noble, who, to prove his loyalty, took and swallowed the *paung* from Shah-Jahen, though he knew it to be poisoned."[1]

The above description of the zenana of Maria Graham was the outcome of a single visit, which did not last for more than a couple of hours. A comparatively sympathetic account of details of the zenana, are provided by Mrs. Meer Hassan Ali, as these were "the

[1] Graham, Maria. *Journal of a Residence in India.* p.17-19.

people with whom twelve years of my life were passed on terms of intimacy and kindness". She was an English woman who spent twelve years in its confines, being in the exceptional position of being the daughter-in-law of, Mir Haji Shah, a Sayyid family of Lucknow. Her descriptions of the zenana are detailed and extensive.[1] In her description of the layout of the zenana she writes, "Imagine to yourself a tolerably sized quadrangle, three sides of which is occupied by habitable buildings, and the fourth by the kitchens, offices, offices, lumber rooms, &c.; leaving in the centre an open court-yard. The habitable buildings are raised a few steps from the court; a line of pillars forms the front of the building, which had no upper rooms; the roof is flat, and the sides and back are without windows, or any aperture through which air can be received. The sides and back are merely high walls forming an enclosure, and the only air is admitted from the fronts of the dwelling-place facing the court-yard. The apartments are divided into long halls, the extreme corners having small rooms or dark closets purposely built for the repository of valuables or stores; doors are fixed to these closets, which is the only place I have seen with them in the zeenahnah or mahul (i.e. mahal, a house or palace occupied by female)"

Gradually over a period of time the mysteries of the *zenana* were put together, along with the nature of their living quarters with their details. After a visit to the *zenana* of the Nawab of Oudh, it was said that the house dedicated for the *zenana* ladies was situated in a *zenana*-garden surrounded by a high stone wall. "The orthodox

[1] Mrs. Ali, Meer Hassan. *Observations on the Mussulmauns of India.* Letter XII.

height for the four walls of a zenana garden is that no man standing on an elephant can overlook them. The building is surrounded by fine trees; and a fountain played before it, in which gold and silver fishes were swimming. Near it was an avenue, in which was a swing, the invariable accompaniment of a *zenana* garden. The season in which the ladies more particularly delight to swing in the open air on it during the rains."[1]

On the zenana it was further more said that, "As they have neither doors nor windows to the halls, warmth or privacy is secured by the means of thick wadded curtains, made to fit each opening between the pillars. Some *zeenahnahs* have two rows of pillars in the halls with wadded curtains to each, thus forming two distinct halls, as occasion may serve, or greater warmth be required: this is a convenient arrangement where the establishment of servants, slaves, &c., is extensive. The wadded curtains are called *purdahs*......Besides the *purdahs*, the opening between the pillars have blinds neatly made of bamboo strips, woven together with coloured cords: these are called *jhillmuns* or *cheeks*.... These blinds constitute a real comfort to every one in India, as they admit air when let down, and the same time shut out the flies and other annoying insects; besides which the extreme glare is shaded by them—a desirable object to foreigners in India. The bedsteads of the family are placed, during the day, in lines at the back of the halls, to be moved at pleasure to any chosen spot for the night's repose; often into the open courtyard, for the benefit of the pure air. They are all formed on one principle, differing only in

---

[1] Parks, Fanny. *Wanderings of a pilgrim*. 28th February 1831, p.183, Vol.I.

size and quality; they stand about half-a-yard from the floor, the legs round and broad at the bottom, narrowing as they rise from the frame, which is laced over by a thick cotton tape, made for the purpose, and platted in checquers, and thus rendered soft, or rather elastic, and very pleasant to recline upon."[1] According to Mrs. Meer Hassan Ali, within the feminine world of the zenana, a hierarchical air pervaded, the highest being "the mistress of the house" who was "easily distinguished by her seat of honour in the hall of the zeenahnah; a *musund* (i.e. *masnad)* not being allowed to any other person but the lady of the mansion". As far as the decorative elements of the zenana, and creature comforts, at par with European standards are considered, they were judged to be lagging far behind. Mrs. Ali continues, "looking-glasses or ornamental furniture are very rarely to be seen in the zeenahnahs, even of the very richest females. Chairs and sofas are produced when English visitors are expected; but the ladies of Hindoostaun prefer the usual mode of sitting and lounging in the carpet; as for tables, I suppose not one gentlewoman of the whole country has ever been seated at one; and very few, perhaps, have any idea of their useful purposes, all their meals being served on the floor, where dusthakhawns (i.e. dastarkhwan, table-cloths as we would call them) are spread, but neither knives, forks, spoons, glasses, or napkins, so essential to the comfortable enjoyment of the meal amongst Europeans. But those who never knew such comforts have no desire for the indulgence, nor taste to appreciate them."

[1] Mrs. Ali, Meer Hassan. *Observations on the Mussulmauns of India.* Letter XII.

As more British ladies settled in India in larger numbers, their interest in their Indian counterparts, especially those within the seclusion of the *purdah* was greatly aroused. This was in strong contrast to the scorn they had for the *bibis*, and the easy familiarity which they shared with the ayahs and others of their ilk. The desire to enter into the mysteries of the *zenana* was overwhelming. "The perusal of Lady Mary Wortley Montague's work has rendered me very anxious to visit a *zenana*, and to become acquainted with the ladies of the East. I have now been four years in India, and have never beheld any women but those in attendance as servants in European families, the low caste wives of petty shopkeepers, and the *nach* women". It was against this background that Fanny Parks eagerly took up the offer of a rich Bengali Hindu while at Calcutta to 'visit his wives and female relatives'. She recounts of her visit that "He led me before a large curtain, which having passed I found myself in almost darkness: two females took hold of my hands and led me up a long flight of stairs to a well-lighted room, where I was received by the wives and relatives. Two of the ladies were very pretty; on beholding their attire I was nc longer surprised that no other men other than their husbands were permitted to enter the *zenana*. The dress consisted of one long strip of Benaras gauze of thin texture, with a gold border passing twice around the limbs, with the end thrown over the shoulder. The dress was rather transparent, almost useless as a veil: their necks and arms were covered with jewels. The complexion of some of the ladies was of a pale mahogany, and some of the female attendants were of a very dark colour, almost black. Passing from the lighted room, we entered a dark balcony, in front of which were fine bamboo screens, impervious to the eyes from without, but from the interior we could look down upon the guests in the hall below, and distinguish perfectly all that passed. The ladies of the *zenana* appeared to know all the gentlemen by sight, and told me their names. They were very inquisitive; requested me to point out my husband, inquired how many children I had, and a thousand questions". [1]While this was a glimpse into the secretive world of the Indian women, this preliminary foray left Fanny Parks 'much disappointed' as 'the women were not ladylike'. She, however, drew consolation from the fact that 'it was only the house of a rich Calcutta native gentleman'.

The details about the inhabitants of the zenana, a royal one, that of the Nawab of Oudh, were exchanged between the memsahibs amongst themselves to satiate their curiosity. The letter written by a friend to Fanny Parks was extracted and recorded in the journal she maintained for her mother. The description of the zenana, as witnessed by the friend on 18th October 1828 was given as follows. "The old *begum* (the king's mother), was the *great lady,* of course, and in her palace we were received; the others being considered her guests, as well ourselves. It was a most amusing sight, as I had never witnessed the interior of a zenana before, and so many women assembled at once I had never beheld. I suppose from the first to the last we saw some thousands. *Women-bearers* carried our *tanjuns,* a regiment of female gold and silver-sticks, dressed in male costumes, were drawn up before the entrance; those men, chiefly Africans, who were employed inside the zenana (and there were abundance of these frightful

[1] Parks, Fanny. *Wanderings of a pilgrim*. 17th April 1826, p.59,Vol.I

creatures), were all of the same class as the celebrated Velluti. The old begum was without ornaments, likewise a very pretty and favourite wife of the late king, and their state of widowhood precluding their wearing them. But the present king's wives were most superbly dressed, looking like creatures of the Arabian tales. Indeed, one was so beautiful, that I could think of nothing but Lalla Rookh in her bridal attire. I never saw anyone so lovely, either black or white. Her features were perfect; and such eyes and eyelashes I had never beheld before. She is the favourite queen at present, and has only been married a month or two: her age about fourteen; and such a little creature, with the smallest hand and feet, and the most *timid, modest* look imaginable. You would have been charmed with her; she was so graceful and fawn-like. Her dress was of gold and scarlet brocade, and her hair was literally strewed with pearls, which hung down her neck in long single strings, terminating in long pearls, which mixed with and hung *as low* as her hair, which was curled on each side her head in long ringlets, like Charles the Seconds beauties. On her forehead she wore a small gold circlet, from which depended (and hung half-way down her forehead) large pear-shaped pearls, interspersed with emeralds. The pearls were this size and form (i.e. about one centimeter in a tear-drop form), and had a very becoming effect, close upon the forehead, between the eyes. Above this was a paradise plume, from which strings of pearls were carried over the head, as we turn our hair. *I fear* you will not understand me. Her ear-rings were immense gold-rings, with pearls and emeralds suspended all round in long strings, the pearls increasing in size. She had a nose-ring also, with large pearls and emeralds; and her necklaces, &c., were too numerous to be described. She wore long sleeves, open at the elbow; and her dress was a full petticoat, some dozens yards wide, with a tight body attached, and open only at the throat. She had several persons to bear her train when she walked; and her women stood behind her couch to arrange her head-dress, when in moving her pearls got entangled in the immense dopatta of scarlet and gold she had thrown around her. How I wished for you when we were seated! you would have been delighted with the scene. This beautiful creature is the envy of all the other wives, and the favourite, at present, of the king and his mother, both of whom have given her titles—the king's is after the favourite wife of one of the celebrated kings of Delhi, "Tajmahul," and Nourmahul herself could not have more lovely. The other newly-made queen is nearly *European*, but not a whit fairer than Tajmahul. She is, in my opinion, plain, but is considered by the native ladies very handsome; and she was the king's favourite until he saw Tajmahul. She was more splendidly dressed than even Tajmahul; her head-dress was a coronet of diamonds, with a fine crescent and plume of the same. She is the daughter of a European merchant, and is accomplished for an inhabitant of a zenana, as she writes and speaks Persian fluently, as well as Hindostani, and it is said she is teaching the king *English*; though, when we spoke to her in English, she said she had forgotten it, and could not reply. She was, I fancy, afraid of the old begum, as she evidently understood us; and when asked if she liked being in the zenana, she shook her head and looked quite melancholy. Jealousy of the new favourite, however, appeared the cause of her discontent, as, though they sat on the same couch, they never addressed each other. ....The mother of the king's children, Mulka Zumanee, did not visit us at the old queen's, but we went to see her at her own palace: she is, *after all,* the person of most political consequence, being the mother of the heir-apparent; and she has great power over her royal husband, whose ears she boxes occasionally. The Delhi princess, to whom the king was betrothed and married by his father, we did not see; she is in disgrace, and confined to her own palace. The old begum talked away to us, but appeared surprised I should admire Tajmahul more than the English begum, as she is called,--*my country women* as they styled her! Poor thing, I felt ashamed of the circumstance, when I saw her chewing *pan* with all the gusto of a regular Hindostanee!"[1]

Thus a zenana was like a microcosm of the world outside, only being different in the fact that all its citizens were women, immune from the outside world, but having their own hierarchical order, which was in a state of continuous flux, depending on who had the greatest proximity to the master of the household. Colonel Gardner, who had married a Muslim noble lady and maintained a zenana of his own, and commented to Fanny Parks: "Nothing can exceed the quarrels that go on in the zenana, or the complaints the begums make against each other. A common complaint is "Such a one has been practicing witchcraft against me." If the husband make a present to a wife, if it only be a basket of mangoes, he must make the same exactly to all other wives to keep the peace. A wife, when in a rage with her husband, if on account of jealousy, often says, "I wish I were married

[1] Parks, Fanny, *Wanderings of a pilgrim*, October 1828, p.87-90, Vol.-I.

to a grass-cutter, " i.e. because a grass-cutter is so poor that he can afford to have only one wife."[1] Fanny Parks, who had access to the zenana of Colonel Gardner, from her own experience calls the zenana "a palace of intrigue, and those who live within the four walls cannot pursue a straight path; how can it be otherwise, when so many conflicting passions are called forth."[2] She further adds, that "Mussulmani ladies generally forget their learning when they grow up, or they neglect it. Everything that passes without the four walls is repeated to them by their spies; never was any place so full of intrigue, scandal, and the chit-chat as a zenana."[3]

In the extract of the letter above, disdain, combined with horror, is apparent for "*my country-woman*", the English begum, who had entered into matrimony with an Indian and adopted their customs with all gusto. The relief is apparent when it was found out that, and rationalized that "the English *begum* was the daughter of a half-caste and an English officer; her mother afterwards married a native buniya (shop-keeper)", and hence the fall was grace could be reasonably explained, along with her deviousness as to how she married a nawab. The story continues in that "she had a sister; both the girls lived with the mother, and employed themselves in embroidering saddle-cloths for the horses of the rich natives. They were both very plain; nevertheless, one of them sent her picture to his majesty, who, charmed with the portrait, married the lady. She had money on profusion at her command: she made her father-in-law her treasurer, and pensioned her mother and sister."

---

[1] *Ibid,* Vol. I; pp.230, 453.

[2] *Ibid*, Vol. I; p.391.

[3] *Ibid*, Vol.I; p 450.

The *zenana* continued to attract the British women increasingly, as it gave a glimpse into the secrets of the Oriental women, but also provided an insight into the real status of women in India. Fanny Parks, while reporting of a bazaar gossip of Allahabad of June 1835, decries the demeaning status of the women in all societies per se, and the Indian in particular. She writes, that 'a native of considerable wealth' found in his *zenana* his two wives with a man, while the man slipped away, the native killed both his wives'. This act brought to her the realization that the position of women, not only in India but in all cultures was subservient to the male, but in India their servitude and lack of freedom and liberty was ensured from a very early age. "A man may have as many wives as he pleases, and mistresses without number; --it only adds to his dignity! If a woman takes a lover she is murdered, and cast away like a dog into a ditch. It is the same all the world over; the women, being the weaker, are the playthings, the drudges, or the victims of men ; a women is a slave from her birth; and the more I see of life, the more I pity the condition of women. As for the manner in which the natives strive to keep them virtuous, is absurd; a girl is affianced at three or four years old, married, without having seen the man, at eleven, shut up and guarded and suspected of a wish to intrigue, which perhaps, first puts it into her head, and she amuses herself with outwitting those who have no dependence upon her, although if discovered, her death generally ends the story".[1]

The seclusion of the women in the *zenana* was absolute, as no tailors were allowed entry into the *zenana* as it would be considered 'indelicate' to make

[1] *Ibid*, 8th June 1835, p.56, Vol.II.

their attire , and the women's clothes were never shown to men 'lest they should be able to judge the form of the lady *purdahnashin*; i.e. behind the curtain'. This was in contradiction to the freedom enjoyed by the women in Britain, and the apparent reaction of the Indian women not accustomed to such liberty, exposed to the merchandising of the feminine attire. "Imagine the disgust of an Asiatic lady would feel if placed in Regent Street, on beholding figures displayed in shop windows, intended to represent English ladies in corsets, bustles, and under petticoats, turning around on poles, displaying for laughter and criticism of the men the whole curious and extraordinary arcana of the toilet of an European!"[1] On the notion of seclusion, which was deeply ingrained into the psyche of the women of the zenana, an incident is cited in the '*Observations on the Mussulmauns of India*', and of the repercussions that devolved upon the feminine mind in the aftermath of a perceived attempt to transgress that invisible boundary. "A lady whose friendship I have enjoyed from my first arrival in India, heard me very often speak of the different places I had visited, and she fancied her happiness very much depended on seeing a river and a bridge. I undertook to gain permission from her husband and father, that the treat might be permitted; they, however, did not approve of the lady being qualified, and I was vexed to be obliged to convey the disappointment to my friend. She very mildly answered me, "I was much to blame to request what I knew was improper for me to be indulged in; I hope my husband and family will not be displeased with me for my childish wish; pray make

---

[1] *Ibid,* 24th April 1837, p.113, Vol.II.

them understand how much I repent my folly. I shall be ashamed to speak on the subject when we meet." [1]

A contradiction is evident in the recollections of Mrs. Meer Hassan Ali, narrator of the above episode, who wrote[2] "At first I pitied the apparent monotony of their lives; but this feeling was worn away by the intimacy with the people, who are thus precluded from generally mixing with the world. They are happy in their confinement; never having felt the sweets of liberty, would not know how to use the boon if it were to be granted to them. As the bird from the nest immured in a cage is both cheerful and contented, so are these females. They have not, it is true, many intellectual resources, but they have naturally good understandings, and having learned their duty strive to fulfil it. So far as I have had any opportunity of making personal observations on their general character they appear to me obedient wives, dutiful daughters, affectionate mothers, kind mistresses, sincere friends, and liberal benefactresses to the distressed poor. These are their moral qualifications, and in their religious duties they are zealous in performing the several ordinances which they have been instructed by their parents or husbands to observe........To the ladies accustomed from infancy to confinement this is by no means irksome; they have their employments and amusements, and those are not exactly to our taste, nor suited to our mode of education, they are not the less relished by those for whom they were invented. They perhaps wonder equally at some of our modes of dissipating time, and fancy we

---

[1] Mrs. Ali, Meer Hassan. *Observations on the Mussulmauns of India.* Letter XII.

[2] *Ibid,* Letter XII.

might spend it more profitably. Be that as it may, the Mussulmaun ladies, with whom I have long been intimate, appear to me always happy, contented, and satisfied with the seclusion to which they were born; they desire no other, and I have ceased to regret they cannot be made partakers of that freedom of intercourse with the world as we deem essential to our happiness, since their health suffers nothing from that confinement, by which they are preserved from a variety of snares and temptations; besides which, they would deem it disgraceful in the highest degree to mix indiscriminately with men who are not relations. They are educated from infancy for retirement, and they can have no wish that the custom should be changed, which keeps them apart from the society of men who are not very nearly related to them."

Within the confines of the zenana, "Female society is unlimited, and that they enjoy without restraint." As Mrs. Meer Hassan Ali observed in her twelve years of residence with Sayyid family, her in-laws, at Lucknow, "The ladies of zeenahnah life are not restricted from the society of their own sex; they are, as I have before remarked, extravagantly fond of company, and equally as hospitable when entertained. To be alone is a trial to which they are seldom exposed, every lady having companions among their dependents; and according to her means the number in her establishment is regulated. Some ladies of rank have from two to ten companions, independent of slaves and domestics; and there are some of the Royal Family at Lucknow who entertain in their services two or three hundred female dependants, of all classes. A well-filled zeenahnah is a mark of gentility; and even the poorest lady in the country will retain a number of slaves and domestics, if she cannot afford companions; besides which they are miserable without society, the habit of associating with numbers having grown up with infancy to maturity: 'to be alone' is considered, with women thus situated, a real calamity."

The memsahibs, among other ideas, imported to India the proselytizing fervor, which was the current flavour in the circles of England. "It has been supposed that commerce is, in the hands of Providence, only one of the means by which distant nations are brought together, in order to the eventual spread of Christianity all over the face of the earth; and it would be a pleasing idea that the coffee of Arabia, the spices of India, and the tea of China, humble plants and shrubs in themselves, but which have now become necessaries of life to all the civilized inhabitants of the world, may ultimately lead to the introduction of the knowledge of the Gospel, in the benighted countries that produce them, by inducing Christian merchant to frequent their shores, for the purpose of trade. Surely we shall have much to answer for, if in pursuit of worldly traffic, we neglect so glorious an opportunity of serving the Lord, and we must expect the vengeance of the Almighty to fall upon us, if we do not our best to convert the Gentiles from their idolatory, when we have an opportunity, in visiting these and other heathen countries."[1]

The Evangelists were of the opinion that it was by the introduction of English education in the zenana, that these native women could become the vehicles for the spread of Christianity in India. Such views were expressed

---

[1] Elwood, Anne Katherine. *Narrative of a journey over land from England.* Vol.-I; p.425-426.

in a private letter written to Mary Frances Billington by one of the editors of a leading newspaper in India, whose name has not been revealed. The content of the letter is as follows; "The chief value in my eyes if the movement has always lain in the promise and hope it afforded of at last invading the seclusion of the zenana, and thus gradually lifting its inmates out of the appalling depths of ignorance and superstition in which they have for centuries been steeped. For what is it at present that hinders all real progress in the county but the overpowering influence of the zenana. Once break down that, or rather shed light on it, and give it a healthy and upward direction, and I believe that progress and enlightenment will make such bounds in this country that the regeneration of India will become a living reality............when the dark recesses of the zenana shall have been penetrated by reason and light, the most powerful lever to progress, and the greatest stimulus to the spread of Christianity throughout the land that it would be possible to discover............when that is done, England's great mission in India would have been accomplished, and it shall be the proudest achievement that was ever entrusted to a great nation to perform in the history of the world."[1]

What significance the zenana had for the Muslim women, the *'purdah'* was the counterpart for Hindu women. However, fundamental difference in the two systems of seclusion was noted by the discerning memsahibs, as Fanny Parks. Eager to explore the unfamiliar surroundings around her and examine the origin of the prevailing customs, she observed that, "The Hindoos never kept their women in *parda*, until

[1] Billington, M. F. *Women in India*, p.110-11.

their country was conquered by the Muhammadans; when they were induced to follow the fashion of their conquerors; most likely, from their unveiled women being the subject to insult."[1] She further adds on the strength of her interaction with Her Highness the Baiza Bai, the deposed Maratha queen of Gwalior, that, "The Mahratta ladies live in *parda*, but not in the such strict seclusion as the Musalmani ladies; they are allowed to ride on the horseback veiled; when the Gaja Raja goes out on horseback, she is attended by her ladies; and a number of Mahratta horsemen ride at a certain distance, about two hundred yards around her, to see that the *kurk* is enforced; which is an order made public that no man may be seen on the road on pain of death."

The 'purdah' system was deeply ingrained in the psyche of Indian women that despite the introduction of female education, even till the last decade of the nineteenth century it was a difficult task to overcome the '*purdah* spirit'. This is illustrated by the incident, when as part of her wedding celebrations in 1889, at Bombay, Mrs. P—y P—n had organized three "at-homes". One was for the Europeans, the second was for the natives, and the third was for the "*Purdah* ladies". In the last gathering no men were allowed, and the household men-servants were dismissed for the day, and in their place some women were employed for assistance. Furthermore, some *purdah*-ladies desired "to see Mr. P—y P—n, and when surprise was expressed as to how such an eventuality could arise, it was suggested by the *purdah*-ladies, who

[1] Parks, Fanny. *Wanderings of a pilgrim*. 6th April 1835, p.6, Vol.II.

said that "he need not see them; he could be put in the light-they in the dark!"[1]

The gender discriminatory stance of the memsahibs vis-à-vis their Indian counterparts was evident in the fact that while the *bibis,* rivals to the claims of affection of their men folk, were ignored, yet their curiosity was aroused in those Indian women who were within the seclusion of the *purdah.* This aroused a great deal of interest in the dynamics of the *zenana,* both within the expatriate community and also with the female audience back home. The *zenanas* were duly investigated and the findings recorded with a very Euro-centric perspective. The first fifty years of the nineteenth century in the historical time-line of the memsahibs was characterized by their increasing interest in the feminine concerns about the Indian women in general, as sati, lack of education and their moral upliftment. These sentiments were to undergo a radical shift in the aftermath of the events that were to reverberate through the dominion of India in 1857.

---

[1] **Ford, Helen C. *Notes of a Tour.* p.157.**

Chapter VIII

Epilogue

The preoccupation of the memsahibs in India was setting up of a 'home' in exile. The home in exile aspired to emulate the idea of the familial bonding, the social customs and practices of the mother-country, in an alien country and environment, though not very successfully. In these settings, the memsahibs wiled away the leisure hours of the long and interminable afternoons of the summer months, in writing down their reflections about India, generally immune from the world of political developments which agitated the Indian minds. The feminine interface with the political establishment being restricted, hence few memsahibs felt qualified to provide a statement on the political affairs of the contemporary times. Despite that, some comments are available, made as they were, by the Lady Governess' or a record of some political episodes by the females accompanying the entourage; or emanating as reactions to reports published in the newspapers.

The political issues, which attracted the memsahibs psyche, had their antecedents in their singular desire to replicate to a very close approximation the 'home' environment. It is against this backdrop that their utterances are to be viewed and studied. The increasing support for free-trade in England was curiously reflected in the sentiments of the memsahibs of India, fuelled by their desire to obtain easily the food items and other commodities from England. "It would be such a convenience to residents in India to be able to procure English articles with facility, that upon their account, independent upon the benefit it would be to our starving manufacturers at home, it appears almost a pity that British tradesman should not rather be invited, than prevented from settling in remote provinces of India."

Lord Hastings (the Earl of Moira) was followed by Lord Amherst in 1823, whose period was notable for military activity: as the first Burmese war (1824-1826); Lord Combermere's storming of the Bharatpur fort; and, the mutiny of the 47th Bengal Native Infantry at Barrackpore. On the Burmese war, Lady Amherst reflected the delight of her husband, as she noted in her diary: "We may fairly say that our foes have been beaten into suing for peace, their insolent language and high pretensions have vanished." Despite the success, the East India Company was not pleased with the Governor-General, as the war had cost £13,000,000, and resulted in the loss of 20,000 lives. Lord Amherst was an anathema in the East India House at Leaden Hall, and a year passed in silence, without the Court of Directors acknowledging the military success in Burma. Lady Amherst complained to her diary, "To this day....Lord Amherst has not received a line from these gentlemen, notwithstanding all the glorious and great events which have occurred." A proud wife, and memsahib, Lady Amherst, recorded on the storming of the citadel of Bharatpur: "The conviction of the impregnability of Bharatpur was held far and wide, and even in Calcutta was so rooted in the minds of its principal native inhabitants as to render them incredulous for a time to the account of its fall. It formed a kind of *point d'appui* for the hopes of all who were hostile to British rule." However, to the Court of Directors in London, Lord Amherst continued to remain an anathema.

The age of Utilitarianism in India really began with the Governor-Generalship of Lord Bentinck, who held office from 1828 to 1835, and he was concerned with administrative and social reform. Bentinck's administration coincided with, and to a certain extent reflected, the climate of evangelical thought then prevailing in England. It was a climate which had resulted in the abolition of slavery, the practices in Hinduism as widow burning, female infanticide and Thugee. But the attitude of mind behind the reforms, encouraged feelings of superiority among the younger servants of the Company, who viewed with horror the older type of administrator who had, it appeared to them, condoned terrible crimes in an attempt to be 'pro-Indian'. This phase then marked the beginning of the belief in the 'white man's burden' and his 'divine ordination in the civilizing mission'. In achieving a pan-Indian level of uniformity between the different parts of the British dominions Bentinck was assisted by the Charter Act of 1833. Under the provisions of this Act, the governor-general was now to become the 'Governor-General of India', and not, as previously, the 'Governor-

General of Fort William in Bengal'. The governor-general was now to exercise supreme authority, and it was expressly stipulated that the Presidency governments no longer had the right to make their own laws. The latter were authorized to submit to the Governor-General in Council 'drafts or projects of any law or regulations which they might think expedient'. This centralization of power was the death knell for the 'sloppy sentimentalists', who opposed a uniform administration for the whole of India. These preservationists of the old order favoured delegation of authority with wide discretionary powers for the local officials, as they were of the firm opinion that codification should be pursued with an intent to provide not a uniform law throughout India, but, a series of comprehensive bodies of law designed to protect local rights and customs from the alien and disruptive effect of English law. But their views were now in a minority, running counter to the general feelings of the British policy makers. By the 1850's, the British in India had virtually institutionalized their contempt for things Indian, urged on by the evangelicals and the utilitarians. The evangelicals believed in God's law, immutable and evident. In their view, all that was needed was to make knowledge of this law available to all. The utilitarians expelled God, to them, sin was not original but a product of poverty, which was in turn a by-product of 'the effect of bad laws and bad government.'

Bentinck was followed for a short period by Sir Charles Metcalfe, one of the most distinguished members of the Company's civil service. But it was a rule that no servant of the Company should hold the highest office in India, and Lord Auckland came to take over in 1836.

Auckland had instructions from Palmerston, the British Prime Minister, that Russia was about to attack India, and consequently encouraged him to engage with Afghanistan in combat, to the most disastrous consequences. Out of the sixteen thousand British and Indian troops, most were killed or taken prisoner. It took bitter fighting for Britain to gain final victory, and this Afghan war was followed by an expedition against the Amirs of Sind then followed in the end of 1845, by the first Sikh war.

Emily Eden makes a telling reference to the growing distance in the attitudes of the officers belonging to the 'old school' and the 'new recruits' coming from London. The incident is mentioned in the letter of 22nd January 1838, written at Bareilly. "There are two officers (European) who command the corps of irregular horses, and dress like natives, with green velvet tunics, scarlet satin trousers, white boots, bare throats, long beards, and everything most theatrical. It does tolerably well for the young adjutant, who is good-looking; but the major, who commanded the regiment, would look better with a neck-cloth and a tight coat. He dotes on his wild horsemen.... The regiment is made up of families. Each Russaldar has at least six sons or nephews in his troop. They are never punished, but sent away if they commit any fault; and they will do anything for their chief if their prejudices of caste are respected. But there have been some horrible tragedies lately, where young officers have come out with their St. James's Street notions of making these men dress like European soldiers. Amongst other things, one young officer persuaded his uncle, a Colonel E., to order them to cut off their beards—a much greater offense than pulling all their noses. The men had idolized this Colonel

E., but the instant they heard this order, they drew their swords and cut him to pieces. There was great difficulty in bringing the regiment to any order again."[1] Runjeet Singh, the 'Lion of Punjab' was held in high esteem by the British, as is apparent from the comment of Fanny Eden, who accompanied Lord Auckland, the Governor-General of India, her brother, who met Runjeet Singh at Ferozepore. Here "Runjeet Singh had a review of his troops yesterday and all our people are in astonishment at his state of discipline, and the very superior way in which they performed their manoeuvres..........but I have a notion from what I can gather that our review was a remarkably poor piece of business, compared to theirs."[2] The Sikhs were however defeated, and Henry Lawrence was appointed to Lahore as the regent for the boy-king.

Lord Ellenborough (1842-1844) who treated the Directors of the East India Company with such disdain, that his appointment was revoked within a short span of two years. He was succeeded by Lord Hardinge (1844-1848), an authoritarian reformer in the utilitarian mould, who expanded the areas under the direct British rule. "He created new, all-India departments to deal with civil engineering works, telegraphs, railways and the post office. Uniformity of management and unity of authority were his guiding principles—and the phrases themselves have an authentic Utilitarian sound."[3] The state of Kashmir was annexed and sold to Gulab Singh. Dalhousie who replaced Lord Hardinge in 1848 faced a revolt on Punjab, where the British forces under Sir Hugh Rose won an

---

[1] Eden, Emily. *Up the Country*. Vol.-I p.108-109.

[2] Eden, Fanny. 6th December 1838; *The Third Journal*; p.176-177.

[3] Edwards, Michael. *British India. 1772-1947.* p.69.

overwhelming victory in 1849 and Punjab was finally annexed. Dalhousie's Governor-Generalship (1848-1856) was a period of intense activity for the British dominions of India, a period of perceived consolidation, which barely concealed the tremors of 1857. The 'Doctrine of Lapse' developed by Dalhousie denied the native rulers of India their immemorial right to adopt an heir in the absence of a natural heir. The first state to fall under this doctrine was Satara, followed by Jhansi and Nagpur. In 1851, the Peshwa of the Marathas died. For thirty-three years, the Peshwa had been a pensioner of the East India Company, but Dalhousie refused to continue paying the pension to his son, Nana Sahib. In 1852 Lower Burma was annexed following a war. In 1853, the first railway was opened and the electric telegraph was introduced. In1856, the kingdom of Oudh was annexed, depriving the Nawab of his privilege to rule, and the sepoys of Oudh who constituted nearly two-thirds of the Company's Bengal army many of their privileges they had enjoyed in their native state by reason of their employment with the East India Company.

By the time the Charter Act came up for renewal in 1853, it was obvious the *raison d'être* of the East India Company was running out, and the day was not far when the Crown would assume direct control over the administration of India. Lord Dalhousie left India in 1856, and his successor Lord Canning, inherited the products of his rule—namely unrest among the princely states of India and unrest among the sepoys, which would find resonance in the events of 1857.

While these political developments were taking place, meanwhile in the last twenty years of the Company's rule the British women were no longer concerned with recording the life of the natives, for curiosity had been replaced by indifference. As they withdrew from active involvement, their desire for participation and contact with the Indians was replaced by an attitude of insularity restricted only to the Anglo-Indian community. This sentiment though was not unanimous, as there were still memsahibs who broke the mould at the Indian scene; but their numbers were rapidly decreasing. This tale would need another narration.

Bibliography

Primary Sources

Acland, T. *A popular account of the manners and customs of India*. London: Murray,1847.

Allen Charles. *A glimpse of the Burning Plain: Leaves from the Indian Journals of Charlotte Canning* . London. 1986.

Ali, Mrs Meer Hassan. *Observations on the Mussulmauns of India: Descriptive of their Manners, Customs, Habits and Religious Opinions. Made During a Twelve Years' Residence in Their Immediate Society.* London 1832. Second Edition, 1917

An Anglo Indian, *Domestic Sketch: A letter from an artist in India to his mother in England*. Calcutta: Thacker, 1849

Bartrum, Katherine. *A Widow's Reminiscences of the Siege of Lucknow.* London, 1858.

Belnos, Sophia Charlotte, *Twenty-Four Plates Illustrative of Hindoo and European Manners in Bengal: Drawn on the Stone by A. Colin from Sketches by Mrs Belnos.* London. 1832.

Bellew, John Francis. *Memoirs of a Griffin, or, a Cadet's first year in India. 2 vols.* W. H. Allen. 1843.

Billington, Mary Frances. *Women in India.* Chapman & Hall, London:1895.

Bower, Ursula Graham. *The Hidden Land.* Murray, London:1953

__________*Nagapath*. Murray, London:1950

Bradley, John. (ed) *Lady Curzon's India: Letters of a Vicerine.* Sidgwick & Jackson: 1967.

Bremner, Christina S. *A Month in a Dandi: A Woman's Wanderings in Northern India.* London: Simpkin, Marhshall, Hamilton, Kent & Co. Ltd. 1891.

Blunt, Whilfried. *Pietro's Pilgrimage: A Journey to India and back, at the beginning of the seventeenth century.* Barrie. London. 1953.

Carpenter, Mary. *Six Months in India* 2 vols. London: Longmans, Green, and Co., 1898.

Chapman, E. F. *Sketches of Some Distinguished Indian Women,* with a preface by the Marchioness of Dufferin and Ava. London and Calcutta: W. H, Allen & Co. Ltd. 1891.

Charters Granted to the East India Company from 1601, Also the Treaties and Grants, made with, or obtained, the Princes and Powers in India, from the Year 1756 to 1772.

Chick, Noah Alfred. *Annals of the Indian Rebellion :1857-1858.* London, Charles Knight & CO. Ltd: 1859.

Clemons, Eliza. *The Manners and Customs of Society in India; including Scenes in the Moufassil Stations; Interspersed with Characteristic Tales and Anecdotes: and Reminiscences of the late Burmese War. To which are added Instructions for the Guidance of Cadets, and other Young Gentlemen, During their First Years Residence in India.* London. 1841.

Coopland, R.M. A Lady's Escape from Gwalior, and Life in the Fort of Agra during the Mutinies of 1857. Smith, Elder, & Co., London: 1859.

Dufferin and Ava, Marchioness of. *Our Viceregal Life in India: Selections from my Journal, 1884- 1888.* 2 Vols. John Murray, London: 1889.

Dunbar, Janet. *Tigers, Durbars and Kings: Fanny Eden's Indian Journals 1837-1838.* London , 1988.

Duncan, Sarah Jeannette. *The Simple Adventures of a Memsahib.* New York. D. Appleton and Co. 1893.

Eden, Emily. *Up the Country: Letters Written to her Sister from the Upper Provinces of India.* Richard Bentley, London: 1866.

________*Portraits of the Princes and People of India, drawn on stone by L. Dickinson.* J. Dickinson, London: 1844.

Elwood, Anne Katharine. *Narrative of a Journey Overland from England by the Continent of Europe, Egypt, and the Red Sea, to India; including a Residence there and Voyage Home, in the year 1825, 26,27 and 28.* 2 vols. London: Colburn and Bentley, 1830.

Anon. *The Englishwoman in India: Containing Information for the use of Ladies Proceeding to , or Residing in, the East Indies, on the Subject of their Outfit, Furniture, Housekeeping, the Rearing of Children, Duties and Wages of Servants, Management of Stables and Arrangements for Travelling, To Which are Added Recipes for Indian Cookery.* London, 1864: 2 nd edn. 1866.

Falkland, Lady Amelia. *Chow-chow; being Selections from a Journal kept in India, Egypt, and Syria. 2 vols.* London: Colburn and Bentley, 1857.

Fay, Eliza. *Original Letters from India; Containing a Narrative of a Journey through Egypt, and the Author's Imprisonment at Calicut by Hyder Ally. To Which is Added, an Abstract of three Subsequent Voyages to India.* Calcutta, 1817.

Fenton, Elizabeth. *The Journal of Mrs Fenton: A Narrative of her life in India, the Isle of France (Mauritius), and Tasmania during the years 1826-1830.* London 1901.

Fort William: India House Correspondence. Vol III 1777-81. National Archives of India. New Delhi. 1981.

Ford, Helen C. *Notes of a tour in India and Ceylon during the winter of 1888-1889.* London: Women's Society, 1889

Fuller, Mrs. Marcus. *The Wrongs of Indian Womanhood,* with an introduction by Pandita Ramabai. Edinburgh and London: Oliphant Anderson and Ferrier, 1990.

Graham, Maria. *Journal of a Residence in India.* Edinburgh: Constable, 1812.

__________*Letters on India. London:* Longman & A. Constable, 1814.

Greathed, *H.H. Letters Written During the Siege of Delhi.* London.1858.

Harris, Lady James P. A *Lady's Diary of the siege of Lucknow. Written for the Perusal of Friends at Home.* London,1858. Asian Educational Services. New Delhi: Reprint 2006.

Harvey, Julia. *The Adventures of a Lady in Tartary, Thibet, China, & Kashmir; through Portions of Territory never before Visited by European (sic). With an Account of the Journey from the Punjab to Bombay Overland, via the Famous Caves of Ajunta and Ellora. Also an Account of the Mahableshwar and Neilgherry Mountains, the Sanatoria of the Bombay and the Madras Presidencies. 3 vols.* London : John Murray. 1853.

Heber, Amelia. (ed), *Narrative of a Journey through the Upper Provinces of India from Calcutta to Bombay 1824-5. (With notes upto Ceylon.) An Account of a Journey to Madras and the Southern Provinces, 1826, and Letters Written in India. 2 vols.* London 1828.

Hoskins, Halford Lancaster. *British Routes to India.* Frank Cass & Co. London. 1928.

Hall, Basil. *Travels in India: Ceylon & Borneo.* London: Routledge and Sons;1931.

Kaye, M.M. (ed), *The Golden Calm: An English Lady's Life in Moughal India.* (Emily Metcalfe). Exter. 1980.

Kindersley, Jemima. *Letters from the East Indies /Letters from the Island of Teneriffe, Brazil, the Cape of Good Hope, and the East Indies.* London 1777.

Lawrence, John, [and Honoria]. *Adventures of an officer in the service of Runjeet Singh.* 2 vols. London 1845.

Lawrence, John, and Woodiwiss, Audrey (eds). *The Journals of Honoria Lawrence: India Observed 1837-1854.* London. 1980.

Leonowens, Anna Harriette. *Life and Travel in India: Being Recollections of Journey Before the Days of Railroads.* Philadelphia: Porter and Coates, 1884.

Lushington, Lady Heneritta. *The Sea-Spirit and other poems.* London 1850.

____________*Almeria's Castle; or, my Early Life in India and England.* London . 1866.

Lushington, Sarah. *Narrative of a Journey from Calcutta to Europe by way of Egypt in the year 1827 and 1828.* London. 1929.

Macrory, Patrick (ed). *Lady Sale: The First Afghan W ar.* Longmans. 1969.

Maitland, Julia, *Letters from Madras, during the years 1836-39, by a Lady* 1843; Reprint London: John Murray. 1946.

Marryat, Florence. *Gup: Sketches of Anglo-Indian Life and Character.* London. 1869.

Mayo, Katherine. *Mother India.* London: Jonathan Cape, 1927

Muter, Doughlas Dunbar. *Travels and Adventures of an Officer's Wife in India, China and New Zealand.* 2 vols. London: Hurst and Blackett, 1864.

Muter, Doughlas Dunbar. *My Recollections of the Sepoy Revolt 1857-1858.* London: John Long Ltd.; 1911.

Mundy, Captain. *The Journal of a Tour in India. 2 vols.* London: John Murray, 1828.

Noble Margaret (Sister Nivedita). *The Web of Indian Life.* 1904; Reprint, Bombay: Longmans, Green 1918.

Parks, Fanny, *Wanderings of a Pilgrim in Search of the Picturesque during four and twenty years in the East ; with Revelations of Life in the Zenana* 2 vols. London: Pelham Richardson 1850.

Postans, Marianne. *Western India in 1838.* 2 vols. London: Saunders and Otley, 1839.

________*Cutch or Random Sketches taken during a residence in one of the Northern Provinces of Western India, interspersed with Legends and Traditions.* London. 1839.

Roberts, Emma. *Scenes and Characteristics of Hindostan, with Sketches of Anglo- Indian Society,* 3 vols. London: W. H. Allen, 1835.

Sherwood, Mary Martha. *The Life of Mrs. Sherwood (chiefly autobiographical with Extracts from Mr. Sherwood's Journal during his imprisonment in France and residence in India,* ed. By her daughter, Sophia Kelly. London: Darton & Co. 1854.

________The Life and Times of *Mrs. Sherwood* (1775-1851) from the Diaries of Captain and *Mrs. Sherwood, ed. F. J. Harvey Darton.* London: Wells Gardner, Darton & Co. Ltd, 1900

Savory, Isabel. *A Sportswoman in India: Personal Adventures and Experiences of Travel in the Known and Unknown World.* London: Hutchinson and Co., 1900.

Spear, Charlotte. Life in Ancient India. London. 1956.

Steel, Flora Annie. India through the Ages: A Popular and Picturesque history of Hindustan. London : Routledge, 1909.

Steel, Flora Annie, and Grace Gardiner. *The Complete Indian Housekeeper and Cook, 1888;* Reprint, London: William Heinemann 1909.

Stocqueler, Joachim Hayward. *Memorials of Afghanistan: Being State Papers and Official Documents illustrative of the British expedition to, and occupation of Afghanistan and Scinde, between the years 1842 & 1842.* Calcutta: Ostell and Lepage, 1843.

Stone, Julia A. *Illustrated India: its Princes and People. Upper, Central and Farther India, up the Ganges and Down the Indus.* Hartford, Connecticut; American Publishing Company: 1877. Reprint 2000.

The Law Relating to India and the East India Company. 2 nd edition London:W.H. Allen & Co., 1841.

Valentia, George. *Voyages and Travels to India, Ceylon, the Red Sea, Abyssinia, and Egypt in the years 1802, 1803, 1805, 1806. 3 vols.* London: William Miller, 1809.

Vansittart, Jane (ed). *From Minnie, with Love : the letters of a Victorian Lady 1849-1861.* (Minnie Wood). London, 1974.

Wagentreiber, Florence. *Reminiscences of the Sepoy Rebellion of 1857.* Lahore, Civil and Military Press Gazette: 1911.

Wilson, Lady Anne Campbell. *Letters from India.* Edinburgh and London: William Blackwood & Sons, 1911.

Wright, Arnold and Sclater, William Lutley. Sterne's Eliza: Some Account of her Life in India: with her Letters Written Between 1757 and 1774. London, 1922.

Secondary Sources

Alloula, Malek. *The Colonial Harem.* Manchester: Manchester University Press, 1987.

Anderson, Nancy Fix. "Bridging Cross- Cultural Feminisms: Annie. Besant and Women's Rights in England and India, 1874-1993, *In Women's History Review,* Vol. 3, No:4, 1994, 563-580.

Armstrong – Hopkins, Saleni. *Within the Purdah: In the Zenana and Homes of Indian Princes and Heroes and Heroines of Zion.* New York, Eaton and Mains, 1898.

Balfour, Margaret, and Ruth Young. *The Work of Medical Women in India.* London: Oxford Unviersity Press 1929.

Ballantyne, Tony and Antoinette Burton, eds. *Bodies in Contact: Rethinking Colonial Encounters in World History.* Durham: Duke University Press 2005.

Ballhatchet, Kenneth, *Race. Sex and Class Under the Raj: Imperial Attitudes and Policies and their Critics, 1793-1905.* London: Weidenfeld and Nicolson, 1980.

Bandhyopadhya Sekhar. "Caste, Widow- Remarriage and the Reform of Popular Culture in Colonial Bengal". In *From the Seams of History: Essays on Indian Women,* ed. Bharati Ray, 8-36, Delhi: Oxford University Press, 1997.

Bannerji, Himani, "Attired in Virtue: The Discourse of Shame (lajja) and clothing of the Bhadramahila in Colonial Bengal", *In From the Seams of History* , ed. Bharati Ray, 67- 106. Delhi: Oxford University Press 1997.

Banerjee, Poompa. Burning Women :Widows, Witches and Early Modern European Travellers in India. New York: Palgrave Macmillian, 2003.

Barr, Pat. *The Memsahibs: The Women of Victorian India.* London: Secker and Warburg, 1976.

Borthwick, Meredith. *The Changing Role of Women in Bengal, 1849- 1905.* Princeton: Princeton University Press, 1984.

Brantlinger, Patrick. *Rule of Darkness: British Literature and Imperialism 1830- 1914.*Itchaca and London: Cornell University Press. 1988.

Buettner, Elizabeth. *Empire Families: Britons and Late Imperial India.* Oxford: Oxford Unviersity Press, 2004.

Buck, Edward J. *Simla: Past and Present.* Bombay:Times Press, 1925.

Burton Antoinette. *Burdens of History: British Feminists, Indian Women and Imperial Culture, 1865- 1915.* Chapel Hill: University of North Carolina Press, 1994.

________*At the Heart of the Empire: Indians and the Colonial Encounter in Late- Victorian Britain.* Berkeley : University of California Press, 1998.

________ed. *Gender, Sexuality and Colonial Modernities.* London: Routledge, 1999.

________*Dwelling in the Archive: Women Writing House, Home, and History in Late Colonial India.* New Delhi, Oxford University Press 2003.

Callan, Hilary and Shirley Ardner. *The Incorporated Wife.* London: Croom Helm, 1984.

Carey, W.H. *The Good Old Days of the Honourable John Company: Being Curious Reminiscences During the Rule of the East India Company from 1600-1858. Compiled from newspapers and other publications.* Calcutta: Quins Book Company, 1882.

Chakravarti, Uma. *Rewriting History: The Life and Times of Pandita Ramabai.* New Delhi: Kali for Women, 1998.

Chakravarty, Suhas. *The Raj Syndrome.* New Delhi: Penguin, 1987.

Chandra Sudhir. *Enslaved Daughters: Colonialism, Law and Women's Rights.* New Delhi: Oxford University Press, 1997.

Chaudhuri, Nupur. "Memsahibs and Motherhood in 19th Century Colonial India". *Victorian Studies 31,* no. 4, Summer, 1988, 517-35.

Chaudhuri, Nupur and Margaret Strobel, eds. *Western Women and Imperialism: Complicity and Resistance.* Bloomington and Indianapolis: Indiana University Press, 1992. Cooper, Eligabeth. *The Harim and the Purdah: Studies in Oriental Women.* London: T. Fisher Unwin Ltd., 1915.

Cowasjee, Saros, ed. *Women Writers of the Raj: Short Fiction From Kipling to Independence.* London: Grafton Books, 1990.

Diver, Maud. *The Englishwoman in India*. Edinburgh and London: William Blackwood & Sons, 1909.

Dalrymple, Willaim. *White Mughals: Love and Betrayal in Eighteenth Century India*. New Delhi: Viking 2002.

__________*The Last Mughal: The Fall of a Dynasty, Delhi 1857*. London: Bloomsbury, 2006.

Dyson, K. K. A Various Universe: *A Study of the Journals and Memories of British Men and Women in the Indian Sub- Continent, 1765- 1856*. 1978; Reprint, New Delhi: Oxford University Press, 2002.

Edwardes, Micheal. *British India 1772-1947 (A Survey of the nature and effects of alien rule)*. London: Sidgwick &Jackson, 1967.

Engles, Dagmar, *Beyond Purdah? Women in Bengal 1890-1939*. Delhi: Oxford University Press, 1996.

Fitzgeralad, Rosemary. 'Clinical Christianity' :The Emergence of Medical Work as a Missionary Strategy in Colonial India, 1800-1914". *In Health, Medicine and Empire: Perspectives on Colonial India*, eds. Biswamoy Pati and Mark Harrison, 88-136, New Delhi: Orient Longman 2001.

Forbes, Geraldine. "'In Search of the Pure Heathen'. Missionary Women in Nineteenth Century India". *Economic and Political Weekly 21*, no. 17, 28 April 1986, WS2-WS8.

________ *Women in Modern India*. Cambridge: Cambridge University Press 1996.

Forrest, G.W. *Selections from the Letters Despatches and other State Papers of the Government of India. 1857-*

1858. Vol. III. Calcutta: Military Department Press, 1902.

Fowler, Mariam. *Below the Peacock Fan: First Ladies of the Raj*. New York: Viking, 1987.

Gardner, Brian. *The East India Company: A History.* London: Granada, 1971.

Garett, G.T. *The Legacy of India*. Oxford, 1934.

Ghose, Indira. *Women Travelers in Colonial India; the Power of the Female Gaze.* Delhi: Oxford University Press, 1998.

________*Memsahibs Abroad: Writings by Women Travellers in Nineteenth Century India.* Delhi: Oxford University Press, 1998.

Ghosh Durba. *Sex and the Family in Colonial India: The Making of Empire.* Cambridge: Cambridge University Press, 2006.

Gilman, Sander L. Black Bodies, White Bodies: Towards an Iconography of 'Female Sexuality in late 19th Century Art, Medicine, and Literature", In *Race, Writing and Difference,* ed. H. L. Gates (Jr.), 223-261. Chicago: Chicago University Press, 1985.

Gilmour, David. *The Ruling Caste: Imperial Lives in the Victorian Raj*. London John Murray,:2005.

Gokhale, Balakrishna G. (ed) Images of India (Asian Studies Two). Bombay:Popular Prakashan, 1971.

Goonetilleke, D. C. R. A *Images of the Raj: South Asia in the Literature of Empire.* Houndmills, Macmillan Press, 1988.

Greenberger, Allen J. *The British Image of India: Studies in the Literature of Imperialism 1880-1960.* New York and Toronto: Oxford University Press, 1969.

Grewel Inderpal. *Home and Harem: Nation, Gender, Empire and the Cultures of Travel.* London: Leicester University Press, 1996.

Grundy, Isobel. British women writers crossing the boundaries: straying, migration, trespass, in *International Review of Eighteenth-Century Studies.* Helsinki & Oxford, 2007.

Hall, Catherine. *Civilizing Subjects: Metropole and Colony in the English Imagination, 1830-1867.* Cambridge: Cambridge University Press 2002.

Hemenway, Stephen. *The Novel of India.* Calcutta: Writers' Workshop, 1975.

Hodges, Sarah, ed. *Reproductive Health in India, History, Politics, Controversies.* New Delhi: Orient Longman, 2006.

Hibbert, Christopher. *The Great Mutiny : India 1857.* London, Penguin Books: 1978

Hirschman, Edwin. *White Mutiny, The Ilbert Bill Crisis in India and the Genesis of the Indian National Congress.* New Delhi: Heritage Publishers, 1980.

Hutchins,Francis G. *The Illusion of Permanence: British Imperialism in India.* Princeton University Press, 1967.

Hyam, Ronald. *Empire and Sexuality: The British Experience.* Manchester: Manchester University Press, 1990.

Jayawardena, Kumari. *White Women's Other Burden: Western Women and South Asia during British Colonial Rule.* New York: Routledge, 1995.

Jones, Mark Bence. *The Viceroys of India.* Constable and Company, Great Britain: 1982.

Karlekar, Malavika. *Voices From Within: Early Personal Narratives of Bengali Women.* Delhi: Oxford University Press, 1991.

Kaye, J.W. *History of the Sepoy War in India 1857-1858.* 3 Vols. London.1880.

Keay, John. *The Honourable John Company: A History of the English East India Company.* London: Harper Collins, 1991.

Kiernan, V. C. *Lords of the Human Kind: European Attitudes Towards the Outside World in the Imperial Age.* London: Weidenfeld and Nicolson, 1969.

Kincaid, Dennis. *British Social Life in India 1608-1937.* London: Routledge, 1938.

Kipling, Rudyard. " Georgie- Porgie", *Life's Handicap: Being Stories of My Own People.* 1891: Reprint Oxford: Oxford University Press, 1987.

_________ *Something of Myself: For my Friends, Known and Unknown.* London: Macmillan & Co. Ltd., 1937.

Kincaid, Dennis. *British Social Life in India 1608-1937.* 1938; Reprint, London: Routledge and Kegan Paul, 1973.

Krishnamurthy, J., ed. *Women in Colonial India: Essays on Survival, Work and the State.* New Delhi: Oxford University Press, 1989.

Krishnaswamy, Ravathi. "Evangels of Empire" *Race and Class* 34, no. 4, 1993, 47-62.

Lal, Maneesha. The Politics of Gender and Medicine in Colonial India: The Countess of Dufferin's Fund, 1885-1888". *Bulletin of the History of Medicine* 68, no. 1, Spring 1994, 29-66.

_________"Purdah as Pathology : Gender and the Circulation of Medical Knowledge in Late Colonial India". In *Reproductive Health in Colonial India*, ed. Sarah Hodges, 85-114, New Delhi: Orient Longman, 2006.

Lewis, Reina. Gendering Orientalism: Race, Femininity and Representation. London and New York: Routledge 1996.

Liddle, Loanna and Rama Joshi. "Gender and Imperialism in British India". *Economic and Political Weekly 20*, no. 43, October 26, 1985, WS72- WS78.

Loomba, Ania. *Colonialism/Post- Colonialism.* London and New York: Routledge, 1998.

Low, Gail Ching Liang. *White Skins/ Black Masks: Representation and Colonialism.* London and New York: Routledge, 1996.

Lutyens, Mary. *The Lyttons in India: An Account of Lord Lytton's Viceroyalty 1876-1880.* London: John Murray, 1979.

Mackenzie, John M. *Propaganda and Empire: The Manipulation of British Public Opinion, 1880- 1960.* Manchester: Manchester University Press, 1984.

Macfarlane, Iris. *Daughters of the Empire: A memoir of Life and Times in the British Raj.* New Delhi: Oxford University Press 2006.

Macmillan, Margaret. *Women of the Raj.* London: Thames and Hudson, 1988.

Malcolm, John. *Sketch of the Political History of India, from the Introduction of Mr. Pitt's Bill, AD 1784 to the Present Times.* London, 1811.

Malhotra, Anshu. *Gender, Caste and Religious Identities: Restructuring Class in Colonial Punjab.* New Delhi: Oxford University Press 2002.

Mani, Lata. "Contentious Traditions: The Debate on Sati in Colonial India", In *Recasting Women* eds. Kumkum Sangari and Sudesh Vaid, 88-126, New Delhi: Kali for Women 1989.

Marston, Annie Westland. *The Children of India, written for The Children of England.* London, The Religious Tract Society. 1883. Reprint 2003.

Masani, Zareer. *Indian Tales of the Raj.* London, B. B.C. Books, 1987,

Mc.Clintok, Anne. *Imperial Leather: Race, Gender and Sexuality in the Colonial Contest.* London and New York; Routledge, 1995.

Midgely, Clare ed. *Gender and Imperialism.* Manchester: Manchester University Press, 1998.

Mill, J. *The History of British India.* London: Baldwin Craddock, and Jay, 1820.

Mill, James. *History of India.* London : Madden, 1840.

Mills, Sarah. *Discourses of Difference: An Analysis of women's Travel Writing and Colonialism.* London: Routledge, 1991.

________*Gender and Colonial Space.* Manchester: Manchester University Press, 2006.

Minault, Gali. Secluded Scholars: Women's Education and Muslim Social Reform in Colonial India. Delhi: Oxford University Press, 1998.

Moon, Penderel. *The British Conquest and Dominion of India,* Duckworth, 1989.

Moore-Gilbert, Bart, ed. *Writing India, 1757-1900, The Literature of British India.* Manchester: Manchester University Press, 1996.

Morris, James. *Heaven's Command: an Imperial Progress.* New York and London: Harvest/ Harcourt Brace Jovanovich, 1980.

Murshid, Ghulam. *Reluctant Debutant: Response of Bengali Women to Modernisation, 1849-1905.* Rajshahi: Sahitya Samsad, Rajshahi University. 1983.

Nair, Janaki. 'Uncovering the Zenana: Visions of Indian Womanhood in Englishwomen's Writings 1813-1940". *Journal of Women's History* 2, no. 1, Spring 1990, 8-34.

Nandy, Ashish. *The Intimate Enemy: Loss and Recovery of Self Under Colonialism. Delhi*: Oxford University Press, 1983.

Nevile, Pran. *Beyond the Veil: Indian Women in the Raj.* New Delhi: Nevile Books, 2000.

________*Rare Glimpses of the Raj.* Somaya, 1998.

Parry, Benita. *Delusions and Discoveries: Studies on India in the British Imagination 1880-1930*. London :Allen Lane, 1972.

Paxton, Nancy, L. *Writing Under the Raj: Gender, Race and Rape in the British colonial Imagination, 1830 – 1947.* New Jersey: Rutgers University Press, 1999.

Pegg, John. *India Cries to British Humanity: Relative to Infanticide, British connection with Idolatry, Ghau Murder, Suttee, Slavery and Colonisation in India.* (third edition)London: Simpkin and Marshall,1832.

Procida, Mary A. *Married to the Empire: Gender, Politics and Imperialism in India, 1883- 1947.* Manchester: Manchester University Press, 2002.

Powell, Avril A. and Siobhan Lambert–Hurley eds. *Rhetoric and Reality: Gender and the Colonial Experience in South Asia.* New Delhi: Oxford University Press. 2006.

Pye-Smith, Charlie. *Rebels and Outcastes. A Journey through Christian India*. London: Viking, 1997.

Ramusack, Barbara N. "Catalysts or Helpers? British Feminists, Indian Women's Rights and Indian Independence". In *The Extended Family: Women and Political Participation India and Pakistan,* ed. Gail Minault, 109-50. Delhi: Chanakya Publications, 1981.

Ray, Bharati ed. *From the Seams of History: Essay on Indian Women*. Delhi: Oxford University Press, 1997.

Ray, Sangeeta. *En-gendering India: Woman and Nation in Colonial and Post – Colonial Narratives.* Durham: Duke University Press 2000.

Rawlinson, H.G. (ed). *Personal Reminiscences in India and Europe 1830-1888 of Augusta Becher.* London. 1930.

Raza, Rosemary. *In their own words, British Women Writers and India 1740-1857.* New Delhi: Oxford University Press 2006.

Renford, R. K. *The Non- Official British in India to 1920.* Delhi: Oxford University Press, 1987.

Ridley, Hugh. *Images of Imperial Rule,* London: Croon Helm, 1983.

Robinson, Jane. *Unsuitable for Ladies: An Anthology of Women's Travellers.* Oxford &New York: Oxford University Press, 1994

________*Angels of Albion.* London: Viking, 1999.

Roy, Parama. *Indian Traffic: Identities in Question in Colonial and Post–colonial India.* New Delhi: Vistaar Publications, 1999.

Said, Edward. *Orientalism,* London and Henley. Routledge and Kegan Paul, 1978

Sangari, Kumkum and Sudesh Vaid, ed. *Recasting Women: Essays in Colonial History.* New Delhi: Kali for Women, 1989.

Sangari, Kumkum. *The Politics of the Possible: Essays on Gender, History, Narratives, Colonial English.* New Delhi: Tulika, 1999.

Sarkar, Tanika. *Hindu Wife, Hindu Nation: Community, Religion, and Cultural Nationalism.* New Delhi: Permanent Black, 2001.

Satin, Anthony (ed). *An Englishwoman In India: The Memoirs of Harriet Tytler (1828-1858).* Oxford . 1986.

Sen, Indrani. *Woman and Empire: Representations in the Writings of British India, 1858 – 1900.* New Perspectives in South Asian History Series, New Delhi: Orient Longman 2002.

______"The Memsahib's 'Madness': The European Woman's Mental Health in Late Nineteenth Century India", *Social Scientist,* Vol. 33, nos. 5-6, May – June, 2005, 26-48.

______"Cruel Oriental Despots': Representations in Nineteenth Century British Colonial Fiction, 1858-1900". *In India's Princely States: People. Princes and Colonialism* eds. Waltraud Ernst and Biswamoy Pati, 30-48. Routledge Studies in the Modern History of Asia Series. London and New York: Routledge, 2007.

_________"Inscribing the Rani of Jhansi in Colonial 'Mutiny' Fiction", *Economic and Political Weekly,* Vol. XLII, No. 19, May 12, 2007, 1754-1761.

________,ed, *Memsahibs' Writings: Colonial Narratives on Indian Women.* New Delhi: Orient Longman, 2008.

Sharpe, Jenny. *Allegories of Empire: The Figure of Woman in the Colonial Text.* Minneapolis: University of Minnesota Press, 1993.

Singh, Jyotsna, G. *Colonial Narratives/ Cultural Dialogues: 'Discoveries' of India in the Languages of Colonialism.* London: Routledge, 1996.

Sinha, Mirinalini. *Colonial Masculinity; The 'Manly Englishman' and the 'Effeminate Bengali' in the late Nineteenth Century.* Manchester: Manchester University Press, 1995.

Stanford, J. K. *Ladies in the Sun: The Memsahib's India 1790-1860*. London: The Galley Press, 1962.

Stoler, Ann. *Carnal Knowledge and Imperial Power: Race and the Intimate in Colonial Rule.* Berkeley: University of California Press, 2002.

Suleri, Sara. *The Rhetoric of English India*. Chicago: University of Chicago Press, 1992.

Sunder Rajan, Rajeswari. *Real and Imagined Women: Gender, Culture and Post- colonialism*. London: Routledge, 1993.

Surtees, Virginia. *Charlotte Canning*. London. 1972.

Teltscher, Kate. *India Inscribed: European and British "Writing on India 1600-1800.* Oxford: Oxford University Press, 1995.

Trollope, Loanna. *Britannia's Daughters: Women of the British Empire.* London: Hutchinson, 1983.

Vicinus, Martha. A. *Widening Sphere: Changing Roles of Victorian Women.* London: Methuen, 1977.

Viswanathan, Gauri. *The Masks of Conquest: Literary Study and British Rule in India*. New York: Columbia University Press, 1989.

Walkowitz, Judith. *Prostitution and Victorian Society: Women, Class and the State.* Cambridge: Cambridge University Press, 1980.

Ware, Vron. *Beyond the Pale: Women, Racism and History.* London and New York: Verso, 1992. Urquhart, Margaret, M. Women of Bengal. *A Study of the Hindu Paradanashins of Calcutta.* 1925; Reprint, Calcutta: Association Press, YMCA. 1927.

Vaughan, Kathleen Olga. *The Purdah System and its Effect on Motherhood; Osteomalacia caused by absence of light in India. Cambridge.* W. Heffer & Sons Ltd. 1928.

Walsh, Judith E. *Domesticity in Colonial India: What women learned when men gave advise.* Oxford University Press. 2004.

Weitbrecht, Mrs. M. *Women of India and Christian Work in the Zenana* London: James Nisbet & Co., 1875.

Index

E

F

G

H

I

J

K

P

R

S

T